TABLE OF CONTENTS

To Karen,

Happy Reading!

Bon Appétit!

Judy Gelman

Vicki L. Krupp

DEDICATION

For our husbands
Peter Krupp
and Peter Zheutlin

TABLE OF CONTENTS

From Breakfast with **ANITA DIAMANT** *to Dessert with* **JAMES PATTERSON**— *A Generous Helping of Recipes, Writings, and Insights from Today's Bestselling Authors*

JUDY GELMAN & VICKI LEVY KRUPP
Creators of BookClubCookbook.com

Avon, Massachusetts

Published by
Adams Media, a division of F+W Media, Inc.
57 Littlefield Street, Avon, MA 02322. U.S.A.
www.adamsmedia.com

ISBN 10: 1-4405-0403-2
ISBN 13: 978-1-4405-0403-7
eISBN 10: 1-4405-0928-X
eISBN 13: 978-1-4405-0928-5

Printed in the United States of America.

10   9   8   7   6   5   4   3   2   1

Library of Congress Cataloging-in-Publication Data
Gelman, Judy
Table of contents / Judy Gelman and Vicki Levy Krupp.
p. cm.
Includes indexes.
ISBN-13: 978-1-4405-0403-7
ISBN-10: 1-4405-0403-2
ISBN-13: 978-1-4405-0928-5 (ebook)
ISBN-10: 1-4405-0928-X (ebook)
1. Cooking. 2. Cookbooks. I. Krupp, Vicki Levy II. Title.
TX714.G4465 2011
641.5—dc22
2010038810

Readers are urged to take all appropriate precautions before undertaking any how-to task. Always read
and follow instructions and safety warnings for all tools and materials, and call in a professional if the
task stretches your abilities too far. Although every effort has been made to provide the best possible
information in this book, neither the publisher nor the author are responsible for accidents, injuries,
or damage incurred as a result of tasks undertaken by readers. This book is not a substitute for professional services.

This book is available at quantity discounts for bulk purchases.
For information, please call 1-800-289-0963.

Contents

OFFERINGS FROM . . .

Introduction

Table of Contents grew out of our ongoing infatuation with books and literature. As ravenous readers with a passion for great literature and delicious food, we are fortunate to have spent much of the last decade immersed in recipes inspired by the pages of our favorite books. Give us a slice of Sue Monk Kidd's honey cake while reading *The Secret Life of Bees*, and we're happy campers. A mojito with Gabriel García Márquez's *Love in the Time of Cholera*—sublime.

Through our early research into book clubs and our website, BookClubCookbook .com, we have confirmed what we had long suspected: we're not the only ones who feel this way. Readers in general are enthralled by food, and many have a strong appetite for recipes connected to the literature they read. Book lovers enjoy being transported to exotic locations and exposed to new cultures in their reading—sampling unfamiliar foods is part of the journey. Some book clubs recreate entire menus to reflect a reading selection, conceive unusual dinner themes based on a book, or research a passing reference made to a dish to serve at their meetings. Countless book club members have shared with us the joy of using food to enhance and enliven their meetings. As one visitor to our website recently wrote, "our greatest pleasures in life include both good books and good food!"

In 2002, we teamed up to create a food and literature resource for book clubs. *The Book Club Cookbook* (Tarcher/Penguin, 2004) matched 100 top book club reading selections with recipes drawn from or inspired by those books. This was followed by a guide for youth book groups, *The Kids' Book Club Book* (Tarcher/Penguin, 2007), which included recipes and activities designed to enhance the reading experience for children and young adults. Our two websites, BookClubCookbook.com and KidsBookClubBook .com, offer recipes and resources for lovers of food and literature. They allow us to stay connected with book clubs and avid readers, offer current resources to book clubs, and help bring authors and readers together. BookClubCookbook.com has become a destination for readers hungry for new and updated author recipes. Here you can find our online "cookbook" of culinary/literary treasures, including Elizabeth Strout's recipe for the doughnuts that her character Olive Kitteridge adores, and the famous Chocolate Pie that Minny bakes in Kathryn Stockett's *The Help*.

Besides tapping the creativity of book clubs, we have frequently turned to authors for recipes inspired by their own writing and this book is the result. Food is often used as a plot device, a way of establishing historical or cultural context, or a method for revealing character in literature. But what we find most fascinating are the stories behind these references. Why did a certain dish appear in a particular scene? Did the author simply imagine the dish? Was it a family recipe? Was it something drawn from the author's travels or life experience? In short, was there a reason a particular food or recipe worked its way into their writing? Authors answered these questions, and through recipes and notes shared their family histories, interests and ambitions, the origin of their characters, or the meaning of their books' settings.

The result is the book you hold in your hands.

For this, our latest book, we chose the fifty authors featured in its pages—from famous and well established writers to a new generation of up and coming literary lights—for their proven appeal to readers. We didn't choose authors simply because their novels or memoirs had culinary themes; we wanted to include authors whose books we know readers and book clubs love.

Many writers were thrilled to participate; they had previously given thought to the role of food in their writing and therefore welcomed the chance to share their culinary creativity with readers. Novelist Barbara Delinsky describes herself as a "noncook," but says "I cook vicariously through my characters. The opportunity to offer readers a recipe is a gift that not only brings attention to a special element of my book, but has drawn in readers who have never read me before." Joanne Harris, author of *Chocolat*, perhaps said it best when she ruminated about the early influences of food and its symbolic and practical role in literature:

> I think tastes and smells are particularly evocative to us because as newborns we first experience the world through those two senses. That means that our *emotional* response to a taste or a smell (think of Proust and his lime-blossom tisane) can act upon us at a very powerful, subconscious level. This is also true in literature, folk tales, and mythology, where food and drink have played an important symbolic role for centuries.
>
> In more recent literature, such references provide a handy means of reflecting different cultures and distant places. It's also a very useful indicator of personality. Eating habits provide us with an insight into a person's background, character, family, and upbringing, as well as their general attitude to life and to other people. Besides, readers *understand* food; in our increasingly diverse and multicultural society, eating remains one of the very few experiences we all have in common; a pleasure, a comfort, and a means of expression.

As writers submitted recipes, we were mesmerized by the stories that accompanied them. For example, characters inspired some recipes. Emma McLaughlin and Nicola Kraus, authors of The Nanny Diaries series, imagine their feisty character, Grandma, serving a Park Avenue Plum Torte to a group gathered in her New York City apartment. Alice, the narrator in Lisa Genova's novel, *Still Alice*, suffers from Alzheimer's disease and can't remember how many eggs belong in the bread pudding she has made so often. The pain of memory loss, explored in Genova's novel, is made palpable as the character struggles to prepare this family recipe.

Some authors linked recipes to their book's setting. Thrity Umrigar set her novel *The Space Between Us* in Bombay, and her recipe for *bhelpuri*—a Bombay street snack made from puffed rice, onions, cilantro, chutneys, and spices—is a culinary parallel to the cultural diversity of the city. Esmeralda Santiago's traditional Puerto Rican recipes conjure the homeland she left behind many years ago—an experience she writes about in *When I Was Puerto Rican*. To make Santiago's recipes—to rub a garlicky *adobo* spice mix onto *pernil* (pork shoulder), and to enjoy the fragrance of a ginger-cinnamon-clove spice infusion as it simmers on the stove—is to be transported to the country that shaped her.

A novel's historical period also offers rich opportunities for culinary creativity. Katherine Howe's novel, *The Physick Book of Deliverance Dane*, is partially set in colonial New England during the Salem witch trials, and her recipes for Fish House Punch and Herb Sallet were gleaned from historical documents of the time. Similarly, Philippa Gregory, author of novels of ancient royal intrigue such as *The White Queen* and *The Other Boleyn Girl*, offers a recipe for Medieval Gingerbread. Although she translates the recipe into modern language, the basic ingredients and procedures remain true to Tudor England.

To our delight, there are many family recipes in this collection—from tried and true favorites handed down through generations to new ones inspired by our request.

Chris Cleave challenged his chef wife, Clémence, to create a recipe combining Nigerian and Western ingredients and flavors to accompany his novel *Little Bee*, a story about the unlikely friendship between a Nigerian girl and an English woman. The result features a delicious and unusual combination of ingredients. In Dolen Perkins-Valdez's historical novel *Wench*, Mawu, a slave, practices magic and makes a stew that she claims can "soften the white man." Many readers have asked the author: what was in Mawu's magical stew? Perkins-Valdez called upon her uncle, whom she calls "the most accomplished cook in my family," to help her create Mawu's Magical Stew for our book. (You'll have to read on to learn what's in the stew!) Abraham Verghese provides three recipes to go with his novel *Cutting for Stone*, all from his Indian-born mother. The cooking scenes he describes in his novel reflect memories of his own childhood in his mother's Indian kitchen. Elinor Lipman offers her mother's noodle kugel as made by aspiring chef Natalie Marx, the narrator of *The Inn at Lake Devine*. And Jayne Anne Phillips contributes two delicious and elegant cake recipes—both of which are her mother's recipes from hand-written notes—that she imagines Lark (from her novel *Lark & Termite*) might prepare.

Table of Contents covers every course, from drinks to desserts and everything in between. Authors offered recipes for every mood and occasion—from Sara Gruen's sophisticated Salmon en Croûte to Jacquelyn Mitchard's down home comfort food of meatballs and gravy. Some recipes call for just three or four ingredients and a few simple steps. Others are more involved, but all can easily be prepared by the home cook. We love the diversity of the recipes, too: their origins span the globe, from Paris to Puerto Rico, from Scandinavia to Syria, from Iowa . . . to Oz. Like our own personal recipe collections, this cookbook contains recipes from authors' family and friends, recipes adapted from their favorite cookbooks, and those well-worn beloved recipes with no known origin.

In addition to their recipes and stories, *Table of Contents* features intimate profiles of these authors. We asked them about their literary influences, what inspires their writing, what they would like readers to know, and questions that readers like you frequently ask. We hope these authors' ideas, anecdotes, and stories will help bring their books alive, encourage thoughtful discussion, deepen the reading experience, and of course, inspire all lovers of good books and good food.

We have spent hours simmering and stewing, kneading and rolling, blending and baking. We learned something about each of these marvelous writers through their stories and their recipes. It's our thrill to share it all with you. Enjoy the feast!

Elizabeth Berg

Photo by Joyce Ravid

SELECTED WORKS

- *Once Upon a Time, There Was You* (2011)
- *The Last Time I Saw You* (2010)
- *Home Safe* (2009)
- *The Day I Ate Whatever I Wanted And Other Small Acts of Liberation* (2008)
- *Dream When You're Feeling Blue* (2007)
- *We Are All Welcome Here* (2006)
- *Open House* (2000)

Inspiration
Lots of things: nature, history, wacky incidents in the news, the yin and yang in everyone's life. But most of all, people: their mystery and charm, their accents and their widely differing points of view, the bigness of their hearts and their resilience. I'm also fascinated by *awful* people.

Readers Should Know
With every book I write, I try to tell the truth. Even though it's fiction, there's an emotional reality I want to get at, and I want to present it with a mix of humor and pathos. *The Last Time I Saw You,* my novel about a fortieth high school reunion, is told from five different points of view: two men and three women. I think readers will find it a lot of fun to read; I certainly had fun writing it.

Readers Frequently Ask
The question that comes up most often is: "How do you know so much about me when we've never met?" And the answer is: I'm *like* you. The first editor for whom I wrote told me, "You have the common touch, and that's a gift." I do feel I have an intimate relationship with my readers. It's an honor and a joy.

Authors Who Have Influenced My Writing
I was galvanized by J.D. Salinger, charmed by E.B. White, and absolutely knocked out by Alice Munro. But influenced? It's more "real people" who do that. They and the extraordinariness of ordinary life.

MY FAVORITE MEATLOAF

Makes 6 servings

I love meatloaf so much I wanted to title one of my novels *The Hotel Meatloaf.* That idea didn't go over so well—the title became *Open House.* But there is still a line in the novel about the Hotel Meatloaf. This is a recipe for meatloaf I found in a woman's magazine that everybody I've served it to *loves.* And it's easy!

I serve this with mashed potatoes, green beans, and apple pie. If there's any left, it's wonderful the next day.

> 8 slices fresh white or whole wheat bread
>   (to make 2 cups fresh bread crumbs)
> 1½ pounds ground beef
> ¼ cup fresh lemon juice
> ¼ cup minced onion
> 1 large egg
> 2 teaspoons seasoned salt, such as Lawry's
> ⅓ cup ketchup
> ⅓ cup light brown sugar
> 1 teaspoon dry mustard
> ¼ teaspoon ground allspice
> ¼ teaspoon ground cloves
> 6 thin lemon slices, for garnish

1 Preheat oven to 350°F. Grease a 9" × 13" × 2" baking pan.
2 Remove the crusts from slices of bread, if desired, and tear slices into 1-inch pieces. Place bread in a food processor and pulse until the bread forms coarse crumbs.
3 In large bowl, combine bread crumbs, beef, lemon juice, onion, egg, and seasoned salt. Mix well. Shape by hand into 6 little meatloaves and place in baking pan. Bake 15 minutes.
4 Meanwhile, mix ketchup, brown sugar, mustard, allspice, and cloves in a small bowl. Spoon sauce over loaves and top each loaf with a lemon slice. Bake 30 minutes more, or until internal temperature registers 160°F on a thermometer.

Sarah Blake

SELECTED WORKS

- *The Postmistress* (2010)
- *Grange House* (2001)
- *Full Turn* (1989)

Inspiration While I was working on *The Postmistress*, I returned to Provincetown, Massachusetts, the outermost town on Cape Cod. One morning I was walking down the single-lane main street and overheard two elderly residents in conversation. "Well," one of them pronounced to the other sagely, "even *good* doctors have their little graveyards."

I already had the character of Dr. Will Fitch firmly in mind, but this comment, and the way it was delivered, sealed his fate. From that moment on the street, I knew what his struggle would be. The woman's phrase went directly into the book. And the image of the tiny hidden graveyards all doctors—even good ones—carry with them was haunting and generative, the way all solid simple truths are.

My writing is always inspired this way: by things overheard that have the nugget of a story in them; or by people I catch a glimpse of whose faces suggest stories or questions. For me, the thrill of writing comes in chasing down those questions—catching the stories latent in scraps overheard or chance encounters held—that rise up over and over in our lives.

The Early Bird Gets Writing When I am in the middle of writing a novel or a story, I like to wake up before anyone else in my house—this is very early!—and simply start where I left off the day before. I do this without thinking, before thinking really, and write as long as I can this way. Then, after lunches have been packed, the kids taken to school, other parents or teachers greeted and talked to, and other stuff of the morning done, I can return to that early morning voice and begin again, like meeting an old friend along the road. It is at that point too, that I like to read a few pages of familiar, beloved writers: Woolf, or George Eliot, Yeats or Calvino, taking in their language, their turns of phrases, like hands I grab hold of in order to pull myself up so I can let go into my own writing.

Readers Frequently Ask Since both of my novels take place in different eras from our own—the late nineteenth century and the 1940s—people often ask about my research: how I go about it, how much I do, and how I know when I'm done.

I like to steep myself in the era I write about, reading history books of course, but also getting my hands on magazines, novels, and poems written in the time period so I can get the diction of my characters just right. And when I decided to set *The Postmistress* during World War II, I knew little about that period and I had to start from scratch. But the wonderful thing about research is that it leads you toward true stories or details that are incredibly generative. When I read that a town in Maine cut down its town flagpole because of fear of U-boats, I knew I had to use that detail. This one fact also suggested a whole series of scenes between Iris and Harry. It's details like these—and there are many that never made it into the finished book—that make it very hard to leave off researching. But you know you're done when the story takes on its own true contours.

....

Authors Who Have Influenced My Writing I return to Virginia Woolf every year, and reread her often to get myself set back on track or if I'm seeking inspiration. Woolf's vivid impressionism—in which shocks of life bolt from the pattern of daily life, "moments of being," as she called them—is my touchstone. *A Room of One's Own; Mrs. Dalloway, To the Lighthouse, Between the Acts; Moments of Being.*

As a child I read Charlotte Brontë's *Jane Eyre* and fell in love with this passionate rebel who talked back. Reading it again as a literature professor, I was able to study the perfect narrative that is the backbone of this book, the three-story structure with a madwoman in the attic. Now as a writer I return to *Jane Eyre*, over and over, dipping in anywhere just to pick up and study this incredible single voice running along the tracks of a well-conceived plot.

FLORENCE (GRANNY) BLAKE'S ROMANCE COOKIES

Makes 16 squares

"We think back through our mothers if we are women," Virginia Woolf wrote in *A Room of One's Own.* Both of my novels, *Grange House* and *The Postmistress*, take her words to heart as I imagine the lives of earlier generations of women to better understand my own life. But I could easily follow Woolf's dictum with this one: we cook back through our mothers, if we are women. I learned as much about making characters as I did about baking, by cooking (or not) with the three women I grew up with.

Though my mother's mother sailed through her kitchen as through foreign waters, leaving all matters culinary to her family's cook, and my mother mostly shooed my sister and me out—cooking being for her a terribly fraught and uncertain operation—my father's mother pulled me into her kitchen, sat me down, and set me going. Granny Blake had been a surgical nurse before she caught my grandfather's eye. She left it all to follow him to Arizona, where she bore him two sons, only to be widowed at thirty-five. Tiny, with a shock of white hair, she was tough-talking and very firm. She wore a skirt every day of her life, and settled at six each evening with her scotch, the news, and two Kent cigarettes. When you cooked with her, you lined up all your ingredients, like soldiers going into battle, and then you began. If Frankie Bard from *The Postmistress* had become a grandmother, this is who she would have been.

Romance cookies are a mouth-watering confection, a two layered cookie, with shortbread on the bottom and butterscotch brownie on top. They were the first things she taught me to make, and making them seemed like an act of derring-do, a high-wire act, a race against time to wash and dry the single bowl from the remnants of the first layer and then assemble and mix the ingredients of the second layer in the ten minutes it took to bake the first. As I would later do as a writer, I learned how to build with her, how to plan and build. And then, when the cookies were pulled from the oven and handed around, I learned the secret life of words. These are Romance Cookies, she'd explain again and again, so-called because they are sticky and sweet—she'd pause—like romance. And the grown-up laughter that greeted her signaled a world I didn't understand or know but that the cookies promised somehow to carry with them, a story unto themselves.

FOR THE DOUGH

1 cup all-purpose flour

2 tablespoons granulated sugar

½ cup (1 stick) unsalted butter, softened

FOR THE TOPPING

2 large eggs

1½ cups dark brown sugar, packed

3 tablespoons all-purpose flour

½ teaspoon baking powder

1 teaspoon vanilla extract

1 cup chopped walnuts

1 Preheat oven to 350°F.

2 To make the dough: In a medium mixing bowl, combine flour, sugar, and butter (you can use an electric mixer if you wish). Use your hands to shape dough into a smooth ball.

3 Place dough in 9" × 9" × 2" baking pan. Press dough into the pan, pushing into the corners so that you make a flat surface, completely covering the pan. Bake for 15–18 minutes so that it is baked but not brown. Don't overbake.

4 While dough is baking, make the topping: Combine eggs, brown sugar, flour, baking powder, vanilla, and walnuts in a medium mixing bowl.

5 Pour mixture on top of shortbread layer and bake for 20–25 minutes, until top layer is set. Cool completely before cutting into 16 squares.

Amy Bloom

Beth Kelly

How My Characters Come to Life Although the specifics change from book to book, it is always the case that there is a story I wish to tell and, even more, there are characters I have created who I wish to set loose in the world. These characters always contain parts of myself, and this gives me a chance to lead 100 other lives.

What I'm Working on Now My new collection of stories is *Where the God of Love Hangs Out*. I have a novel, expected out in 2012, about two sisters in the 1930s.

Readers Frequently Ask I think most readers have questions either about a plot detail that puzzled them or a choice I made that they want me to explain. Very often the questions are more personal. How did I choose an aspect of a character? Why did I let these bad things happen to a character they loved? I answer people both as personally and with as much detail as I can. Usually I can explain why I made the literary decision I did. I can't explain why it affected them the way it did.

Books That Have Influenced My Writing I think writers are most influenced by people they read when they are young, when they are reading only for pleasure and fun, not instruction. The three books that most influenced me as a young reader were:

- Charles Dickens's *A Tale of Two Cities*
- Louisa May Alcott's *Little Women*
- Willa Cather's *My Ántonia*

These are all books with both great scope and great attention to the interior lives of characters who are whole and engaging and real.

These are three of my favorite recipes, none of which I ever make when I'm working hard. But for brunch to celebrate finishing a book, for bringing a new baby into the world, or for any other occasion of great satisfaction and relief, these are the best recipes I know.

Two of my favorite characters in *Where the God of Love Hangs Out* are William and Clare, middle-aged friends who become lovers. Clare is what I call a "secret cook," one of those people who cooks for loved ones but who doesn't like to make a big "dinner party" deal out of it. I imagine that William makes a fire and coffee strong enough to peel the paint off your walls on a Sunday morning while Clare makes these eggs and this hash and this drink and they stay in their pajamas all day.

IDIOT-PROOF SCRAMBLED EGGS WITH LOX, LEEK AND DILL

Makes 4–6 servings

3 tablespoons good quality unsalted butter, divided (unsalted Plugra comes to mind)
8 large eggs
Pinch of salt
½ teaspoon ground pepper
1 medium leek, white part only, thinly sliced or diced
1–2 ounces cream cheese, smooshed into pea-sized pieces
5–6 ounces lox, cut into narrow strips or square inches
1 tablespoon chopped fresh dill (if you can't get fresh dill, use parsley or nothing at all)

1 Melt 2 tablespoons of butter in large skillet. Whisk eggs, salt, and pepper in large bowl. Add eggs to buttered skillet and scramble over low heat, until almost set.
2 At the same time in a separate skillet, melt 1 tablespoon of butter over low heat and sauté leek in butter for 5 minutes, until wilted. Toss into eggs. Add cream cheese and lox. Stir 1 more minute. Transfer to plates and sprinkle with dill.

RED FLANNEL HASH

Makes 2–4 servings

Note: Allan Benton's Smoked Country Bacon from Madisonville, Tennessee, is as good as it gets. It has a hearty flavor and, if you can't find it, I recommend doubling the amount of regular bacon you'll use in the recipe.

4 slices Allan Benton's Smoked Country Bacon or 8 slices regular bacon (see note)

1 cup chopped Vidalia or red onion

2 large potatoes (Yukon Gold or Baby Bliss are nice), steamed or boiled, cooled and diced (leave skin on)

1 15-ounce can whole, skinned beets, drained and diced (If you want to boil your own and remove the skins, God bless you.)

½ cup whole milk

1 Cook bacon on medium low heat in a large skillet until brown but not crispy. Drain bacon on paper towel. Crumble.
2 Sauté onion in bacon grease until soft. Mix in crumbled bacon, potatoes, diced beets, and milk. Flatten with a spatula to shape like a giant pancake. Cook until heated through, stirring up the bottom crust a couple of times. Make sure there is substantial crust all around; this takes longer than you'd think (about 15 minutes).
3 Serve. (Some people will really appreciate it if there's a bottle of hot sauce and a few extra strips of Benton's bacon on the side.)

THE VELVET SWING

Makes 1 drink

6 ounces champagne
½ ounce port
½ ounce cognac
1 raspberry

Pour champagne, port, and cognac into a glass with a stem (I recommend a champagne flute) and drop in the raspberry.

Jenna Blum

Marcia Perez

The Power of Emotion I always write about subjects that have fascinated me since childhood and pair them with an emotional question. For instance, I've always been fascinated with the Holocaust, so it made sense that my debut novel, *Those Who Save Us*, was set during that time period. The emotional key in the ignition was the relationship between the novel's primary heroine—a German woman trying to save herself and her daughter—and her sadistic captor, the *Obersturmfuhrer* of Buchenwald. The question this book asks is: "How far would you go to save your child?"

Storm chasing is the world in which my novel, *The Stormchasers*, is set. I got into storm chasing partially because I've been enthralled by tornadoes since I was a child and saw one in my grandmother's farm hometown. I've become a storm chaser as an adult. Yes, I'm like the guys on Discovery Channel who chase tornadoes, except I'm a lot more cautious and subdued about it! The storyline of *The Stormchasers* is about bipolarity; I've had loved ones who are bipolar and watched them struggle with the disorder. *The Stormchasers* centers on twins: a storm chasing brother who is bipolar, and his sister who acts as his caretaker. How does the disorder, and the events it triggers, twist their relationship? How far does one go to protect a sibling? These are the questions I'm exploring in this novel.

Readers Should Know I'm what one reader kindly called a "method writer." When I'm writing, I'm 100 percent committed to a project, to the exclusion of everything else except walking my black Lab, Woodrow. I try to immerse in the world of the book as much as possible. When I wrote *Those Who Save Us*, I listened to German music, read everything I could about Germany, baked every recipe that appears in the novel, and even dressed like my heroine, Anna, with my hair in braids…though only inside the house! For *The Stormchasers*, I lived within the setting of the book. Working at home in Boston proved too distracting for me—so much shopping potential to lure me away from my deadline—so I went to the small Minnesota farm town where my characters are born and lived in a motel for two months, until the draft was finished. It was a dreamlike, surreal time that I utterly treasure.

....

Readers Frequently Ask Readers often ask why I left quotation marks out of *Those Who Save Us*. The answer, along with much more information about both novels, is on my website (*www.jennablum.com*), but the short version is this: I wanted the novel, which is so much about the persistence of memory, to have an austere, almost sepia atmosphere. The quotation marks, which are very lively pieces of punctuation, were like little firecrackers on the page and disturbed the book's tone, so I left them out. Some readers loved this. Others are much happier that my second novel, *The Stormchasers*, has quotation marks in it.

One of my favorite in-person reader questions was posed at an event for which I'd gotten a big swirly updo. A woman in the audience stood up and asked, "Is that your real hair?" There are absolutely no questions I won't answer! (Yes, it was and is my real hair.)

....

Books That Have Influenced My Writing

- *Sophie's Choice*, William Styron: I aspire to be Styron because his novels wed beautiful writing with moral substance.
- *The Stand*, Stephen King: Actually I like any of the very early King works, not because of the horror component but because he does such a great job of portraying what happens to people's psyches under duress. His imagination is so vivid and so extensive—and the man knows how to tell a story. Without a story, you've got only a bunch of pretty words. What I aim to do is provide my readers with a good story well told.
- *Shining Through*, Susan Isaacs: I love this book about a peppy everygirl-turned-spy in New York City and Germany during World War II. Another example of great storytelling—not letting the telling of the story get in the way of the story itself.

LUVERNE JOERG'S *ROMMEGROD*

Makes about 12 (1-cup) servings

Traditionally made at Christmas, with lots of cursing and complaining
by the cook that her arms are about to fall off.

My recipe is for a Norwegian Christmas pudding called rommegrod (pronounced
"room-a-grout," and indeed it could be mistaken for and function as grout). Rommegrod
appears in my recent novel, *The Stormchasers*, as a favorite dessert of the novel's heroine
and hero, Norwegian twins, Karena and Charles Hallingdahl.

Legend has it that, in pioneer days on the plains, rommegrod was served not only at
Christmas but also as a strengthener and curative. Norwegian settler women would give birth,
be given a bowl of rommegrod, then get up out of bed and resume working in the fields.

I would think this story was apocryphal if I had not myself witnessed the miraculous
powers of rommegrod in action. In her late eighties, my grandmother Luverne Joerg
broke her hip while living in farm-town Minnesota. Of course, this unhappy event would
normally be seen as the beginning of the end, and indeed my grandmother developed
pneumonia while she was in the hospital. It was the first time I had heard firsthand what
is known as a "death rattle," which sounded like a bicycle chain in her lungs every time she
took a breath. She was failing fast, so much so that she was not expected to live the night.
We called the family members in from New York and Arizona, as well as other parts of
Minnesota, to say their goodbyes.

While we were waiting, I said to my mom, Luverne's daughter, "Why don't we go to
Decorah and get some rommegrod for her and see what happens?"

Decorah, Iowa, is a Norwegian town that prizes its heritage, and one of the cafés there
still offers the pudding. We drove three hours from Rochester, Minnesota, bought a takeout bowl of rommegrod, and returned to the hospital.

I crushed my grandmother's medicines, which she had been otherwise unable to take,
and stirred them into the rommegrod. Then I coaxed her to eat a bite, and another bite,
and another. She managed about half a bowl.

By the next morning, when my aunts and uncles arrived—with my uncle Lowell weep-
ing and saying, "Goodbye, little Mother!"—my grandmother was sitting up in bed.

"Why, hello," she greeted everyone. "So nice to see you here!"

Luverne lived to be ninety-eight years old. Thanks, rommegrod!

Note: This pudding can be reheated beautifully. My mom has it for breakfast for several days after Christmas!

1 quart heavy cream
¾ cup flour
1 quart whole milk
Cinnamon, for sprinkling
Sugar, for sprinkling

1　In a large saucepan, bring cream to a boil over medium heat, stirring continuously. Boil for 15 minutes, stirring all the while.
2　Add flour and stir. (It's okay if the flour clumps up.) When mixture becomes a soft ball and the liquid has separated in the bottom of the pan (this will take about 30 seconds), remove from heat. Transfer mixture to a strainer and allow liquid to drain off. Reserve liquid, and return solids to the saucepan.
3　In a separate medium saucepan, bring milk to a boil over medium heat. Add milk to cream solids, and bring to a boil over medium-low heat, stirring constantly. Reduce heat and simmer until thick and velvety, stirring until arms are indeed about to fall off, 15–20 minutes. Use hand-held electric mixer set on low, if possible (but it's okay if you don't have one; the old Norwegian ladies didn't either).
4　Serve either hot or cold. Top with cinnamon and sugar, and drizzle with some of the reserved liquid. Refrigerate any leftovers.

ADELINE ELLINGSON'S NORWEGIAN HAM BALLS

Makes 6½ dozen large meatballs

This is a traditional Christmas Eve recipe from the Norwegian side of my family—specifically from my grandmother's best friend. The Hallingdahl twins in *The Stormchasers* would eat these sweet, sinful meatballs as an entrée with their holiday rommegrod on the side.

Note: Any kind of ham will work, as long as it's precooked. I like smoked ham myself, but even a canned ham will do.

FOR THE MEATBALLS
1 pound ground ham (use a food processor to grind fairly fine) (see note)
1½ pounds ground pork
2 cups plain dry bread crumbs
2 large eggs, beaten
1 cup whole milk

FOR THE SAUCE
2 cups brown sugar
1 cup white vinegar
2 tablespoons prepared nongrainy mustard of your choice (such as plain yellow or nongrainy Dijon)
1 cup water

1 Preheat oven to 325°F.
2 **To make the meatballs:** Place all ingredients in a large bowl, and knead with hands until completely combined. Shape into meatballs between the size of a walnut and a ping pong ball. Place in one 9" × 13" × 2" baking dish, and one larger pan, such as a shallow roasting pan or jelly roll pan, leaving a little space between meatballs.
3 **To make the sauce:** Place all ingredients in a small bowl. Stir mixture together until sugar is dissolved. Pour over meatballs.
4 Bake 1½ hours. Remove pans from oven and turn meatballs to coat them with the candied sauce. Meatballs will keep a week in the fridge, longer in the freezer. To reheat meatballs, cover with aluminum foil and place in preheated 300°F oven for 15 minutes. Check a meatball to see if interior is warm. If not, continue heating for another few minutes.

Adeline Ellingson's Potato Salad

Makes 6–8 servings

This is a family recipe provided by my grandmother Luverne's best friend, Adeline. The two ladies were inseparable lifelong friends, so this salad is a staple at family picnics and signifies summer to me. Potato salad appears in *The Stormchasers* as a favorite food of the twins. I will probably be taken out by a Norwegian hit man for confessing this, but the secret is in the sugar.

Note: The flavors of this salad intensify after 24 hours, so it's best when made a day or two ahead of time.

For the salad
3 pounds Idaho potatoes, peeled and cut
  into ½-inch cubes
3 teaspoons salt, divided
¾ cup mayonnaise (Hellman's or
  Miracle Whip)
1 tablespoon prepared plain yellow
  mustard
1 tablespoon sugar
¾ teaspoon pepper

Dash Worcestershire sauce
3 large hard-cooked eggs, diced small
⅓ cup finely chopped onion

For the garnish
3 large hard-cooked eggs, sliced into rings
Dried parsley flakes, for sprinkling
Paprika, for sprinkling

1 Place potatoes in a large pot, cover with water, and bring to boil over high heat. Add 2 teaspoons of salt, reduce heat to medium, and boil gently for 4–5 minutes, or until potato cubes are just tender. (Check cubes often while cooking by fishing one out and tasting it. As soon as they're tender enough to bite through easily, drain them. The potatoes will continue cooking a bit after being drained, so it's better to err on the side of too firm than risk mushy potatoes.) Drain potatoes, and pour into a large bowl.

2 Whisk together the mayonnaise, mustard, sugar, remaining teaspoon of salt, pepper, and Worcestershire sauce in a separate bowl. Pour on the warm potatoes, and combine gently with a wooden spoon. Add the diced eggs and onion, and stir to combine. Chill.

3 When ready to serve, arrange the egg rings on top of the salad, and sprinkle with parsley and paprika.

Ethan Canin

Fred Gerr

Inspiration

Two things inspire me as a writer. The first is reading. Not just any book, but a book that *makes* me read it, and only one in ten books *makes* me read it. The second is the great fear of not being productive as a human being. I like to make things, work in the garden, cut firewood, or build furniture. The fear of not producing something is a fear of life passing by. I should add that it feels very good to be devoted to something, as well. When you're writing a book, you are utterly devoted to it.

Like many writers and artists, I go from ecstasies to despondencies, and the trick to making a career of writing is to make more shallow the depths of the despondencies and, in some ways, to level out the heights of the ecstasies.

Readers Should Know

I spent a number of years trying to figure out what I find inspiring. I've traveled, lived in the jungle, hitchhiked, put myself in dangerous situations, gambled. But after all that, I've discovered that I write best sitting in my office looking out over a familiar view: a shed in my backyard and some chickens plucking at the grass.

Readers Frequently Ask

Who is the guy at the beginning of *America, America* at the funeral with the cane?

That question has a very specific answer: a character who is identifiable later by that same cane.

People always ask, too, whether *America, America* is based on Ted Kennedy. The plot of the novel obviously derives from certain incidents in Kennedy's life, but the character of the senator was more deeply inspired by Lyndon Johnson, by his public idealism set against his personal ruthlessness.

People wonder what impact teaching has on my writing. I'm lucky because I teach at the University of Iowa Writers' Workshop and I have fabulous students. Their writing moves and goads and inspires me. To teach good students is a deep delight.

People also ask about my being a doctor and wonder whether I'm ever going to write a medical novel. My strong belief is that if you don't invent everything, you can't invent anything. A novel about medicine would be the last book I'd write.

Influences on My Writing

I can't remember the details of all the books I've loved and been inspired by, only the emotion I had when reading them. I love funny books but I remember sad ones.

- *The Stories of John Cheever*. This is the book that first made me want to be a writer.
- *The Deptford Trilogy*, by Robertson Davies. The scope of imagination, both outward and inward, stuns me. One novel in the trilogy, for example, is about the life of circus performers, while another is the transcript of a Jungian analysis.
- *Open Secrets*, by Alice Munro. This book really expanded my idea of the short story.
- *Tell Me A Riddle*, by Tillie Olsen. This is not an ornate book, but it certainly is a searing one. As I've grown older as a writer, I've become more interested in content than style. I've come to believe, in fact, that a writer must choose between psychological realism and poetic prose. In my opinion, the two simply cannot fully coexist, for either writer or reader.

ANNA SIFTER'S
STRAWBERRY RHUBARB PIE

Makes 1 (9-inch) pie; 8 servings

An original 1960s recipe from Kathy's Pies of Cedar Rapids, Iowa, a family bakery.
The strawberry rhubarb pie remains a bestseller.

The scene that got me started on my most recent novel, *America, America*, is the
one that features a strawberry rhubarb pie. Though it did not end up being the first
scene in the book, it was the first one I wrote, long before there was a presidential
candidate, a love affair, or even a fully formed family story in my mind. Though one
is unconscious of this kind of thing when writing, I realize now that the humble, old-
fashioned gesture of baking a pie seemed to emphasize the differences between, on
the one hand, working-class Corey Sifter and his diligent mother Anna (who actually baked the pie) and, on the other, the wealthy girl who invites Corey sailing. I also
must have thought that the combination of something beautiful and luscious—the
strawberry—and something lowly, sour, and common—the rhubarb—would work well
in a novel that in many other ways juxtaposes opposites.

I myself am a berry lover, blueberries and strawberries especially, so much so
that my wife believes I must have been a brown bear in another life. The recipe here
is from a long-held family business in Cedar Rapids, Iowa, which is about a half
hour from where I live, in Iowa City. To my delight, people in Iowa still give home-
baked pies as gifts, so this recipe is also a suitable representative of my adopted
home state.

FOR THE FILLING
*1 pound rhubarb (fresh or frozen), cut into
½-inch pieces*
1 cup sugar
3 cups hulled and sliced strawberries
Dash of salt
5 tablespoons cornstarch

FOR THE CRUST
*2½ cups all-purpose flour, plus additional
for sprinkling the board*
*2 tablespoons granulated sugar, plus addi-
tional for sprinkling on the crust*
½ teaspoon salt
*¾ cup (1½ sticks) cold unsalted butter, cut
into 1-inch pieces*
½ cup cold vegetable shortening
6–8 tablespoons ice water
Milk, for brushing on dough

1 **To make the filling:** Place rhubarb in a medium bowl, add sugar, and stir to combine. Cover with plastic wrap. If using fresh rhubarb, refrigerate for 2–3 hours. If using frozen rhubarb, refrigerate overnight.

2 **To make the crust:** In a food processor, pulse the flour, sugar, salt, butter, and shortening until the mixture resembles coarse crumbs. Add the water all at once, and pulse again until dough just begins to come together, but doesn't form a ball.

3 Turn the dough out onto a lightly floured board, and knead gently until it comes together. Press the dough into a ball. Divide the dough into 2 pieces, one slightly smaller than the other. Flatten into disks and wrap in plastic. Refrigerate at least 1 hour or overnight.

4 Strain rhubarb in a colander and reserve juice (you should have approximately 1 cup of juice).

5 Place ½ cup rhubarb juice into a large stockpot. Add strawberries and salt, and bring to a boil over medium-high heat. Mix cornstarch into remaining juice and add to boiling mixture. As soon as the juice has thickened and becomes clear, turn off the heat and add the rhubarb. Remove from heat and cool cooked fruit completely.

6 Preheat oven to 350°F. Allow each dough disk to sit at room temperature for approximately 10 minutes.

7 Place bigger ball of dough on a lightly floured surface (you will need a surface at least 15 inches square). With a lightly floured rolling pin, roll from the center outward into a circle roughly 14 inches in diameter. Carefully fold in half, then again to form a triangle. Place in an ungreased 9" pie plate, positioning it so the point of the triangle is in the center of the pie plate. Gently unfold.

8 Trim edges to within 1½ inches of edge and pour cooled fruit mixture into shell. Roll remaining ball of dough into slightly smaller circle as described above. Lay the rolled pastry over the filling and then roll the edges inward, pressing lightly. Seal edges of dough with your thumb, indenting at regular intervals to form a single fluted edge. Lightly brush the center of pie (not edges) with milk and sprinkle generously with sugar. With the tip of a sharp knife, cut several vents in the center of the top.

9 Place a sheet pan on oven shelf below the pie to catch any dripping juices. Bake for 45 minutes. Turn pie around in oven and continue baking until top crust is golden, about 15 minutes. Cool on a wire rack for several hours until pie reaches room temperature or is just barely warm.

Kate Christensen

Giulia Fitzgerald

Getting Started
A character or situation comes into my head and begins to expand and take on weight and dimension and color. I become increasingly curious and interested, and eventually I have to write it down to see what happens.

Like Riding a Bike? Not Quite . . .
Writing a novel does not become easier with each book. Each new book is like starting all over again.

Readers Frequently Ask
"Where do your characters come from?" is a common question. My characters very often come from potential parts of myself that I haven't ever fully explored or realized, which isn't the same thing as writing about myself. It's as if, with each new book, I get to experience glimpses of other lives I might have had.

Books That Have Influenced My Writing
Jane Eyre by Charlotte Brontë, *The House of Mirth* by Edith Wharton, and *The Horse's Mouth* by Joyce Cary. All three novels have unforgettable, complex, amazingly vivid protagonists who live on in the reader's imagination long after the closing of the books' covers. This to me is the hallmark of all the greatest novels and my highest aspiration.

Mexico City Taco Stand Chicken Tacos

Makes 4–6 servings

Adapted from caloriecount.about.com

In *Trouble*, Josie, a Manhattan therapist whose marriage has just ended, goes down to Mexico City for a five-day vacation with her best friend, Raquel, a Los Angeles rock star who has become enmeshed in a sordid tabloid scandal. Josie and Raquel, who are in their mid-forties, both feel that their lives are at some kind of crisis point. They drink tequila and feast on tacos and allow themselves to get caught up in that strange and exotic city.

Note: Wear plastic or rubber gloves while handling the chiles to protect your skin from the oil in them. Avoid direct contact with your eyes, and wash your hands thoroughly after handling.

This is a moderately spicy dish. You can use just 1 jalapeño chile if you prefer a milder sauce.

For the filling	For the garnish
3 pounds bone-in chicken breasts (3–4 breasts)	Sliced avocado
2 jalapeño chiles (see notes)	Minced red onion
2 cups finely chopped tomatoes (fresh or canned)	Chopped cilantro leaves
⅓ cup finely chopped onion	Green and red salsas
3 tablespoons minced garlic	Sour cream
3 tablespoons chopped cilantro leaves	Lime wedges
1 teaspoon salt	Pickled jalapeño chiles
1 teaspoon pepper	Thinly sliced radishes
18 corn tortillas	

1. **To make the filling:** Place the chicken breasts in a large pot and cover with at least 1½ inches of water. Bring to a boil and cook, uncovered, for 30–40 minutes. Use a large metal spoon to occasionally skim the scum that rises to the surface. Remove chicken and reserve 1½ cups of chicken broth. When chicken is cool enough to handle, shred it into bite-size pieces, discarding the skin and bones. You should have about 5 cups of shredded chicken.

2. If you have a gas range, roast the chiles over an open flame until tender and blackened on all sides. If you have an electric range, place the chiles on a broiling tray covered with foil and broil, turning occasionally, until skin is blackened and blistered on all sides. Place chiles in a small bowl, cover tightly with plastic wrap, and let sit for 5 minutes. Remove stems and peel off blackened skin.

3. Place reserved broth, chiles, tomatoes, onion, garlic, cilantro, salt, and pepper in a blender and purée for 1–3 minutes (depending on the efficiency of your blender).

4. Place shredded chicken and puréed sauce in a skillet or saucepan and simmer for 45 minutes on low heat, stirring occasionally.

5. Preheat oven to 300°F.

6. **Warm the tortillas:** Place tortillas on two baking sheets (they can overlap slightly). Spray both sides lightly with cooking spray. Bake until tortillas are soft and pliable, about 4 minutes.

7. **To assemble the tacos:** Place a few tablespoons of chicken mixture into a warm corn tortilla, and garnish with avocado, red onion, cilantro, green and red salsas, sour cream, lime wedges, pickled jalapeños, and radishes.

FRUIT FOR A LONG-DELAYED LOVE SCENE

Makes 4–6 servings

This recipe is for a dish mentioned in Chapter Ten of *The Great Man*. Teddy, the seventy-four-year-old former mistress of the "great man" (who has been dead for five years when the novel opens) cooks breakfast for her former boss, Lewis, who has been in love with her for many decades. She brings all the ingredients one hot summer morning in a basket from her house in Greenpoint, a neighborhood in North Brooklyn in New York City, to his apartment on the Upper East Side. She serves this fruit salad with a kielbasa omelet, the perfect combination to inspire the tender but spicy love scene that follows.

> 4 cups ¾-inch watermelon chunks (about 3 pounds with rind)
>
> 2 cups (1 pint) fresh blueberries, washed
>
> 2 cups perfectly ripe sliced plums (½ inch thick at curved end) (2–3 plums)
>
> ¼ cup fresh lime juice (2–3 limes)
>
> 1 teaspoon honey
>
> 3 tablespoons minced fresh mint leaves
>
> Whipped cream (optional)

1 Place the watermelon chunks, blueberries, and plums in a large bowl. Mix gently with a wooden spoon.

2 In a measuring cup, whisk together the lime juice, honey, and mint leaves. Pour the dressing over the fruit salad and toss. Serve right away or chill first. Add whipped cream if you like.

HUGO'S NEIGHBORLY VISIT SHRIMP NEWBURG

Makes 4–6 servings

Adapted from About.com: Southern Food

In *The Epicure's Lament*, Hugo, a hermit who is determined to smoke himself to death and cook as many meals as he can along the way, spontaneously cooks the following dish for his sister-in-law, Marie, and her *au pair*, Louisa, on a bucolic evening. He shows up at Marie's house one night when he knows his brother has the kids. He arrives with groceries and wine, finds the two women sitting outside in the grass, and goes inside and gets right to work in the kitchen.

Hugo uses canned shrimp, but please feel free to use fresh. He serves this Newburg on white rice with a side of buttered green beans.

My mother made this recipe for a very festive dinner party in my honor after I gave a reading near her house in Woodstock, New York. It was absolutely delicious.

Note: You may purchase cooked or uncooked shrimp for this recipe. You will need about 1½ pounds shrimp cooked in shell, or about 2 pounds uncooked in shell. To prepare uncooked shrimp: boil shrimp for 5 minutes exactly, then plunge into ice water (and peel if necessary).

¼ cup (½ stick) butter	3 tablespoons dry sherry
2½ tablespoons all-purpose flour	2 egg yolks, lightly beaten
¾ teaspoon salt	3 cups (about 1 pound) cooked and peeled
1 pinch ground cayenne pepper	large shrimp (see note)
1 dash nutmeg	Steamed white rice, for serving
1¾ cups half-and-half	

1   In a medium saucepan, melt butter on medium heat. Blend in flour, salt, cayenne pepper, and nutmeg with a wire whisk. Cook, stirring, for about 1 minute. Gradually add half-and-half and sherry; stirring constantly with the whisk to keep the sauce smooth. Cook sauce until thickened and smooth, about 5 minutes.

2   Stir about ⅓ of the hot sauce into the egg yolks, and then pour the egg yolk-sauce mixture into the remaining sauce in the saucepan. Add shrimp and heat through, stirring constantly. Serve over white rice.

Jill Ciment

- *Heroic Measures* (2009)
- *The Tattoo Artist* (2005)
- *Teeth of the Dog* (1999)
- *Half a Life* (1996)
- *The Law of Falling Bodies* (1993)

Arnold Mesches

Inspiration Lost dog and cat flyers invariably catch my attention, and I make a special effort to look out for those missing pets. I remember one such flyer—a lost gray cat—adhered to a lamppost in my old neighborhood, the East Village in New York City. The next day was 9/11 and in the aftermath, flyers for missing persons—photographs, which tower, what floor—began to share the lamppost. At first, nobody covered the lost cat poster, but eventually it was plastered over: the human tragedy consumed the animal's plight. If a novel can be reduced to a single image of conception, then the lost cat poster is responsible for *Heroic Measures.*

The novel takes place in a fraught, post 9/11 New York on panic alert. An aging couple, Alex and Ruth, must sell their East Village walk-up at the same time their beloved dachshund, the emotional center of their childless marriage, is hospitalized and fighting for her life.

The dachshund's paralysis and miraculous recovery were borrowed from my late dog Sadie, a seven-pound dachshund whose medical file weighed more than she did.

The old couple is entirely imaginary except for the collage series based on Alex and Ruth's old FBI files. The artwork was borrowed from my husband Arnold Mesches' series, *The FBI Files.*

The five-flight staircase leading up to the apartment, however, is real. Over the eighteen years I climbed it I was always aware that there were elderly all over the city, as marooned in their walk-ups as shipwrecked sailors on desert islands.

....

Third Draft's the Charm My novels generally evolve over three separate drafts; I call it the Jane Goodall writing process. I'm in a jungle during my first draft; it's hot and I'm terrified, following these beasts around just writing down everything that they do. Then, my second draft takes place back at the shack; I've taken a shower, made some tea, and considered what I witnessed in the jungle. I start to think about motivation. I basically ask, "Why did one chimpanzee hit the other chimpanzee over the head?" After that, I put the manuscript away until the story transforms itself into memory. My third draft is written as if I'm an old lady looking back at the drama, knowing the whole of my chimp's stories, from birth to death.

....

Readers Frequently Ask   How did you get into the mindset of a little dog?

I found it interesting in writing from a dog's point of view that the animal's reactions felt flat until I invented a specific dog: a hypochondriac, gourmand, twelve-year-old dachshund named Dorothy, a soul as complex and emotional as any of my human characters. In other words, I had to allow myself to be as surprised by her individual quirks as any other fictional character. Anyone who lives with a dog, as I do, comes to understand the uniqueness of their dog's spirit and nature.

....

The Author Who Has Most Influenced My Writing   Chekhov.

He is mentioned throughout *Heroic Measures* since Ruth, one of the protagonists, is reading his short stories. I chose Chekhov because he is the most humane writer I know. He does this extraordinary thing that only great fiction writers can do—he gives us access to another person's consciousness. Fiction is the only art in which you can spy on the way another person thinks. It's what I strive to do: write books that allow other people to see that the human character is tricky and selfish, but also really compassionate and highly complex.

Rainbow Room's Manhattan

Makes 1 drink

From *New York Cookbook* by Molly O'Neill (Workman, 1992)

Like me, Ruth from *Heroic Measures* may not cook or bake, but we both make a fabulous cocktail. What better drink to sip while reading about New York than a Manhattan?

1½ ounces blended whiskey
½ ounce sweet vermouth
Dash of aromatic bitters
1 maraschino cherry

Pour whiskey, vermouth, and bitters into a large mixing glass with ice cubes. Stir well. Strain into a chilled cocktail glass. Garnish with a cherry.

BLUE SKY BAKERY'S BRAN MUFFINS

Makes 18 muffins

Recipe courtesy of Blue Sky Bakery in Brooklyn, New York,
owned and managed by Erik Goetze and George Mason

Heroic Measures is set in Manhattan; my characters, Alex and Ruth, and their dachshund, Dorothy, are all quintessential New Yorkers. Like many New Yorkers, myself included, Ruth and Alex don't cook, but love to eat.

In one of the novel's pivotal scenes, Alex and Ruth stop for a quick breakfast at a Lower East Side bakery on their way to the animal hospital to visit their beloved Dorothy. I have Alex order a bran muffin because I wanted him to taste and be sated by the most earthly of flavors. "Alex yanks down his muffin's wax-paper skirt and takes a big bite. He's stunned at how good it tastes. It's as saturated with flavors as the air is with scents."

Note: Wheat bran is available at natural food stores. It is also available in supermarkets in boxes labeled Quaker Unprocessed Bran.

You can add almost any fruit to these muffins, as long as it's unsweetened and fairly dry (no citrus or pineapple). Blueberries, raspberries, apples, and bananas, or any combination of these fruits, work well. You can use either fresh or frozen berries. For apples, core, peel, and dice the fruit. For bananas, peel and dice.

2⅔ cups buttermilk

2 large eggs

⅔ cup vegetable oil

3 cups wheat bran (see note)

2 cups unbleached all-purpose flour

1 tablespoon baking powder

1 tablespoon baking soda

½ cup dark brown sugar, lightly packed

½ teaspoon salt

1½–2 cups fruit (see note)

4 teaspoons granulated sugar, divided

1   Preheat oven to 425°F. Coat 18 muffin cups (in 2 12-cup muffin tins) with butter or vegetable cooking spray.
2   Mix buttermilk, eggs, and oil in a medium bowl. In a separate large bowl, combine wheat bran, flour, baking powder, baking soda, brown sugar, and salt.
3   Pour wet mixture into dry mixture. Mix just until combined.
4   Place about 2 tablespoons of batter into each muffin cup (the batter will expand to fill about ⅓ of cup). Place a generous flat layer of fruit (about 2 heaping teaspoons) into each cup. Measure 2 teaspoons of the granulated sugar into a small bowl. Taking pinches with your fingers, sprinkle the sugar over the fruit. Divide remaining batter evenly among the muffin cups. Place remaining 2 teaspoons of sugar into bowl, and pinch and sprinkle the sugar over tops.
5   Bake for 5 minutes. Rotate muffin tins from front to back to ensure even cooking, and bake another 11–13 minutes, until test toothpick comes out clean, or with a few moist crumbs sticking to it. Do not overbake. Allow to cool on wire rack for 10 minutes, then remove muffins from tin. Serve warm.

BLUE SKY BAKERY'S
CHICKEN GARLIC DOG BISCUITS

Makes approximately 1 baking sheet of biscuits, assorted sizes

Recipe courtesy of Blue Sky Bakery in Brooklyn, New York,
owned and managed by Erik Goetze and George Mason

Alex isn't the only character in *Heroic Measures* who enjoys his food. Dorothy, the dachshund, is a gourmand as well. After her surgery, when her first bowl of dog food is set before her, she eats with relish. "The circumference of her bowl might as well be the whole globe . . . while she's eating, nothing else is real."

Note: Wheat bran is available at natural food stores. It is also available in supermarkets in boxes labeled Quaker Unprocessed Bran.

Nutritional yeast is an inactive yeast with a nutty, cheesy flavor. It is popular with vegans because of its similarity to cheese when added to food, and because it's a reliable source of protein and vitamin B12. Nutritional yeast is available at natural food stores and online.

FOR THE BISCUITS
1¼ cups unbleached all-purpose flour
1 cup whole wheat flour
⅓ cup cornmeal
⅔ cup wheat bran (see note)
1¼ teaspoons salt
1 teaspoon nutritional yeast (see note)
1 cup chicken or turkey stock, or 1 small chicken bouillon cube dissolved in 1 cup hot water

FOR THE EGG WASH
1 egg
¼ cup milk
1 tablespoon garlic powder

1   Preheat oven to 325°F. Line a baking sheet with parchment paper.
2   To make the biscuits: In a large bowl, combine both flours, cornmeal, wheat bran, salt, and yeast. Add ⅔ cup of the chicken or turkey stock (or dissolved bouillon). Mix, and continue to add stock, one or two tablespoons at a time, until the batter forms a ball with the consistency of bread dough.
3   Roll out dough to ¼-inch thickness on a lightly floured board. Use a knife or cookie cutter to cut out shapes. (Bone shapes, about 3½ inches long, work well.) Place shapes on baking sheet.
4   To make the egg wash: Whisk together the egg and milk. Stir in garlic powder. Brush egg wash on shapes.
5   Bake for 40–45 minutes until shiny and golden brown. Turn off heat, and leave baking tray in oven for 6 hours (or overnight) to allow biscuits to harden.

Chris Cleave

Niall McDiarmid

Inspiration   Real events, often communicated to me by friends who are reporters, inspire my writing. I write fiction about real themes in contemporary life. My belief is that real life is exciting and engaging, and that it is an admission of defeat to turn from it to fantasy or escapist genre. I try to go out with a reporter's eyes or, failing that, to borrow a reporter's eyes and find what I feel is the biggest story in town. Then I try to tell that story in the most unexpected way for the most adventurous readers. I like to write in the first person and to use quite intimate narration of ordinary people living through extraordinary events.

Readers Should Know   I think readers should know that I have two sides to my writing. My main work is the novels, but I have a lighter side too, which comes out on Fridays when I write a comedy column about my family for *The Guardian* newspaper. You can check it out on my website at *www.chriscleave.com.* I also write stories for my kids, just to make them laugh, and one day I might publish some of them. Writing novels is a very committed and serious undertaking, and I find that having the lighter side too helps keep me happy and sane. I also ride my bike and swim a lot, because you go mad very quickly as a writer if you don't get physical exercise every day.

Readers Frequently Ask   The question I'm asked most often is how and why, as a man, I write from the point of view of female characters. There are many ways of answering the question. Sometimes I pretend that I lived as a woman until my early twenties. Other times I try to get closer to the truth, although in all honesty what writer can ever know the reasons for the stories that come out of him? I think I have always really liked women and found them good company, and because of that I've had the kind of conversations with women that have given me things to write about. Men don't talk so easily, so they're more of a closed book to me. That isn't to say that men aren't just as interesting, or just as complex. I simply haven't worked out a way to write about men yet.

....

Avoiding Influence With the work of other writers (as with drugs and alcohol), I try never to work under the influence. Of course there are writers whose work I hugely admire. If I am to list just three books then I would choose *Great Expectations* by Charles Dickens, *Germinal* by Émile Zola, and *Treasure Island* by Robert Louis Stevenson. Dickens because he used entertaining fiction to examine uncomfortable emotional truths in the make-up of the society he lived in; Zola for the same reason, and also because of his fanatical commitment to his project; and Stevenson because he knew how to tell a yarn in such a way that one's own brain endlessly chews over the story, filling in all the details and imagining plots, subplots and backstories within his narrative.

POST-COLONIAL PIE

Makes 6 servings

A recipe by my wife Clémence Cleave-Doyard, CookingwithClem.blogspot.com

When different cultures meet, their cuisines, like their stories, join. *Little Bee* is the story of the friendship between a Nigerian girl, the eponymous Little Bee, and an English woman, Sarah. My wife, who is a chef, created this recipe to celebrate that friendship.

Fish pie is a traditional and comforting British dish. Since Britain now has a thriving and successful Nigerian community, the traditional recipe is revisited here to give it a Nigerian twist, replacing the potato with yam, using tilapia for fish, seasoning it with lots of pepper, and livening it up with a hint of chile.

Here is how Little Bee and Sarah would cook it:

Note: Wear plastic or rubber gloves while handling chiles to protect your skin from the oil in them. Avoid direct contact with your eyes and wash your hands thoroughly after handling.

---

3 cups milk

1 small onion, quartered

1 carrot, roughly chopped

1 celery stalk, roughly chopped in 4-inch chunks

1 bay leaf

1 bunch parsley

10 peppercorns

1⅓ pounds tilapia fillet (or other firm white fish such as cod or haddock)

⅓ pound smoked undyed haddock or cod fillet (if unable to find the smoked fish, you may use skinned salmon steak)

1 large yam, approximately 2 pounds

Pinch of salt

11 tablespoons butter, divided, plus extra for buttering dish and topping

Freshly ground black pepper to taste

½ cup all-purpose flour

1 fresh red or jalapeño chile, finely chopped

1 In a large shallow sauce pan combine the milk, onion, carrot, celery, bay leaf, a few parsley stalks, and the peppercorns.

2 Place the pan on low heat and add both types of fish fillets. When the milk begins to simmer, turn off the heat and leave the fish to poach gently for 2 minutes. With a slotted spoon, remove the fish from the milk. Strain the fish milk, saving the milk for the béchamel sauce. Discard the vegetables and herbs.

3 Peel the yam and cut it into even, small chunks. Place in a large pot, cover with water, add a pinch of salt and bring to a boil. Once boiling, cook for roughly 10 minutes until tender. Drain the water. Return to the pan and mash the yam adding 5½ tablespoons butter in cubes and pouring in a bit of the strained fish milk in order to get a nice textured mash. Season generously with lots of freshly ground pepper to taste. Set the mash aside.

4 Preheat the oven to 400°F. Make the béchamel sauce: In a large saucepan, on medium heat, melt the remaining 5½ tablespoons butter. Add the flour and stir well, leaving it to cook for a couple of minutes when starting to bubble. Pour in the fish milk, whisking constantly, reduce the heat and cook for 5 minutes until it thickens into a creamy sauce. Season with freshly ground pepper and a bit of salt. Roughly chop the remaining parsley. Add parsley and chile pepper to the béchamel.

5 Check for bones in the fillets and place the big chunks of fish into the béchamel, stirring them in gently so the fish doesn't break up too much.

6 Butter an ovenproof dish. Pour the fish and béchamel sauce into the dish and cover with spoonfuls of yam mash, gently spreading mash on top. Sprinkle a few cubes of butter on top. Place the dish in the oven, and cook for 20–30 minutes until it has a nice golden color and is bubbling.

Helene Cooper

SELECTED WORKS

- *The House at Sugar Beach* (2008)

Inspiration   I like to read, I like to travel, I like to eat, and I like to live. I guess all of that inspires my writing.

....

Readers Should Know   Since my book, *The House at Sugar Beach*, came out, I've switched back to newspaper writing, the antithesis of memoir writing. I'm now the White House reporter for the *New York Times*.

....

Readers Frequently Ask   The question most people ask me is how my family members are doing, particularly my sister Eunice. And to that, my answer remains the same: great.

....

Authors Who Have Influenced My Writing

- Chinua Achebe. This Nigerian writer was the first African writer I ever read. I had a Western education which didn't include African literature, so when I discovered Achebe on my own I was thrilled. He is so evocative, and an amazing storyteller, in the classic West African sense of the word, to boot. There's a lot of imagery and spirituality in his writing. Reading his books, from *Things Fall Apart* to *No Longer at Ease*, put me right in the middle of my home continent in the best way possible. I thought about him a lot when I was working on my book.
- Alexandra Fuller. I read her memoir, *Don't Let's Go to the Dogs Tonight*, while on the plane flying back to the United States from Iraq. Her writing is lyrical and her story, while completely different from my own, felt like my story at the same time. Her book was the model for my own. I kept going back to it, again and again, while I was work- ing on *The House at Sugar Beach*. I so admire her honesty, and her ability to render her family in such a stark way while at the same time leaving the reader with no question of how much she loved them, warts and all.
- Jane Austen. I know. Such a cliché. But come on, who can resist a happy ending?

My recipes are all family recipes, and the recipes I've included represent classic Liberian cooking. This is the food I grew up on.

I was posted to the *Wall Street Journal*'s London bureau the year I turned thirty, where, suddenly, I was deluged with invitations to dinner parties. There were these four to five-hour affairs that came complete with dessert wines and cheese courses; far more well-thought out than the pot of chili dinners I was used to having with my friends back in Washington.

After a few months of this, I realized that at some point, I would have to reciprocate. I was terrified—my cooking skills, at that point, veered toward spaghetti and mashed potatoes.

I was on the phone long distance with my mother, trying to come up with a menu, when she suggested I go Liberian. "I'll help you," she said. "And even if it doesn't turn out well, they won't know the difference anyway."

So, coached by my Mom, I had my first formal sit-down dinner party, in my one-bedroom apartment in Notting Hill, with eight folding chairs crowded around the rough pine table I had bought from Ikea. I had exactly eight plates, eight wineglasses, eight forks, eight knives.

About an hour before my guests were to arrive, one of them, Danny, called me to ask if he could bring a friend, who was visiting him. "I only have eight plates!" I said.

"So I'll bring a plate," he replied. Which he did (along with a chair, knife, fork, and wineglass).

I served: potato greens, Shrimp Creole, rice, fried plantains, and ripe mangoes (peeled and sliced). This last dish served as a perfect dessert after this heavy meal.

POTATO GREENS

Makes 4 servings

Note: Although this dish has greens, it's more of a substantial main dish with chicken and beef. I couldn't find sweet potato leaves in London, so I substituted spinach.

When cooking the chicken, be careful of splattering oil.

4 tablespoons olive oil

1 medium (4-pound) chicken, cut into 8 pieces

½ pound beef stew meat, cut into bite-size cubes

1 large onion, chopped

1 green bell pepper, chopped

1 habañero chile, minced

4 10-ounce bags prewashed baby or regular spinach

4 small chicken bouillon cubes

Salt to taste

Ground black pepper to taste

About 20 button mushrooms, halved

White rice, for serving

1 Heat oil in a large stockpot or saucepan over medium high heat and sauté chicken pieces, in two batches if necessary, for about 10 minutes, until browned on each side. Remove chicken from pot and set aside. Add beef, and sauté until brown, about 5–10 minutes. Remove beef and set aside.

2 Add onion, bell pepper, and chile, and sauté for 5 minutes. Add the spinach, one bag at a time, until all four bags are incorporated. Add bouillon cubes and salt and pepper to taste. Return chicken and beef to the pot. Bring to a boil, then lower heat and simmer, covered, for 30 minutes. Add mushrooms and simmer for 10 more minutes.

3 Serve over white rice.

SHRIMP CREOLE

Makes 4 servings

Note: You can buy fresh shrimp, or pick up frozen shrimp and thaw them. We leave the shell on for cooking and serving shrimp because that helps retain the flavor. It's peel and eat while on your plate, but I highly recommend first licking all the lovely Creole juice off the shrimp before peeling it.

Wear plastic or rubber gloves while handling chiles to protect your skin from the oil in them. Avoid direct contact with your eyes and wash your hands thoroughly after handling.

1 pound raw large shrimp, shell on, deveined (see note)
1 teaspoon paprika
1 teaspoon salt
½ teaspoon seasoned salt, such as Lawry's
½ teaspoon freshly ground black pepper
3 tablespoons olive oil
1 large onion
1 green bell pepper
1 habañero chile
2 cups whole okra (can use frozen)
1 cup diced carrots (can use frozen)
1 cup water or chicken broth
1 cup frozen peas
White rice, for serving

1 Season shrimp with paprika, salt, seasoned salt, and pepper, and toss to coat shrimp evenly.
2 Heat 2 tablespoons of olive oil in a large saucepan over medium-high heat, and sauté shrimp on both sides until opaque, about 5 minutes.
3 Add remaining tablespoon of olive oil, onion, bell pepper, and chile, and sauté until softened, about 5 minutes. Add okra, carrots, and water or broth. Simmer, stirring frequently, about 15 minutes. Add peas, adjust seasoning, and simmer another 10 minutes.
4 Serve over white rice.

FRIED PLANTAINS

Makes 6–12 servings

6 very ripe (almost black) plantains
Salt to taste
½ cup vegetable oil

1 Peel and slice plantains thinly (about ⅛-inch) lengthwise. Salt slices.
2 Heat oil in a sauté pan and fry plantain slices, about 2–3 minutes per side, until golden.
   Drain on paper towels and serve hot.

Barbara Delinsky

Tsar Fedorski

Inspiration

My greatest inspiration is real life, which hit me in the face with my mother's death when I was eight. The fairy tale ended for me then, but it wasn't all bad. Without a mother, I became a more self-reliant, confident person. I had faced the worst and survived.

Not all people do, so what makes some of us survivors and some not? This is the back story of each of my books. I write about family crises, subjecting my characters to upheaval and then watching them cope. Do they make it? Most do. I absolutely believe in that silver lining.

What real life occurrences have inspired books of mine? Well, 9/11 inspired *The Summer I Dared*, in which three survivors of a ferry accident have to deal with why they've been spared. The death of Grace Kelly of Monaco inspired *The Secret Between Us*, which involves a car crash and a lie that takes on a life of its own. The idea for *Not My Daughter* came from news of a high school pregnancy pact in Gloucester, Massachusetts, but my writer's mind went past the girls to their moms, and the good mother issue became the focus of my book.

Readers Should Know

Readers should know three things. First, I don't write romances. Yes, my very first books were in that genre, but I haven't written a romance in nearly twenty years. I wasn't the best romance writer; my books were too realistic. I only built a following once I left the genre.

Second, I couldn't produce a book without Post-its.

And third, I keep learning. I've had the privilege to work for the last four years with an editor who truly edits. She has taught me how to keep my prose fresh and my pacing swift. Each book is stronger, better written than the last. This means the world to me. I do believe life is about growth—both in my characters and in me.

Readers Frequently Ask The one question nearly every book group asks is whether I write from personal experience. The answer is no . . . and yes. Though I've never based a plot on my life, I often use snippets of familiar people or events. For instance, I've never lived the dramatic arc of *The Secret Between Us*, but the protagonist, Deborah Monroe, has been shaped by a perfectionist father she adores. I know about fathers like that because mine was one.

Likewise, I have neither been pregnant at seventeen nor had a child who was, as in *Not My Daughter*. But I am an avid knitter of hand-painted yarn, just like the moms in my book.

Since my publisher wants a book a year, I typically finish one and quickly start on the next. But after completing *Not My Daughter*, I was mentally drained, and absolutely beat. At that moment, the only story I wanted to write was of a woman who was so tired of being so busy that, on a whim, she just walks away. Leaves everything. Vanishes.

That's my fantasy. I'd never actually do it, but to watch a character do it would be fun. What do you think?

....

The Lone Influence on My Writing Honestly? I was never an avid reader. Nor did I ever think to be a writer. I was kicked out of Honors English in high school because I couldn't keep up. So I remember few of the books I read back then that might have influenced my writing.

Except, that is, Laura Ingalls Wilders Little House on the Prairie series. I remember reading every one as a child and being totally immersed in another life and time. Though I don't do series work myself, I try to make my characters similarly compelling so that my readers, too, will be immersed.

CRAB AND CORN CHOWDER

Makes 6 servings

Recipe courtesy of Keith Marden of Captain Marden's Seafoods
of Wellesley, Massachusetts

The protagonist in *Not My Daughter*, Lily Tate, is seventeen and pregnant. This has not gone over well with her mom, Susan, who, as a seventeen-year-old mom herself, wanted better for her child. After a long, hard struggle for education and respect, Susan is now principal of the local high school. With her own daughter pregnant, though, parents are questioning whether she is the best role model for their kids.

Lily hadn't anticipated that her mother's job would be at risk. In a gesture of conciliation on a day when Susan has worked late doing damage control, Lily makes dinner. She knows that her mom loves Crab and Corn Chowder, and though Lily doesn't eat seafood much during her pregnancy, she makes a pot.

Have I ever made Crab and Corn Chowder myself? Never had to, since Captain Marden's fish market is seven minutes from my house. We buy it by the quart, my husband and me, and make a dinner of it.

That said, I was thrilled when the Captain agreed to share his recipe. Sinfully smooth and savory, his Crab and Corn Chowder is one of the shop's biggest sellers. Come the time when I can't get there—perhaps a snowy day or one when I'm at the lake, three hours away—this recipe will be a nifty thing to have.

Note: A double boiler works best to avoid burning the chowder, but you may cook soup in a large soup pot or saucepan in place of a double boiler.

2 slices bacon, diced	*1 medium potato, steamed until tender,*
2 tablespoons margarine	*and diced in ½-inch pieces*
½ medium onion, diced	*¼ pound fresh crab meat*
¼ cup all-purpose flour	*½ tablespoon salt (or more to taste)*
2¼ tablespoons cornstarch	*½ teaspoon ground black pepper*
1 quart whole milk	*1½ teaspoons dry parsley, or parsley flakes*
2 cups light cream	*⅛ cup or more chicken stock (optional)*
1 ear corn, cooked (remove kernels and	*Hot cayenne pepper sauce (such as Frank's*
reserve cob and kernels)	*Red Hot) (optional)*

1   In a medium skillet, cook bacon over medium heat until crisp. Remove from pan and drain on paper towels. Add margarine to pan, and sauté onions in margarine and bacon fat until translucent. Remove onions with a slotted spoon and set aside.

2   Add flour and cornstarch to make a roux; stir into bacon fat and margarine slowly over low heat until mixture thickens and is bubbly.

3   If using a double boiler, fill the bottom half full of water. Bring water to a boil over medium heat. Pour milk and cream in top of the double boiler and add the corn cob. Place gently over boiling water; upper pan should not touch the water. Stir for 10 minutes over medium heat. Do not let the liquid boil.

4   Remove cob and stir in roux as needed for desired thickness. Add diced bacon, onions, corn kernels, potatoes, crab meat, salt, pepper, and parsley. Stir and heat through. Add chicken stock (to add flavor and thin chowder if desired) and/or cayenne pepper sauce for flavor.

HOT MULLED CIDER

Makes 8 servings

From *Better Homes and Gardens New Cook Book* (Meredith Corporation, 1981)

I'm a sucker for comfort food. I mean, it's not just that I like certain foods, but that they do bring comfort. When I'm feeling lousy, a fried egg on toast gives me a lift; I swear it does. On a cold, rainy night, there's nothing like Sloppy Joes to drive away the chill. And macaroni and cheese? That's comfort food any time.

What makes comfort food comfort food? In some instances, it's food from our childhood that reminds us of home. In others, it's food that is just fattening enough to be a splurge when we need to break the rules. In still others, it's food that has traditionally been associated with relaxation, celebration, or encouragement.

Hot mulled cider represents satiation and warmth. It fills us up, body and spirit, and this is exactly what the Snow family in *While My Sister Sleeps* needs in those final pages of the book.

This family has lived a nightmare. Its thirty-two-year-old daughter—the oldest of three children, an elite marathoner, and the star of the family—has had a massive heart attack and is on life support. Her powerhouse of a mom is paralyzed, her dad takes his usual backseat, and her brother is preoccupied with marital woes. Molly, the baby of the family at twenty-seven and, up to that point, very much a background person, is the only one who can speak for Robin. But the voice that comes out offers surprises, and, for that, comfort is needed.

Hence, hot mulled cider. I imagine it simmering in a pot on the stove in the kitchen at the end of the book. The smell fills the room. The Snow family has come a long way by now and is actually seeing the cloud's silver lining, but this ultimate comfort food will ensure an ongoing sense of hope. Enjoy!

FOR THE SPICE BAG
2 3-inch cinnamon sticks
1 teaspoon whole allspice
1 teaspoon whole cloves

FOR THE CIDER
8 cups apple cider
½ cup packed brown sugar
Dash ground nutmeg

FOR THE GARNISH
8 thin orange slices
8 whole cloves

1 **To make the spice bag:** Place cinnamon sticks, allspice, and cloves in a piece of cheesecloth and tie tightly. Set aside.
2 **To make the cider:** In a large saucepan combine apple cider, brown sugar, and nutmeg. Add spice bag. Bring to boil over medium-high heat. Reduce heat, cover, and simmer for 10 minutes. Remove spice bag and discard.
3 Serve cider in large mugs with a clove-studded orange slice in each.

SoMa Stickies (Sticky Buns)

Makes 20 sticky buns; 2 pull-apart loaves

Contributed by Enriqueta Villalobos, Head Baker
at the Ventana Inn & Spa, Big Sur, California

I'm a lousy cook. Well, maybe lousy is too strong a word. I am a competent cook who can perform in the kitchen when necessary. But I have no history of cooking. There have been no recipes passed down through the generations, not even a favorite recipe from my childhood. There is definitely a void in my personal history when it comes to food. That's probably why my books so often include kitchen goodies. It's compensation, sweet and simple, for what I don't have in real life.

In the case of *The Secret Between Us*, the kitchen goodies are produced in a bakery. Here's another thing about my books: they often include little pockets of sanity to which my characters and I go when we need grounding. In *The Secret Between Us*, that little pocket of sanity is Sugar-On-Main, the bakery owned by the sister of the main character. The parking outside is easy, the tables inside perfect for reading the paper or talking with a friend. And the smells? Warm, buttery, and sweet. To die for.

How to write about a bakery when I don't bake myself? Easy. All I had to do was to create a place that serves my favorite goodies. SoMa Stickies are definitely that.

SoMa stands for Sugar-On-Main, and Stickies are pecan rolls, a.k.a. sticky buns with pecans on top. I have always loved pecan rolls. Yeah, some are dry and not very sticky. But when I find a good one, I indulge. This is precisely what I do each time my husband and I vacation at the Ventana Inn in Big Sur, California. Breakfast there is strictly Continental style, but absolutely wonderful. At one end of a long table are fresh berries, hard boiled eggs, and yogurt. At the other end, along with juices, coffees, and teas, are breads, English muffins, and . . . sticky buns.

We regularly return to Ventana for the hiking, the fresh air and incredible flower smells, and, yes, the sticky buns. I have one for breakfast each morning I'm there. They aren't huge, but they're worth the trip!

FOR THE DOUGH

4 cups unbleached bread flour, divided,
  plus extra for dusting

½ cup granulated sugar

1 teaspoon salt

1 ¼-ounce package quick-rise yeast (2¼
  teaspoons)

½ cup milk

½ cup water

¼ cup (½ stick) unsalted butter, at room
  temperature

2 large eggs, at room temperature

FOR THE FILLING

¼ cup (½ stick) unsalted butter, at room
  temperature

½ cup firmly packed brown sugar

1 teaspoon ground cinnamon

⅔ cup raisins

FOR THE TOPPING

¼ cup (½ stick) unsalted butter, at room
  temperature

½ cup firmly packed brown sugar

⅔ cup coarsely chopped pecans

1 **To make the dough:** In a large bowl or the bowl of an electric stand mixer, combine 1½ cups of flour, the granulated sugar, salt, and yeast.

2 In a medium saucepan over low heat, combine the milk, water, and butter and heat to lukewarm (110°F.) Gradually beat the milk mixture into the flour mixture. Beat in the eggs, and then gradually stir in remaining 2½ cups of flour to make a soft dough that holds its shape.

3 Knead dough by hand or with a dough hook, adding additional flour as necessary. If using your hands, knead until dough is smooth and elastic, about 10 minutes. If using a dough hook, knead until dough is not sticky and pulls cleanly from the bowl sides, or 6–7 minutes.

4 Grease a large bowl with butter. Form the dough into a ball. Cover with plastic wrap and let rise in a warm place until doubled in size, 1½–1¾ hours.

5 Turn out the dough onto a lightly floured work surface. Cut dough in half. Using a rolling pin roll out each half into an 8" × 15" rectangle.

6 **To make the filling:** Spread the rectangles with the butter, dividing it equally. In a bowl, mix brown sugar, cinnamon, and raisins, and sprinkle mixture over the dough. Starting with the long side facing you, roll each dough rectangle tightly. Pinch the seams to seal. Cut each roll crosswise into 10 equal slices.

7 **To make the topping:** Grease one 9-inch round and one 8-inch square cake pan. Stir butter and brown sugar together. Add the pecans and sprinkle mixture over pan bottoms. Place 9 dough slices, cut-side down and almost touching, in the square pan. Place 11 dough slices in the round pan. Cover with a kitchen towel and let rise until doubled in size, 60–75 minutes.

8 Preheat oven to 350°F. Uncover the loaves, place in oven and bake until golden brown, about 30–35 minutes. Invert the pans onto wire racks set over aluminum foil. Remove the pans and serve.

Anita Diamant

Mark Ostow

Dancing to Write
One of the things that moves me to sit down at my computer and create is modern dance, which inspires me in powerful and joyful ways. I love being introduced to the insights of movement, rhythm, music, and sound as the imagination becomes physical. I treasure the adrenaline rush and the challenge to think anew. It reminds me of the honor it is to be a member of the species that dances.

Readers Should Know
I depend upon my writing group a lot. I cofounded a group when I started writing fiction in the mid 1990s. I had not felt the need to be a part of a group as a journalist and nonfiction writer, but the isolation of working without colleagues or a waiting editor made me long for feedback and support. The group has changed over the years and now numbers three dear friends who are trusted editors and necessary cheerleaders.

Readers Frequently Ask
"Where do you get your ideas for novels?" I can't give a generic answer because it's different every time. *The Red Tent* grew out of many sources, including *midrash,* an ancient and imaginative form of Jewish biblical interpretation, and Virginia Woolf's *A Room of One's Own. Good Harbor* was a response to the fact that so many friends were undergoing breast cancer treatment, and my love for Cape Ann (Gloucester and Rockport, Massachusetts). That was also the setting for *The Last Days of Dogtown*, which was inspired by a local pamphlet about the history of the place. The seed for *Day After Night* was planted in 2001 while visiting Atlit, the "living history" museum where Holocaust survivors were interned by the British in Palestine.

Influences on My Writing *A Room of One's Own* by Virginia Woolf. I first read it as an undergraduate and I am still inspired by Woolf's clear-eyed message that women's stories need to be told, and also by her style, conviction, and wit. M.F.K. Fisher, author of many books about food and travel, is a master of clear, clean writing and I am always refreshed by her prose. And speaking of refreshment, I find it in poetry (i.e., Mary Oliver, Yehuda Amichai, Billy Collins, Pablo Neruda) that invites me to slow down and savor the weight and texture of words.

SHAYNDEL'S APPLE KUCHEN

Make 8 generous servings

Adapted from *Pies & Tarts* by Maida Heatter (Cader Books, 1997)

There is nothing like a dessert to call up a baker, a kitchen table, and the sweetness of childhood. (Proust knew what he was doing with that madeleine.) For the young Holocaust survivors in *Day After Night*, memories of food are a visceral connection to everything they lost. And yet, biting into a delicious piece of cake among friends is also an affirmation of the senses, of community, of life.

Kuchen, or coffee cake, was popular among German bakers, Jews and Gentiles alike, from the nineteenth century on. There are dozens of varieties, from yeast-based doughs topped with fruit or cheese to quick breads and cakes. Although this version employs yeast, no rising time is required, and the result is a sweet, sticky cake full of the apples and almonds that delight Shayndel at the Rosh Hashanah feast described in *Day After Night*.

Note: This is equally good with peaches, pears, blueberries, or a combination of fruits. If you use apples or pears, they should be peeled, quartered, cored, and cut into wedges about ½-inch thick at the curved edge. If you use peaches, they should be peeled and halved, with the pits removed, and then sliced into wedges about ½-inch thick at the curved edge.

FOR THE TOPPING
½ cup chopped or slivered (julienned) blanched almonds
3 tablespoons unsalted butter
½ cup light or dark brown sugar, firmly packed
1 teaspoon ground cinnamon
¼ cup all-purpose flour

FOR THE CAKE
2 tablespoons warm water (105–115°F)
1 teaspoon plus ½ cup granulated sugar
1½ teaspoons active dry yeast
2 cups all-purpose flour
1 tablespoon baking powder
½ teaspoon salt
½ cup (1 stick) unsalted butter
2 large eggs
½ teaspoon vanilla extract
¼ teaspoon almond extract
Finely grated peel of 1 large lemon
¼ cup milk
4–6 cups peeled, cored, and sliced apples (3–4 medium apples) (see note)
¼ cup raisins (optional)

FOR THE ICING
1 cup sifted confectioners' sugar
1½ teaspoons fresh lemon juice
1 tablespoon boiling water

1 Preheat oven to 350°F. Butter a 9" × 13" × 2" cake pan and place it in the freezer (it is easier to press out a thin layer of dough if the pan is frozen.)

2 To make the topping: Place the almonds in a shallow pan in the oven and bake for about 5 minutes, until hot but not colored. Set aside to cool.

3 In an electric mixer's small bowl, beat the butter until soft. Add the brown sugar and cinnamon and combine, then add the flour and beat only until the mixture is crumbly. Stir in the cooled almonds. Set topping aside.

4 To make the cake: Place the warm water in a small bowl, and add 1 teaspoon of sugar (set aside the remaining ½ cup sugar) and the yeast. Stir briefly with a knife just to mix. Set aside.

5 Sift together the flour, baking powder, and salt and set aside.

6 In an electric mixer's large bowl, beat the butter until soft. Add the remaining ½ cup of sugar and combine. Add the yeast mixture, eggs, the vanilla and almond extracts, and the lemon peel, and combine. (It is fine if the mixture looks curdled now.) On low speed, mix in half of the sifted dry ingredients, then the milk, and finally the remaining dry ingredients. Beat until well mixed.

7 Spread half of the mixture (about 1¼ cups) into a very thin layer over the bottom of the buttered, frozen pan (a frosting spreader works well.)

8 Place the prepared apples in rows, each slice just barely touching the one before it. Or, if you wish, the amount of fruit can be increased slightly and the slices can just barely overlap. Sprinkle raisins over the fruit, if desired.

9 Using two teaspoons—one for picking up with and one for pushing off with—place small spoonfuls of the remaining cake mixture over the fruit and the bottom layer. Try to cover as much surface as possible, although it's okay if some fruit shows through. Then, with your fingers, carefully sprinkle the prepared topping to cover as much of the cake as possible.

10 Bake for 35–40 minutes until the top is nicely browned.

11 Prepare icing just a few minutes before cake comes out of oven to prevent icing from stiffening. To make the icing, combine the confectioners' sugar, lemon juice, and water in a small bowl. Use a rubber spatula to mix until icing is smooth and thick.

12 As soon as the cake is removed from the oven, use the spatula to drizzle thin lines of the icing every which way over the cake.

13 Serve warm. Cut into large squares and use a wide metal spatula to transfer the portions.

ISRAELI SALAD

Makes 3–4 servings

Adapted from *Cooking with Love* by Ruth Sirkis (R. Sirkis Publishers, 1984)

Chopped vegetables for breakfast? This takes the European characters in *Day After Night* by surprise. A staple on breakfast buffet tables in modern Israel, these vegetables offer a bright wake-up call to the palate—though the dish remains a bit of a culinary shock for many tourists to this day.

Note: Israeli pickles can be purchased online or at specialty stores. Lebanese pickles are an excellent substitute, but do not substitute traditional American pickles. Pickles bring some saltiness to the salad so, if you add them, use the lesser amount of salt.

1 carrot, peeled and shredded
2 medium tomatoes, diced
1 cucumber, peeled and diced
2 small radishes, diced
2 Israeli pickles, diced (optional) (see note)
2 scallions, minced
2 tablespoons finely chopped fresh parsley
2 tablespoons olive oil
¼ cup fresh lemon juice
½–¾ teaspoon salt (see note)
Ground black pepper to taste

Combine carrot, tomatoes, cucumber, radishes, pickles (if using), scallions, and parsley in a large salad bowl. Add olive oil, lemon juice, salt and pepper to taste and toss gently. Serve immediately.

BARLEY BREAD

Makes 3 (6- or 7-inch) loaves

From *Gourmet Magazine* (May 2006)

Yeast and ovens were not a part of the era and landscape of *The Red Tent*. Bread was flat, cooked very quickly on top of a heated surface. And yet, there might have been barley flour and there certainly was olive oil, seeds, honey, water and perhaps even salt—some of the ingredients in this earthy recipe. The rustic, homey taste of this bread goes well with olives and other simple fare. This is not a dainty loaf; rip off a hunk to sop up the leavings of goat stew—or whatever is on your menu.

Note: Barley flour and semolina flour can be found at health food stores, or online. Nigella seeds, also labeled *kalungi* or black caraway seeds or mislabeled "black onion seeds," are available at Indian and Middle Eastern grocers, or online.

You will need a large pizza stone for this recipe.

1 ¼-ounce package active dry yeast (2¼ teaspoons)

1 tablespoon mild honey

1¾ cups warm water (105-115°F)

3 cups all-purpose flour, divided, plus additional for dusting

1 cup barley flour (see note)

1 cup semolina flour (see note)

1 tablespoon nigella seeds (see note)

1½ teaspoons salt

¼ cup olive oil, divided, plus additional for dipping

3 tablespoons cornmeal

1   Combine yeast, honey, and 1 cup warm water in a small bowl, and stir gently with a fork. Let stand until foamy, about 5 minutes. (If mixture doesn't foam, discard and start over with new yeast.)

2   While yeast mixture stands, stir together 2⅓ cups all-purpose flour with barley and semolina flours, nigella seeds, and salt in a large bowl. Make a well in flour mixture and add yeast mixture, 3 tablespoons olive oil, and remaining ¾ cup water, then stir until a soft dough forms. Turn dough out onto a lightly floured surface and knead, working in just enough of remaining ⅔ cup all-purpose flour to keep dough from sticking, until dough is smooth and elastic, 6–8 minutes.

3   Put pizza stone on lowest rack of oven and preheat oven to 450°F.

4   Divide dough into 3 equal pieces and form each into a ball. Sprinkle a baking sheet with cornmeal and arrange balls of dough on it. Firmly flatten balls into 5-inch rounds (leave about 2 inches between each), then brush dough with remaining tablespoon of oil. Cover rounds loosely with plastic wrap and a kitchen towel, and let stand to rise in a warm, draft-free place for 1 hour.

5   Transfer loaves, one at a time, using a wide spatula, to pizza stone and bake until well browned and loaves sound hollow when tapped on bottoms, about 20 minutes. Transfer to a rack to cool. Serve warm, with olive oil for dipping.

Chitra Banerjee Divakaruni

Anand Divakaruni

SELECTED WORKS

- *One Amazing Thing* (2010)
- *Shadowland* (2009)
- *The Palace of Illusions* (2008)
- *The Mirror of Fire and Dreaming* (2005)
- *Sister of My Heart* (1999)
- *The Mistress of Spices* (1997)

Inspiration What I see in the world around me inspires me. For instance, *Sister of My Heart,* a story about two cousins living in a traditional family in the city of Kolkata, was inspired by an ancient mansion I saw being demolished on one of my visits back to that city. I recreated that mansion in my novel—it became the home of the cousins. *One Amazing Thing,* a novel about grace under pressure, came out of the traumatic experience of being evacuated from my home in Houston when Hurricane Rita was approaching.

My latest novel, *One Amazing Thing* is about a group of people trapped by a major earthquake, and how they manage their desperation by telling each other an amazing story from their lives. It comes out of an idea that has been important to me in much of my writing: the power of stories to affect our lives and to save us. It is unlike my other books because instead of a single protagonist, it has nine equally important characters.

I Don't Play Favorites People often ask me if I have a favorite among the books I wrote. Not really, I tell them, the books are like my children, each a labor of love in a different way. With each one I set myself a different kind of challenge. But perhaps because of that reason, I'm always a little fonder of the latest because it contains the most difficult challenge I could think of. For instance, in *One Amazing Thing,* I set myself the challenge of having the characters trapped in an office lobby with nowhere to go. I therefore had to work very hard to not let the setting get monotonous. I did this by describing in detail the many worlds of the stories being told.

Books That Have Influenced My Writing A book that greatly influenced me when I began writing was Maxine Hong Kingston's *The Woman Warrior.* Maxine also writes about the challenges of being an immigrant in America. Her book resonated with me and inspired me to try and tell the stories of my own people, immigrants from India and their children growing up in America.

Following are three recipes, each taken from a dish mentioned in one of my books, and modified to fit my lifestyle, one which requires balancing many roles. The first is an appetizer, the second a main dish, and the third a dessert. Together they constitute a well-rounded Indian vegetarian dinner.

AMAZINGLY EASY POTATO *PARATHAS* (A FAMILY RECIPE)

Makes 4–6 servings

Parathas appear in *One Amazing Thing* in the story of Jiang, a Chinese woman living in the city of Kolkata, who falls in love with an Indian man. He takes her to eat the foods he loves in clandestine cafés where they can meet without the knowledge of their families. The dough for traditional parathas has to be kneaded and rolled out, but I've substituted tortillas, which taste just as good. Sorry, Mom!

Note: You can prepare the *raita* while the potatoes are boiling. If you don't want to make the raita, these parathas taste pretty good with salsa or ketchup. That's how my children like them.

Make sure to use the red chili powder found at an Indian grocer, as it has a different flavor from typical commercial chili powders.

> 4 medium russet potatoes
> Salt to taste
> ½ teaspoon ground red chili powder (less if you prefer milder spice) (see note)
> ½ teaspoon ground cumin
> ½ teaspoon ground coriander
> 2 tablespoons chopped cilantro leaves (if you like the taste)
> 8 large flour or whole wheat tortillas
> Canola oil for frying (approximately 2 teaspoons)
> Raita (see recipe)

1. Quarter potatoes and boil until soft. Peel and mash. Add salt to taste, chili powder, cumin, coriander, and cilantro (if desired) and stir to combine.

2. Spread ¼ of the potato mixture on a tortilla. Cover with another tortilla and press down carefully so the mix spreads to the edge of the tortillas. Repeat with remaining tortillas.

3. Warm a large skillet over low heat. Add a small amount of canola oil. Place paratha in pan, drizzle top with ¼ teaspoon oil, and fry until golden brown, about 3–5 minutes. Flip and fry other side until golden brown. Cut each paratha into four pieces with a pizza cutter and serve with raita.

RAITA (YOGURT SAUCE)

Makes 2–2½ cups

1 medium cucumber
2–2½ cups plain yogurt
Salt to taste
Ground black pepper or red chili powder to taste

Peel and chop cucumber. In a medium bowl, lightly beat yogurt with salt to taste, and pepper or chili powder to taste. Fold in the cucumber. Serve on the side with the parathas.

PANCHAALI'S EGGPLANT *BHARTA*

Makes 4 servings

Panchaali, the main character in my novel *The Palace of Illusions*, is given a test by her mother-in-law soon after her marriage. She is asked to cook an eggplant (*brinjal*) without any oil or spices. Panchaali, who has been trained by a sorceress, is able to conjure up the necessary ingredients, but I've included a list of spices for those of us who might lack such special skills.

Note: Garam masala is a ground mix of spices such as cumin, coriander, black pepper, cinnamon, cardamom, and clove and can be purchased at an Indian grocery.

Wear plastic or rubber gloves while handling chiles to protect your skin from the oil in them. Avoid direct contact with your eyes and wash your hands thoroughly after handling.

1 large eggplant

Approximately ½ teaspoon salt

3 tablespoons canola oil

1 onion, chopped

4 garlic cloves, chopped

1 ½-inch piece fresh gingerroot, peeled and chopped

1 teaspoon chopped serrano or jalapeño chile (less if you don't want it spicy; more if you want an added zing) (see note)

1 teaspoon ground coriander

1 teaspoon ground cumin

1 teaspoon garam masala (see note)

2 large tomatoes, chopped

Hot rice or roti (rolled bread similar to tortillas), for serving

1 Chop eggplant into 1-inch cubes. Sprinkle with salt and toss. Set aside for 10 minutes.
2 In a skillet, heat oil over medium heat. Add onion, garlic, ginger, chile, coriander, cumin and garam masala, and sauté until the onions are golden brown, about 10 minutes. Add tomatoes, and sauté until well-cooked, about 5–10 minutes.
3 Add the cubed eggplant. Cover pan and simmer until eggplant is fully cooked, 10–20 minutes. As the eggplant softens, remove cover, turn heat to low and cook until any liquid dries up (it should not be watery when finished). Mash the entire mix together (it should be fairly thick).
4 Serve with hot rice or roti.

A *Sister Of My Heart* Special: *Payesh* (Bengali Rice Pudding)

Makes 4–6 servings

When Anju and Sudha, the cousins who are the protagonists in my novel *Sister of My Heart*, are little girls, their aunt, Pishi, cooks several special desserts for them. This one, payesh, is very traditional in Bengal, the part of India where I come from and where *Sister of My Heart* is set. It is also a dish that my mother was famous for. But whereas hers used to take a half-day to make, I've given you a shortcut recipe.

Note: The payesh consistency should be fairly thick, and it may take a little longer than indicated to achieve this thickness. Keep in mind that the payesh also thickens as it cools. The almonds in the payesh give it a crunchy texture.

3 cups half-and-half (nonfat or whole)
1 cup whole milk
¾ cup basmati rice, washed
1 2–2½ inch stick cinnamon
¾–1 cup granulated sugar or brown sugar, according to your taste
½ cup raisins
½ cup blanched almonds
Rose petals (if desired)

1   In a heavy bottomed pot, bring half-and-half and milk to a boil over high heat.
2   Add rice and cinnamon stick. Reduce heat to medium-low and cook, stirring often to prevent sticking, until rice is soft and milk thickened, 20–30 minutes.
3   Add sugar, raisins, and almonds. Cook on low heat another 15–20 minutes until the mixture is thick (see note). Remove cinnamon stick.
4   Payesh can be eaten warm or chilled. Sometimes we sprinkle rose petals on the chilled version just before serving. If refrigerated, it keeps for 5–6 days.

Heidi Durrow

Timothi Jane Graham

Inspiration I was inspired to write *The Girl Who Fell From the Sky* by a newspaper article I read around fifteen years ago about a girl who survived a terrible accident that killed her family. I became obsessed with the girl: what would her survival look like? How would she grow up with her grief? *The Girl Who Fell From the Sky* was my attempt to give that girl a voice and a future.

Readers Should Know Nothing inspires me to write more than my morning coffee, which I drink with a bendy straw. I write first thing in the morning in longhand in my Moleskine journal. It's raw, wild writing; no rules or forms. It's the only time I'm not afraid of the blank page.

Readers Frequently Ask People often ask me whether the story of Rachel, my young, biracial, and bicultural character in *The Girl Who Fell From the Sky*, is autobiographical. And the answer is yes and no. What happens to Rachel did not happen to me, but the emotional center of her struggle is something that I can relate to.

Poetic Influence I have a lot of favorite writers, but I turn to poetry when I am looking for inspiration. It helps attune me to language in a different way. Some of my favorites are William Stafford, Audre Lorde, Mary Oliver, Sharon Olds, and Shakespeare's sonnets.

HEIDI'S MORNING FRANSKBRØD (WHITE BREAD)

Makes 1 loaf

The Girl Who Fell From the Sky is the story of Rachel, a young biracial/bicultural girl who survives a tragedy in which her family dies. Rachel is half-black and half-Danish and ends up living with her strict African-American grandmother in Portland, Oregon. In the early chapters, Rachel is struck by the fact that the bread she loves—the bread that her mother used to make—isn't anywhere to be found in her new community. Wonder Bread bought from the Wonder Bread Factory is the staple in her new neighborhood. Like Rachel, I missed hearty Danish breads when we moved to the United States from overseas. This recipe is my mother's homemade bread, and it takes me "home" every time I make it.

My favorite way to eat this bread is with a little butter, a slice of Danish Havarti cheese with caraway seeds, and a good cup of coffee. This is possibly my favorite meal of all time. Also, try it with a good jam or the Danish way with butter and a dark chocolate wafer. This is something I've only ever seen in Denmark, so I buy a few packs of wafers each time I get back.

Note: This bread can be hand stirred; just use clean hands as a tool. Brush the dough with egg for a shiny crust or coffee for a deep golden brown crust.

1⅓ cups warm water (105–115°F.)
1 ¼-ounce packet active dry yeast
½ teaspoon sugar
3½ cups all-purpose flour, plus additional as needed
¾ teaspoon salt
Vegetable oil, for greasing bowl
1 lightly beaten egg, or 1 tablespoon egg substitute or cold coffee (see note)

1 Measure water, yeast, sugar, flour, and salt into large bowl of electric mixer fitted with the paddle attachment. Start mixing at low setting; when all dry ingredients are moist increase speed to medium high. Mix until well combined, about 1 minute. Switch to dough hook and mix at low speed for 10 minutes. Dough should form a smooth lump. If dough is sticky, add additional flour, 1 tablespoon at a time, until dough no longer sticks to bottom or sides of bowl.

2 Turn dough onto lightly floured work surface, and knead for about 1 minute.

3 Lightly grease a medium bowl with oil. Place dough in bowl, and turn over to coat the top. Cover bowl with moist dish towel or plastic wrap sprayed on the inside with cooking spray or rubbed with oil. Put in warm place and let dough rise until double in size, 25–30 minutes.

4 Preheat oven to 425°F. Lightly coat a 9" × 5" × 3" loaf pan with cooking spray or oil.

5 Turn dough onto lightly floured work surface, and punch dough down to original size. Knead lightly and shape into a 9-inch long roll.

6 Place in loaf pan. Cover pan with dish towel and allow dough to double in size, 25–30 minutes.

7 Brush with lightly beaten egg, egg substitute, or coffee (see note). Poke several times with fork, or slice 5–7 slits in top (no deeper than ¼ inch). Place in oven and bake 40–45 minutes. Bread is ready when golden brown, and a light tap on crust gives a knocking sound.

8 Tip loaf onto cooling rack. Wait 10–15 minutes before slicing with a very sharp bread knife. Serve and enjoy your favorite way.

MOR'S *PANEKAGER* (CREPES)

Makes about 12 crepes

In *The Girl Who Fell From the Sky*, the big special "breakfast" that Aunt Loretta makes for Rachel when she comes to live in Portland, Oregon, is pancakes, the big fluffy kind. "There is something dangerous about pancakes," Rachel says when she notices her grandmother watching her eat. I grew up on Danish style pancakes (or panekager). Later in life, I learned that Danish pancakes—served with applesauce and sugar in my house—were called crepes in the United States. I simply call them delicious!

Our favorite way to serve these is to slather applesauce on them (each person does their own) and either sprinkle sugar on before rolling them up, or dip the rolled crepe into sugar and then applesauce. My mother makes the applesauce from scratch generally, and she also sometimes will serve them with other jams if there's a feeling for adventure in the room! We also like savory fillings such as Chicken à la King, broccoli and cheese, seafood, and cottage cheese garnished with tomatoes and cucumber slices.

Note: My mom's favorite pan for these crepes is a 10-inch cast iron pan, but she also uses a nonstick at times. The crepes should be thin, similar to French crepes, so pour just enough batter into the pan to cover the bottom. Mor sometimes uses a gravy spoon to scoop the batter, and that's just about the right size.

FOR THE CREPES
1 cup milk (skim or 2%)
1¼ cups all-purpose flour
5 large eggs
½ teaspoon ground cardamom or
  1 teaspoon vanilla extract
2 tablespoons sugar
½ cup (1 stick) margarine or unsalted
  butter, melted and cooled slightly

FILLINGS (OPTIONAL)
Applesauce
Sugar
Strawberries and whipped topping
Blueberries and whipped topping
Chunky applesauce with cinnamon
Favorite jam or jelly

1 In a large bowl, mix the milk, flour, eggs, cardamom or vanilla, and sugar vigorously by hand or with an electric mixer. Slowly stir in melted margarine or butter.
2 Heat an ungreased 10-inch crepe pan or cast iron skillet over medium heat. It's hot enough when a few drops of water sprinkled onto pan disappear in a rapid dance.
3 Pour about ¼ cup of batter in the center of sizzling pan (see note). Immediately swirl pan until the entire surface is covered. Tiny bubbles will appear on top of the "almost-ready-to-be-turned-over" crepe. Another sign is that edge gets slightly curly. (If ridges form on batter while cooking, reduce heat slightly.) Flip crepe over with a spatula. Use common sense in cooking time on the other side. It is very brief, about 1 minute.
4 Serve with desired fillings.

PECAN PIE À LA DANE

Makes 1 (9-inch) pie; 8 servings

Because my mom, like my character Rachel's mom, is Danish, her signature dishes are all made from Danish recipes. But my mom also worked hard to incorporate some American foods into her repertoire. Pecan pie became one of her specialties even though it would seem quintessentially Southern and not at all Danish. This recipe is perfection and even the very Southern Grandma Doris character in *The Girl Who Fell from the Sky* would agree.

I am a pecan pie purist. I like vanilla ice cream beside the pie on the plate, and maybe I will wet a bite or two of the pie with the melty part of the ice cream. My mom likes ice cream on the pie.

FOR THE CRUST
1¼ cups all-purpose flour
½ cup solid vegetable shortening, chilled
1 large egg yolk
1 teaspoon white vinegar
2 tablespoons ice water, or more as needed

FOR THE FILLING
⅓ cup packed light brown sugar
⅓ cup granulated sugar
⅔ cup light corn syrup
3 large eggs
⅓ cup (5⅓ tablespoons) margarine or butter, melted
1⅓ cups pecan halves
Vanilla ice cream, for serving (optional)

1. **To make the dough by hand:** Place flour in a mixing bowl. Add shortening in small amounts. Use a pastry cutter or your fingertips to crumble flour and shortening together until mixture reaches the consistency of grated cheese. In a separate bowl, combine the egg yolk, vinegar, and water. Pour into flour mixture. Stir lightly with a fork just until dough forms a ball. Do not overmix or pound dough. If dough is not coming together, sprinkle on additional ice water, 1–2 teaspoons at a time. **To make the dough in a food processor:** Pulse the flour and shortening until the mixture resembles coarse crumbs. Add the egg yolk, vinegar, and ice water, and pulse again until dough begins to mass together. Add extra water, 1–2 teaspoons at a time, if the dough seems crumbly or dry.
2. Shape dough into a flat disk, wrap in plastic or wax paper, and refrigerate for 20–30 minutes.
3. Preheat oven to 350°F.
4. **To roll the dough:** Place dough on lightly floured surface. With a lightly floured rolling pin, roll from the center outward into a circle roughly 13 inches in diameter. Carefully fold in half, then again to form a triangle. Place in an ungreased 9" pie plate, positioning it so the point of the triangle is in the center of the pie plate. Gently unfold.
5. Trim dough to within ½ inch of edge of plate. Roll edges of dough inward, pressing lightly. To decorate, press the tines of a fork firmly into the dough rim, repeating around entire edge.
6. **To make the filling:** Combine the sugars, corn syrup, eggs, and margarine or butter in a food processor, or beat vigorously by hand.
7. Pour pecan halves into the unbaked pie shell. Pour filling mixture over pecans. Bake for 65–70 minutes, until edge of crust is golden brown. Filling will not be set, but will do so as it cools off.
8. Serve lukewarm or cold as desired. Filling will become firmer after refrigeration. Serve with vanilla ice cream if you wish (see note). Pie also freezes well for later use.

David Ebershoff

Edith Sanchez

Inspiration   Several years ago I was talking to a professor of nineteenth-century women's history. In this conversation she mentioned someone called the nineteenth wife. I said, The nineteenth what? Who was this nineteenth wife? And what kind of life did she lead? These are the questions that started me on the long, long process of writing *The 19ᵗʰ Wife*.

....

Readers Should Know   If you're a dog person, you'll understand this. If you're not, you'll find this corny, so forgive me. My dog, Elektra, helps me write. She's ten now, and for the last decade she's always been at my feet as I've written my books. She's so present in my writing process that she worked her way into my last novel. One of the characters in *The 19ᵗʰ Wife* has a dog named Elektra who is shamelessly based on the real Elektra. To my great delight, Elektra now has fans.

....

Readers Frequently Ask

Q: What are you working on next?

A: Unfortunately my answer is a little lame because I don't like to talk about a book while I'm writing it. I can tell you it's a new novel set in the recent past about a family you might have heard of.

....

Influences on My Writing

- The Brontë sisters because they revolutionized the novel and wrote books that captivated my imagination when I was young, precisely when I needed books to take me away.
- E.M. Forster because his novels are both serious and ironic, often simultaneously, and because he bravely wrote gay men into literature.
- Leo Tolstoy because everything a novelist needs to know can be found in his work.

PEACHES À LA ANN ELIZA

Makes 3-4 servings

Pioneers learned to make do with what they had in nineteenth-century Utah. The high desert climate was harsh (hot in summer, frigid in winter) and the natural vegetation was scant. When I was researching *The 19th Wife*, I encountered many mentions of peaches in women's letters and diaries. The abundant sunshine and dry air were ideal for fruit and nut orchards, and many pioneer women had at least one or two peach trees on their property. These women proved ingenious at using all of a tree's fruit, never letting a peach go to waste. Of course, they made peach pies, jams, and preserves, but they also made peach sauce, which was used as a sauce or added to other recipes as a sweetener. I found a number of references to "peach leather," a peach jerky made by drying peach strips in the sun. That technique isn't practical in New York City, but after I read an article about grilled desserts in *Men's Health* magazine, I figured grilling peaches was the next best thing.

Note: This recipe works best late in summer when peaches are at their sweetest. Soft, ripe peaches work best because their juices release more quickly and caramelize better. I leave the pit in, but you don't have to. In winter, when good peaches are scarce and the grill sits under a heap of snow, you can broil canned peaches in your oven.

A good summer peach should be sweet enough to serve by itself, but some people like their grilled peaches drizzled with maple syrup.

For a more substantial dessert, serve with Greek yogurt or vanilla ice cream.

FOR GRILLED FRESH PEACHES
Ripe peaches (1 per person)
Vegetable cooking spray for the grill

FOR BROILED PEACHES
1 15-ounce can sliced peaches, or 1
*   16-ounce bag frozen sliced peaches,*
*   thawed*
Olive oil, for greasing the broiler pan
Salt for sprinkling

FOR THE TOPPINGS
Maple syrup, for serving (optional)
Greek yogurt or vanilla ice cream, for serv-
*   ing (optional)*

FOR THE GARNISH (OPTIONAL)
Dried cranberries
Raisins
Walnuts

1. **To make grilled peaches:** Wash and dry the peaches, and cut them in half.
2. Coat the grill with vegetable cooking spray and preheat for 10–15 minutes at medium-high heat. If you're grilling the peaches after grilling your main course, scrape the grill of any clinging meat or fish. You shouldn't need to re-spray.
3. Grill the peach halves for about 5 minutes, face down. You want the peaches to become soft and the juice to bubble. Blackened edges and grill marks are a good sign of when to turn them.
4. Turn the peaches over and grill for about 3 minutes, or until the peach skin has blackened in places.
5. If desired, drizzle with maple syrup, serve with Greek yogurt or vanilla ice cream, and garnish with dried cranberries, raisins, or walnuts.

1. **To make broiled peaches:** Set your broiler to high. Rinse canned sliced peaches, or thawed frozen peaches in a colander under cold water, and drain. If using canned peaches, you want to remove as much of the sugar water as possible.
2. Grease the bottom of a broiling pan with olive oil. Pour the peaches into the pan and lightly salt. Broil the peaches for 5–6 minutes, or until the edges and points are blackened. Turn the peaches and broil for 2–3 minutes, or until blackened to your liking.
3. If desired, drizzle with maple syrup, serve with Greek yogurt or vanilla ice cream, and garnish with dried cranberries, raisins, or walnuts.

KNIPLINGSKAGER
(DANISH LACE COOKIES)

Makes 3 dozen cookies

From *The Great Scandinavian Baking Book* by Beatrice Ojakangas (Little Brown, 1988)

Several years ago I was in Copenhagen researching my first novel, *The Danish Girl*. That makes it sound like a more organized and systematic trip than it actually was. I had heard about the remarkable Lili Elbe—a woman all but forgotten to history—and I went to Denmark on a hunch that there was a story to be found. Every day I went around the city, looking for signs of her life—at the Royal Academy of Arts, in the rolls of microfiche at the library—and then, in the afternoon, I'd go back to my little hotel room near the train station and write down what I had seen and learned. On the way, I'd stop at a bakery for a cup of coffee and a few Danish cookies to revive my mind for an evening of work. I've always liked cookies that aren't especially sweet. Something about the flour or, in this case, the oats, I find more satisfying than chips of chocolate or ginger or M&Ms. In any case, I'd buy a few cookies and think about the character I was trying to recover from history's blank memory. Standing at the bar in the bakery window, I'd nibble on the little cookies and sip my coffee and watch the pedestrians pass by on the street. A man walking a little white dog; a woman with a woven basket over her arm; a girl in a summer dress standing on the pedals of her red bicycle. It was in these moments that I began to find the heart of my novel, that I began to discover the heart of this Danish girl. The book would be about many things, but during those afternoons, alert with coffee and cookies, I came to realize that above all it would be about love.

Note: Try to make the cookies on a dry day. On a humid day, the cookies will absorb too much moisture and be chewy instead of crispy.

½ cup (1 stick) butter, melted
1½ cups old-fashioned rolled oats
¼ teaspoon ground ginger
1 large egg
⅔ cup sugar
1 teaspoons baking powder
1 tablespoon all-purpose flour

1 Grease two baking sheets and line with parchment paper. Preheat oven to 350°F.

2 Place melted butter in a small bowl. Stir in rolled oats and ginger.

3 In a large mixing bowl, beat the egg with sugar, by hand or with a mixer, until foamy.

4 In a small bowl, stir together the baking powder and flour, and then stir into oatmeal mixture along with the egg mixture. Drop by generous teaspoonfuls onto baking sheet, leaving 2–3 inches between cookies.

5 Bake for 8–10 minutes or until golden. Remove from oven, cool for 1 minute, and gently remove from sheet with a spatula. Store in an airtight container.

Jamie Ford

Inspiration   History. I love doing the research for my books—digging in the past, sifting through forgotten or discarded moments that meant so much to the people who lived through those times—and bringing those moments to life, connecting them to today.

Readers Should Know   I try to write with all five senses in mind so naturally food plays an important role in my fiction—from the descriptions of dim sum in my first novel to a formal Japanese tea ceremony in my new book. It's no wonder I'm always hungry after a day of writing.

Readers Frequently Ask   Book groups always ask about the Panama Hotel from my novel *Hotel on the Corner of Bitter and Sweet.* Yes, it's a very real place. And yes it's still there. In fact, they have a lovely tearoom that's become a popular venue for book clubs to meet.

Authors Who Have Influenced My Writing

- Harlan Ellison. He's known for science fiction (or speculative fiction), but his essays are where his true brilliance lies. They're honest, irreverent, caustic, and delicious.
- Sherman Alexie. A powerful and subtle writer whose poetic language never gets in the way or distracts from the story.
- Nikki Giovanni. An amazing poet who reminds us that the work of our hearts is at least as equal to the work of our hands.

HENRY'S FAVORITE *HUM BAO* (CANTONESE BARBEQUE PORK BUNS)

Makes 22 buns

Food is everywhere in my debut novel, *Hotel on the Corner of Bitter and Sweet*. I don't know if that's because I was always hungry while writing it, or because Chinese food is such an important cultural ingredient that it's impossible to leave out. It's probably a little of both, honestly.

In one particular scene, Henry and his son Marty go out for dim sum—an early lunch of steamed and baked dumplings, egg tarts, and chicken feet. After lunch, Henry sends his son off with a to-go box of a dozen hum bao—one of my personal favorites and something my own grandparents did for me on many occasions.

Basically, there are two major kinds of hum bao: steamed or baked. Both are made with the same pillowy dough and succulent pork filling. Eileen Yin-Fei Lo's *The Dim Sum Dumpling Book* has a fantastic multi-day recipe if you want to go all out, but here's a short-cut version if you're in a hurry.

Note: The dough is where I cheat. (Sorry Grandma!) Instead of making dough from scratch, I used Rhodes Bake-N-Serv White Dinner Rolls, found in the freezer section. (Do not use Pillsbury Dinner Rolls or other rolls that are found in the refrigerated section because the consistency differs from that of the frozen rolls.) Thawing the dough and allowing it to rise will take several hours.

Chinese five-spice powder is available in the spice aisle of most grocery stores.

You can use ground pork in place of minced pork loin. Be sure to purchase pure ground pork and not seasoned sausage. These buns are also delicious made with beef. Substitute 1 pound of ground beef for the pork loin.

FOR THE DOUGH
22 Bake-N-Serv rolls (see note)

FOR THE FILLING
½ small onion
1 pound pork loin (see note)
1 tablespoon vegetable oil
2 tablespoons whiskey

1½ tablespoons soy sauce
1½ tablespoons honey
1½ tablespoons oyster flavored sauce
2 tablespoons hoisin sauce
½ teaspoon Chinese five-spice powder
  (see note)
½ teaspoon salt
Dash of pepper

1 Thaw rolls and allow dough to rise, following the thawing and rising instructions on the package. Cut 22 2-inch squares of wax paper, and set aside.

2 To make the filling: Mince onion. If using pork loin, trim fat from pork and then mince pork (see note).

3 Heat oil in a wok or sauté pan on high heat. Add onions, reduce heat to medium, and cook until onions turn brown, about 3 minutes. Add pork and stir-fry until brown, about 5 minutes. Reduce heat to low and add the whiskey. Cook for 1 minute, then add the soy sauce, honey, oyster flavored sauce, hoisin sauce, five-spice powder, salt, and pepper. Remove from heat and let cool to room temperature.

4 To make the bao: Place a dough ball on a flat surface. Press the dough by hand into a disk about 4 inches across. (If your hands stick to the dough, place a sheet of wax paper on top before flattening.) Place a tablespoon of filling in the center of the dough. Pinch two sides shut, then the opposite two sides. Pull the open corners together and pinch to seal. Place the bao sealed side down on a 2-inch square of wax paper. Repeat until all dough balls are prepared.

5 Let rest in a warm spot for about an hour to allow the dough to rise.

6 Transfer several buns with wax paper to a steamer, spacing them so they are not crowded. Steam over lightly boiling water 15–20 minutes. Repeat until all buns are cooked. Peel wax paper before eating.

7 For baked bao, brush each bao with a beaten egg after they've risen, and bake at 350°F. for 15–20 minutes, until the tops are golden brown. Enjoy!

Lisa Genova

Christopher Seufert

Inspiration

Life! I only have about fifteen hours a week to write (and often less as minutes here and hours there are siphoned off to my kids, *Still Alice* promotion, and Alzheimer's speaking events), so that leaves lots of time for living. I believe that a fully lived life is a blessing for the author and the best inspiration for writing that is fully alive.

Getting Unstuck

I read and reread books that keep me psychologically "on path" when I write. I read books like *The Artist's Way* by Julia Cameron, *Fearless Creating* by Eric Maisel, *Bird by Bird: Some Instructions on Writing and Life* by Anne Lamott, *Writing Down the Bones: Freeing the Writer Within* by Natalie Goldberg, *Wild Mind: Living the Writer's Life* by Natalie Goldberg, and *On Writing* by Stephen King. And if I'm feeling stuck, I get out a notebook and write a couple of pages of unedited stream of consciousness. That usually works to break things open. Get the pen moving, and sometimes some great pieces of wisdom come out. One day recently, stuck and somewhat terrified about writing *Left Neglected*, I scribbled this:

> *Lisa, write your book. Let it come through you, however imperfectly. Don't judge it yet. Just get it down. Believe in this story. Have faith that it will come through you. Write it down. Don't be afraid. Don't think about all 300 pages. Think only about the next scene, the next five pages. Don't make it hard. Enjoy it! Be brave and write the next scene.*

Readers Frequently Ask

The question I receive most from readers about *Still Alice* really isn't so much a question, but rather a comment that then sparks many heated questions and comments. The comment has been made in many ways, but the gist of it is, "I'm still really mad at John," and then the conversation really gets going. Was he too selfish? Did he make the right decision? Did he make a fair decision? Did he and Alice have a good marriage? Did he truly love her? What would you have done? I always tell readers to remember that, like all of us, John is flawed. But I have great empathy for John, and I understand his love for Alice, his denial, his suffering as a caregiver, and his rational if flawed decision.

··

Authors Who Have Influenced My Writing

- Oliver Sacks. In fact, *The Man Who Mistook His Wife For a Hat* was really the spark that ignited my interest in neuroscience to begin with. He has said, "In examining disease, we gain wisdom about anatomy and physiology and biology. In examining the person with disease, we gain wisdom about life." That's what I hope to accomplish with my writing.
- Brunonia Barry. She originally self-published her riveting novel, *The Lace Reader*, and then went on to obtain a huge book deal with William Morrow. *Still Alice* was self-published when I heard about her book deal, and so she gave me a concrete example of success. Her achievement fueled my perseverance and gave me the courage to dream big.
- Julia Fox Garrison. I love her memoir, *Don't Leave Me This Way*. Her writing is honest and deeply moving. Her words can make me laugh out loud on one page and go looking for Kleenex on the next.

ALICE'S WHITE CHOCOLATE
CHALLAH PUDDING

Makes 6 servings

From *The Figs Table: More Than 100 Recipes for Pizzas, Pastas, Salads, and Desserts* by Todd English and Sally Sampson (Simon & Schuster, 1998)

This is the dessert in *Still Alice* that the title character forgot how to make on Christmas Eve. I chose this particular recipe for a couple of reasons. The first is that my friend Judy and I have been obsessed with this dessert from Todd English's Figs restaurant for years. It's rich, smooth, and luscious. I don't care for white chocolate, and I'm not crazy for bread pudding, but somehow the combination is divine!

I also selected it because of my own experience with forgetting. It's an easy recipe to make and an easy one to memorize, especially if you make it often. But every time I make this pudding, I get hung up on the number of eggs. *Seven? Eight? Nine? How many are yolk only? Hold on, let me check.* And I have to look it up.

Throughout *Still Alice*, I tried to illustrate the difference between normal forgetting and forgetting due to Alzheimer's. When is forgetting a name, a word, an appointment, or a recipe normal, and when is it not? I realize this can be a scary and troubling question to pose, but I promise there is nothing scary or troubling about this dessert. Enjoy!

7 large egg yolks
2 large eggs
2 teaspoons vanilla extract
3 cups heavy cream
1 cup milk
½ cup sugar
10 ounces white chocolate (about 2 cups chopped)
4 cups challah cubes, approximately 1½ inches square (about 1 loaf, crusts removed)

1 Preheat oven to 350°F.
2 Place the egg yolks, eggs, and vanilla in a small bowl and mix to combine. Set aside.
3 Place the cream, milk, and sugar in a 2-quart saucepan over medium-high heat and cook until scalded (when bubbles begin to form around the edges and it begins to steam, but has not quite come to a boil), about 7 minutes. Add the white chocolate and mix until fully melted. Gradually add the egg mixture in a slow, steady stream, whisking continuously.
4 Place the bread cubes in an 8" × 8" × 2" pan. Slowly pour the egg-cream mixture over the bread cubes. (If cubes bob to the top, pour more slowly to allow time for the mixture to soak into the bread.) Use your hands or the back of a spoon to press the cubes down and let rest for 15 minutes, or until mixture is entirely absorbed.
5 Cover with aluminum foil and place in a larger pan filled halfway with very hot water. Transfer to the oven and bake until firm and the custard does not show up on your finger when you touch the middle, about 1 hour and 15 minutes. After 30 minutes, check on the water level, and replenish water if necessary to keep the level at the halfway point. Serve warm with fresh berries, caramel sauce, or raspberry sauce (see recipe).

RASPBERRY SAUCE

Makes 1 cup

From *The Figs Table: More Than 100 Recipes for Pizzas, Pastas, Salads, and Desserts* by Todd English and Sally Sampson (Simon & Schuster, 1998)

4 cups fresh or frozen raspberries, thawed
2 teaspoons fresh lemon juice
6 tablespoons sugar

1 Purée the raspberries, lemon juice, and sugar in a blender and process until smooth. Pour the mixture into a strainer and press the solids through to strain the liquid. Discard the solids.
2 Add water to thin sauce if necessary. Serve immediately, or cover and refrigerate up to one week.

NANA'S CREAM PUFFS

Makes 24 cream puffs

Still Alice was inspired by my grandmother, Angelina Genova, who was diagnosed with Alzheimer's Disease when she was eighty-five. Although she lost her history and couldn't understand who we were or why we were there (she told people her daughter Mary was a homeless woman who'd wandered in to live with her), there were parts of my grandmother that never left her. As she always had, she loved lively company. We're a loud, Italian family. She delighted in having us there, sitting around her kitchen table, eating, laughing to tears, telling stories. And she remained good-natured and good-humored, willing to participate. Here's one of my favorite exchanges:

Aunt Mary: Come on, Ma, we're going to the movies.

Nana: Okay, I don't know who you are, but I'm coming!

The reasons why her family loved her, the reasons why we are connected, disappeared for her, but they didn't for us. We continued to love her, and she accepted it. She understood our hugs and kisses and smiles and returned them with great enthusiasm. I know she felt included and loved until the moment she died.

My grandmother made the best cream puffs. In fact, she won $25 from *Parade Magazine* in 1969 for her recipe. Someone in my family makes her cream puffs for every holiday, and we still fight over who gets the last one.

Note: These will keep if made in the morning and served later in the day, but they become soggy after a day or two in the fridge.

One stick of butter may be substituted for the shortening.

If you're pressed for time, you can make a quick version of the filling. Cook 1 box of vanilla pudding (not instant; with whole milk), and let cool in the refrigerator. Add 1 teaspoon of vanilla to 1 cup of heavy cream, and beat until thick. Fold cream into pudding. Done!

FOR THE PUFFS

1 cup all-purpose flour

¼ teaspoon salt

½ cup butter flavor solid vegetable shortening (see note)

1 cup water

4 large eggs, at room temperature

FOR THE CUSTARD FILLING

½ cup granulated sugar

5½ tablespoons cake flour

½ teaspoon salt

2 cups whole milk

2 large eggs, at room temperature

1 teaspoon vanilla extract

1 cup heavy cream

Confectioners' sugar, for sprinkling (optional)

1 Preheat oven to 425°F. Line two baking sheets with parchment paper.

2 **To make the puffs:** Combine flour and salt in a small bowl. Place shortening and water in a medium saucepan, and bring to a boil. Add flour mixture all at once and stir vigorously until mixture balls up and becomes quite dry. Remove from heat.

3 Transfer mixture to medium bowl of electric mixer. Add eggs one at a time and beat at high speed until mixture becomes a smooth paste.

4 Drop batter by tablespoonful on baking sheets, placing 2 inches apart. Bake for 15 minutes, then reduce heat to 375°F and bake for an additional 15 minutes. Do not open the oven during cooking, except during final minutes if needed to check on puffs. Puffs are done when they are well browned, and moisture can no longer be seen on the tops. Transfer puffs to wire rack to cool.

5 **To make the custard filling:** Sift together sugar, cake flour, and salt. In medium saucepan, heat milk over medium heat. Whisk flour mixture into warm milk and heat, stirring, until thick and bubbly, about 3 minutes. Remove from heat.

6 In a separate medium bowl of an electric mixer, beat eggs until frothy. Add milk mixture to eggs, and mix well. Return mixture to saucepan and cook over medium heat for 3 minutes.

7 Remove from heat and transfer mixture to clean bowl. Whisk in vanilla. Rub butter on piece of plastic wrap and place wrap butter side down on top of the custard (to prevent a skin from forming). Chill thoroughly in refrigerator.

8 In separate bowl of an electric mixer fitted with a whisk attachment, beat cream on high speed until thick. Fold whipped cream into custard.

9 To assemble the cream puffs: Use a serrated knife to slice the top third from each puff. Remove any excess "skin" from inside of puff. Fill with about 2 tablespoons of filling, until full but not overflowing, and replace top. (Any extra filling is wonderful on fresh fruit.) Sprinkle with confectioners' sugar if desired. Serve immediately (see note).

Julia Glass

Dennis Cowley

On My Characters

Every piece of fiction I write begins with a single character, one who generally occurs to me out of the blue so I'm never really sure where he or she came from. Of course, that character is always in a pickle of some kind. The trouble may come from inside or outside the character, but trouble there always must be. That's the genesis of the story. Other characters "sprout" from the first one—mates, children, parents, coworkers—and often I'm surprised which ones grow in importance. For instance, *The Whole World Over* began as a "he said, she said" tale about the marriage of Greenie Duquette and Alan Glazier. Two characters I created only as foils to this couple—Walter, the restaurateur for whom Greenie makes desserts; and Saga, the woman who's struggling with a damaged memory and who captivates Alan—loomed far larger than I originally intended. Basically, they stole my heart. That's what I love about forging ahead into the territory of a novel without a map in hand. Only when I've written several chapters do I begin to see where the journey may end.

....

Readers Should Know

The lion's share of writing fiction is, for me, the day-dreaming that takes place during the margins of my daily life: traffic jams, long lines at the post office, showers, walking the dog, idling through the produce aisle. That's when I make essential decisions about my characters' choices and relationships, about what accidents will befall them. I may go two or three weeks without getting any of these imaginings down on the page, but finding space for this interior process every day is crucial. You cannot write good fiction without spending significant time alone, marinating in your own thoughts, listening to those accidental inner voices, and nurturing the souls who populate your stories. You must be unreachable by phone, untethered by an iPod, and steeped in a private silence. Our culture is increasingly impoverished by a collective dependence on media gadgets and all electronic forms of communication that saturate our minds in facts, opinions, political prophecies, and the so-called news. We may be living in a golden age of invention, but that kind of creativity is not synonymous with, or a substitute for, imagination.

....

Readers Frequently Ask

People express amazement that I can so intimately portray people who seem so different from me—most notably, a gay Scottish man (Fenno, the central character in *Three Junes*). I explain that I always have a great deal in common with my main characters. Like Fenno, I adore books, I lived in Greenwich Village, and for much of my youth I was overly cautious when it came to taking emotional risks. Like Greenie Duquette, I love to immerse myself in making people happy by feeding them. At the time I wrote *The Whole World Over*, I also had a verbally precocious young son and lived in a very small apartment with makeshift sleeping quarters. That old chestnut "write what you know" goes only so far, however. Without setting challenges for oneself—stretching far to know what you want to know about human nature—the imagined world would quickly become predictable, the experience of writing myopic. In every new story, I take on at least one character or experience I'm initially doubtful I can pull off (but definitely want to). Take the make-believe governor of New Mexico in *The Whole World Over*; Clement Jardine's work with endangered grizzly bears in *I See You Everywhere*; and, in *The Widower's Tale*, an illegal Guatemalan immigrant who works as a gardener.

....

Influences on My Writing

Daniel Deronda, the last novel by George Eliot (the pen name of Mary Anne Evans), made me realize I wanted to write fiction. I was in my late twenties then, working primarily as a painter (even though I was paying the rent with my editorial and writing skills). The heroine of that book, Gwendolen Harleth, remains my favorite character in all the literature I've read, primarily because she is utterly contemptible at the outset, and yet wins (and breaks) the reader's heart by the end of the story after she faces the complex consequences of her vain, foolish choices. I found the experience of this emotional transformation haunting and provocative. Yes, Eliot's language is gorgeous, her characters rich, and her plotting brilliant, but this novel's gift to me was a profound understanding of how great fiction exerts its power by instilling empathy. It teaches us viscerally, again and again through endlessly diverse stories, how to stand in the shoes of people we might otherwise ignore, dismiss, or condemn. It opens our eyes and hearts to worlds beyond our own. What can be more important than that?

BASQUE CHOCOLATE CAKE WITH CHERRY PRESERVES

Makes 8–10 servings

Adapted from *Food and Wine* (October, 1998)

The heroine of my second novel, *The Whole World Over*, is Greenie Duquette, a pastry chef whose signature dessert is an elaborate coconut cake. It will come as no surprise to readers that I have a treacherously irrepressible sweet tooth, but sadly I rarely have time to make complicated desserts.

This chocolate cake is outrageously rich, pretty when garnished, and easy to make. (The sour flavor of the crème fraîche is essential; don't substitute whipped cream.)

Note: I find that the surface of the cake cracks slightly, making the cake fragile, so I cool it in the pan on a rack. When ready to serve, I cut the pieces straight from the pan, then plate and garnish them in the kitchen.

12½ tablespoons unsalted butter
5½ ounces bittersweet chocolate
3 large eggs
½ cup sugar
⅓ cup all-purpose flour
½ cup black cherry preserves
Crème fraîche, for serving

1 Preheat oven to 350°F. Lightly butter and flour a 9" round cake pan.
2 In a heavy medium saucepan, combine the butter and chocolate. Melt over low heat, stirring frequently, until smooth, about 4 minutes. Remove from the heat and let cool slightly.
3 In a medium bowl, use an electric mixer and beat the eggs with the sugar at high speed until smooth, about 3 minutes. Add the flour and beat at low speed just until combined. Fold in ⅓ of the melted chocolate, then gently fold in the remaining chocolate; do not overmix.
4 Pour the batter into the prepared pan and bake for about 35 minutes, or until a toothpick stuck into the center comes out clean. Place the cake on a rack and let cool.
5 Meanwhile, in a saucepan, warm the cherry preserves over moderate heat. Cut the cake into wedges (see note) and serve with the cherry preserves and crème fraîche.

TOURTE DE BLETTES (APPLE, SWISS CHARD, AND PINE NUT PIE)

Makes 1 (10- or 11-inch) pie; 8–10 servings

Adapted from *The Cuisine of the Sun: Classical French Cooking from Nice and Provence* by Mireille Johnston (Fireside, 1990)

My first novel, *Three Junes*, features several meals lovingly prepared by chef Dennis McLeod, brother to Fenno. Though he's Scottish, Dennis is married to a Frenchwoman and owns a restaurant in Provence. Readers never get to visit the restaurant, but I'm certain Dennis would serve this unusual pie, a favorite of mine that always earns raves. It is a savory-sweet dish, a marriage of healthy and indulgent, and the perfect centerpiece for a brunch. It tastes good warm, cool, or even cold, so you can make it well ahead.

Note: While the pastry should be made by hand, I use a food processor, taking care not to overmix.

FOR THE PASTRY
3 cups unbleached all-purpose flour
2 large eggs, beaten
1 cup (2 sticks) unsalted butter, softened
½ cup granulated sugar
About 1 tablespoon salt

FOR THE FILLING
4 large Golden Delicious or Granny Smith apples
3 tablespoons raisins
2 tablespoons dark rum or dry apple brandy, such as Calvados

1 cup Swiss chard, ribs removed, blanched for a few minutes and thoroughly drained (you can substitute about 2 pounds fresh spinach, blanched for 1 minute)
4 tablespoons pine nuts
½ cup confectioners' sugar, plus 3 tablespoons for sprinkling (optional)
¼–½ pound bland cheese, such as Gouda or mild Cheddar, diced
2 large eggs, beaten
Grated peel of 1 lemon
2 tablespoons currant jelly

1 **To make the pastry:** Place all ingredients in the bowl of a food processor (see note). Pulse repeatedly only until coarsely blended. Turn the dough onto a large floured board and press away from you with the heel of your hand to complete the blending. Shape into a ball, cover with a clean cloth, and leave for 2 hours at room temperature.

2 **To make the filling:** Peel and core the apples and cut two of them into small cubes. Put the raisins and liquor in a small saucepan and bring to a boil. Simmer 2 minutes.

3 Preheat oven to 375°F. Butter a large (10"–11") pie dish.

4 In a large bowl, mix the Swiss chard (or spinach), apple cubes, raisins, pine nuts, confectioners' sugar, cheese, eggs, and lemon peel.

5 Divide the pastry into two unequal parts, the smaller about a third the size of the larger part. On a floured surface, roll the large part into a circle (as thin as possible) and lay it in the buttered pie dish; it should hang over the edges a bit. Prick all over with a fork. Spread the jelly on the bottom and add the filling. Slice the remaining two apples and mound evenly over the filling.

6 Roll out the remaining dough and fit carefully over the top of the filling. Trim and crimp the edges. Prick the surface with a fork or make a decorative vent at the center. Bake 30 minutes, or until golden. Remove from the oven and sprinkle with confectioners' sugar, if desired.

BLACK BEAN CHILI
WITH CAYENNE-GLAZED TOFU

Makes 8 cups

Chili recipe adapted from *The Greens Cookbook* by Deborah Madison (Bantam, 1987)

To atone for the indulgences of the other recipes I've offered, here's an extremely healthy recipe that would meet with the approval of Zip, one of Clem Jardine's many colorful boyfriends in *I See You Everywhere*. Zip loves to cook, but there's a catch: everything is aggressively virtuous, from the "hijiki salads, brown rice breakfasts, and daikon root stews" that drive Clem crazy to his "black bean chili with tiny cubes of roasted tofu glazed with cayenne," which she knows she will miss if she leaves him. My favorite black bean chili comes from Greens, the legendary San Francisco vegetarian restaurant; the toasted herbs give it an exceptional flavor. The added cubes of tofu roasted with a cayenne glaze are courtesy of Zip.

Note: Wear plastic or rubber gloves while handling chiles to protect your skin from the oil in them. Avoid direct contact with your eyes and wash your hands thoroughly after handling.

FOR THE CHILI

2 cups black turtle beans, soaked overnight (or 4½–5 cups cooked black beans)
1 bay leaf
4 teaspoons cumin seeds
4 teaspoons dried oregano
4 teaspoons ground paprika
½ teaspoon ground cayenne pepper
1 chile negro or ancho chile, for homemade chili powder (or 2–3 tablespoons commercial chili powder)
3 tablespoons corn or peanut oil
3 medium yellow onions, diced
4 garlic cloves, coarsely chopped
½ teaspoon salt
1½ pounds ripe or canned tomatoes, peeled, seeded, and chopped; juice reserved
1–2 teaspoons chopped chipotle chiles
About 1 tablespoon rice wine vinegar to taste
4 tablespoons cilantro, chopped
Cayenne-Glazed Tofu (see recipe)

FOR THE GARNISH

Poblano or Anaheim green chiles, or 2 ounces canned green chiles, rinsed well and diced
½–¾ cup grated Muenster cheese
½ cup crème fraîche (or sour cream)
8 sprigs cilantro

1 **To prepare the chili:** Sort through the beans and remove any small stones. Rinse the beans well, cover them generously with water, and let them soak overnight.

2 The next day, drain the beans, cover them with fresh water by a couple of inches, and bring them to a boil with the bay leaf. Lower the heat and let the beans simmer while you prepare the rest of the ingredients.

3 Heat a small heavy skillet over medium heat. Add the cumin seeds. When they begin to color, add the oregano, shaking the pan frequently so the herbs don't scorch. As soon as the fragrance is strong and robust, remove the pan from the heat and add the paprika and cayenne. Give everything a quick stir; then remove from the pan (the paprika and cayenne only need a few seconds to toast). Using a mortar and pestle or spice mill, grind into a coarse powder.

4 Preheat oven to 375°F. To make the homemade chili powder, put the negro or ancho chili in the oven for 3–5 minutes to dry it out. Cool it briefly; then remove the stem, seeds, and veins. Tear the pod into small pieces and grind it into a powder in a blender or spice mill.

5 Heat the oil in a large skillet, and sauté the onions over medium heat until they soften. Add the ground herbs, chili powder, garlic, and salt, and cook another 5 minutes. Add the tomatoes, their juice, and about 1 teaspoon of the chipotle chiles. Simmer everything together for 15 minutes; then add this mixture to the beans, and if necessary, enough water so the beans are covered by at least 1 inch. Continue cooking the beans slowly until they are soft, an hour or longer, or pressure cook them for 30 minutes at 15 pounds of pressure. Keep an eye on the water level and add more, if needed, to keep the beans amply covered.

6 When the beans are cooked, taste them, and add more chipotle chiles if desired. Season to taste with the vinegar, additional salt if needed, and the chopped cilantro.

7 **Prepare the garnish:** If using fresh green chiles, and you have a gas range, roast the chiles over an open flame until tender and blackened on all sides. If you have an electric range, place the chiles on a broiling tray covered with foil and broil, turning occasionally, until skin is blackened and blistered on all sides. Place chiles in a small bowl, cover tightly with plastic wrap, and let sit for 5 minutes. Remove stems, peel off blackened skin discard the seeds, and dice.

8 Serve the chili ladled over a large spoonful of grated cheese. Top with slices of Cayenne-Glazed Tofu (see recipe), and garnish with the green chiles, crème fraîche (or sour cream), and a sprig of fresh cilantro.

CAYENNE-GLAZED TOFU

Makes 8 servings

1 pound firm tofu
2 tablespoons honey
1 tablespoon canola oil
1 tablespoon warm water
½ teaspoon salt
⅛ teaspoon ground cayenne pepper, or more to taste

1 Preheat oven to 400°F. Drain the water from the tofu. Slice into ½-inch thick pieces, and then cut into smaller rectangles (approximately 1" × 1½"). Set aside on a paper towel while you make the glaze.

2 In an oven-safe glass pie plate or baking dish, mix together the honey, oil, water, salt, and cayenne. Place the tofu into the glaze and turn a few times to coat. Lay the tofu flat in one layer. Place in the oven and bake for 12 minutes. Carefully remove the dish from the oven and turn the tofu to coat again.

3 Place the dish back in the oven and bake for 10 more minutes. Remove the dish from the oven and again turn the tofu, positioning it with a different point up to get even browning. Bake for 10 more minutes.

Amy Greene

Amy Smotherman Burgess

Inspiration So much of my inspiration comes from the Appalachian landscape, the farmland and mountains and creek banks of home. I spent most of my childhood playing outdoors, exploring the wooded hills around our house. In *Bloodroot*, Byrdie talks about loving the land as much as she does any of her kin, and that's very much how I feel about East Tennessee.

The Intimacy of Writing Longhand I wrote the first draft of *Bloodroot* longhand, spending hours shut away in my bedroom with a notebook and pen, emptying the story from my head onto paper. I've always written like this, going back all the way to first grade. Somehow I feel more of an intimacy with the story and the characters by putting pen to paper rather than sitting in front of a computer screen confronted with a blinking cursor.

Readers Frequently Ask I'm often asked if I did research before writing *Bloodroot*, and the truth is that I didn't. The story began with an image of a woman with black hair and vivid blue eyes living in the mountain woods with her twins, hiding from some kind of danger. I was interested first in exploring the characters, unsure whether or not a story would evolve. Finally I just picked up my pen and wrote, appropriating the voices of the people I've known and loved my whole life for my characters.

Influences on My Writing I consider both Toni Morrison and Cormac McCarthy major influences. I discovered Morrison's *Beloved* when I was in my early twenties. I was in awe of her lyrical prose, and the novel's magic realism spoke to me as a native of Appalachia, where there's a rich culture of mysticism and folklore. *All the Pretty Horses* by McCarthy is another inspiring book for me. I was enamored with the way he wrote dialogue that rang so true to a fellow native Appalachian from Knoxville.

APPALACHIAN CATHEAD BISCUITS

Makes 6 large biscuits

Adapted from *Smokehouse Ham, Spoon Bread, & Scuppernong Wine*
by Joseph E. Dabney (Cumberland House, 1998)

In Southern Appalachia, where I grew up and still live, there's a rich tradition of coming together around the kitchen table. Homecomings and church picnics and Sunday dinners are a big part of our culture, with good food serving as a catalyst for fellowship and family togetherness. In *Bloodroot*, Myra tells how she appeased her cruel husband by feeding him well: "I served him steaming plates heaped with meatloaf, okra, pork chops, soup beans, pickled beets, country fried steak and cathead biscuits. I stuffed him with banana pudding and coffee cake and cobbler, all the things Granny had taught me to make." Later, Myra's children first sense her troubled state of mind when they wake up without the smell of breakfast, and Johnny tries to make biscuits to comfort his twin sister Laura. For me, of all the home-cooked meals I grew up loving, cathead biscuits and white gravy are the most symbolic of warmth and safety and home. Each Saturday morning of my childhood I woke to the smell of my mother's biscuits and gravy waiting for me on the table, just as my mother walked into that same kitchen to eat her own mother's cooking when she was a girl. The love and skill of home cooking has been handed down through generations of the women in my family, making these recipes almost like genetic traits, as much my ancestral inheritance as the color of my eyes. I like to think that I'm sharing a piece of my history by passing them on, and a little taste of what home is to me.

Note: Light, fluffy biscuits require a low-protein, low-gluten flour, such as White Lily all-purpose flour, long a staple of southern baking. White Lily flour can be difficult to find outside the South. Use 2 cups of White Lily all-purpose flour if you can. If not, the best substitute is a combination of a lower-gluten "northern" all-purpose flour, such as Pillsbury, and cake flour.

These biscuits are best served hot, straight from the oven. My mom makes the gravy while the biscuits are baking.

> 1 cup all-purpose flour (see note)
> 1 cup cake flour (see note)
> ½ teaspoon salt
> ½ teaspoon baking soda
> 2 teaspoons baking powder
> 5 tablespoons unsalted butter or solid vegetable shortening, chilled
> ¾ cup cold buttermilk, plus an additional 1–2 tablespoons if needed

1 Preheat oven to 450°F.
2 Mix both flours, salt, baking soda, and baking powder together in a medium-sized mixing bowl.
3 Add the butter or shortening in small amounts, then mix it into the dry mixture thoroughly with a pastry cutter, two butter knives slicing in a scissor fashion, or your fingertips. The finished mixture should have the consistency of course-ground cornmeal, with a few larger lumps of butter remaining.
4 Add the buttermilk all at once. Stir quickly with a fork until mixture forms into a soft ball, about 30 seconds. If dough feels firm and dry bits are not gathering into a ball, sprinkle with an additional tablespoon of buttermilk. Do not overmix. Using your hands (you might want to coat them lightly with flour), gently knead the dough in the bowl about 3 times.
5 Divide dough in half. To make cathead biscuits (so called because they are large, about the size of a cat's head), simply pinch dough into thirds and shape pieces into thick patties. Place the shaped dough on an ungreased cookie sheet or in a large cast iron skillet (it's fine if the biscuits are slightly crowded). Bake for 15 minutes or until the tops of the biscuits are a light golden brown.
6 Serve immediately with butter, jam, honey, or white gravy (see recipe). If serving with white gravy, open the biscuit and smother with gravy.

WHITE GRAVY

Makes 1 cup

This recipe comes from a falling-apart Watkins recipe book from the 1940s, passed down from my great-grandfather, who sold Watkins products back then. It was difficult to reach stores at that time in rural Appalachia, so families relied on traveling salesmen from the Watkins Company, offering everything from vitamins to pie filling, for the supplies they needed.

Note: We eat sausage or bacon with our meal of gravy and biscuits, usually with fried eggs and a slice of fresh tomato from the garden on the side.

Any kind of milk is fine, but use whole milk if you like your gravy rich, or cream if you like it extra rich.

About ½ pound sausage or bacon, for frying (or as much as you wish) (see note)
2 generous tablespoons all-purpose flour
1 cup milk or cream (see note)
Salt to taste
Freshly ground black pepper to taste

1   In a skillet, fry sausage or bacon. Place 2 tablespoons of drippings (or more if you plan to double or triple the recipe) in a medium saucepan. If there aren't enough drippings, add oil or solid vegetable shortening.
2   Whisk flour into the hot drippings over low heat. Raise heat to medium and stir constantly until the mixture bubbles and turns light brown.
3   Slowly whisk in milk or cream. Continue to cook and stir mixture constantly to keep it from getting lumpy, until it thickens and becomes smooth, 2–3 minutes. Season to taste with salt, and sprinkle generously with pepper. If mixture gets too thick, add a little milk or cream to reach desired consistency.

Philippa Gregory

James Stewart

My Writing Process
My writing always starts with the discovery of a character or, sometimes, an event that seems to me so extraordinary that it releases a train of thought. I then research for more than a year on the topic before I even think of writing, then I have the intense pleasure of letting the research suffuse my thinking until I get to the point where I can visualize everything and even hear the voices of the characters in my head. Then I am ready to write.

Readers Should Know
I am so excited that *The White Queen* is the start of a six-book series that will span the period of the Wars of the Roses. They were called the Cousins' War at the time, so that's the title of the series. The joy of the series is that each book stands quite alone and can be read in isolation, and each book is from the point of view of one of the key players—all of them women—at the heart of the warring world of England.

Readers Frequently Ask
Many people ask me about my writing routine and my technique and I tell them that I have very little routine except to always reread or write something every day. This way I keep in touch with the novel and with the creative flow. But it can be any time of day, and it can be anywhere! I carry my laptop with me everywhere I go and I can write wherever I am; I don't need quiet or a lovely view (though that is a pleasure). Only when I am starting the writing process do I need to be surrounded with reference material; later on it is better if the novel does not read as if it was written in an old library!

Writers I Love The first books I loved were the children's classics by Beatrix Potter; I loved the attention to detail and the passion for the countryside. She was a writer who lived in the north of England in the country, as I do now, and the landscapes in her book are like the one outside my window. I am influenced, as every English novelist must be, by Jane Austen. I think she created an austere, spare, cool narrative voice which has the merit of being very analytical and very, very funny. Her understanding of female rivalry and snobbery is supreme. Another great novelist (and there are so many) would be E.M. Forster. He has such compassion and underwrites drama with such a deft light touch, but the pathos that he can wring from a little scene! He's another lover of the countryside, and I like that too.

MEDIEVAL GINGERBREAD

Makes 3 dozen (2-inch) shapes, or 30 balls

Adapted from a Medieval recipe (see below)

First let me say that being able to cook is not, in my view, an intrinsic part of female nature and being unable to cook is not a symptom of gender crisis. It is unreasonable to expect all women to cook, unreasonable to expect them to cook well, and absolutely out of the question that they should have to clear and wash up too. That having been said, and observing that I would rather read a book than cook a meal (sometimes even though I am hungry), I offer you this gingerbread recipe.

Gingerbread was one of the great treats of the medieval feast. First it was spiced with ginger, an incredibly expensive and rare taste that was imported from the Mediterranean countries and from the cuisine of Islam. Perhaps the Crusaders got the taste for it and brought it home to their castles, along with the other spices and herbs that helped sweeten and spice the bland cooking of the northern countries. The spices helped to hide the taste of meat which was "on the turn," or going bad, in the days before refrigeration, as well as add flavor to drinks, scent to rooms, and contribute to perfume. As such, gingerbread was a real treat.

Its appearance was enhanced at times of special celebration by being cut into special shapes: stars and moons, perhaps even crafted into little models like the gingerbread house of the fairytale. The medieval and Tudor diners loved when food was presented extravagantly. Gingerbread was often gilded, sometimes with real gold leaf, sometimes with sprinkles of sugar.

My mother used to eat gingerbread spread with butter as a tea time treat, and it was recommended to me as a cure for nausea in pregnancy. I have to say that it didn't work at all, but it was an interesting experiment. In less extreme circumstances, you might try it while reading my series of books set in medieval times, The Cousins' War, with hot sweetened wine.

This is a recipe for gingerbread as it appears in a fifteenth-century cookery-book, Harleian ms. 279 (ab. 1430).

Gyngerbrede. Take a quart of hony, & sethe it, & skeme it clene; take Safroun, pouder Pepir, & þrow ther-on; take gratyd Brede, & make it so chargeaunt þat it wol be y-leched; þen take pouder Canelle, & straw þer-on y-now; þen make yt square, lyke as þou wolt leche it; take when þou lechyst hNyt, an caste Box leaves a-bouyn, y-stkyd þer-on, on clowys. And if þou wolt haue it Red, coloure it with Saunderys y-now.

Note: The flavor of medieval gingerbread resembles that of traditional gingerbread, but its consistency is quite different. It's more like dense, rich, chewy candy, but with a little kick.

Because honey is a main ingredient, the type you use will affect the flavor of the gingerbread. Use a high-quality flavored honey, such as orange blossom, or organic honey, if possible.

Gingerbread was traditionally molded into shapes, but it's also delicious served in balls coated with ground cloves and sugar. During the Middle Ages, gingerbread was sometimes decorated with whole cloves and box leaves (the leaves of boxwood hedges). You can use candied leaves, boxwood, or another nontoxic shrub with tiny leaves, as decoration.

1 pound plain white sandwich bread, sliced
1 pound (1¼ cups) honey, preferably flavored or organic (see note)
1¼ teaspoons ground ginger
1 teaspoon ground cinnamon
¼ teaspoon ground white pepper
Few drops red food coloring (optional)

FOR DECORATION
5 teaspoons sugar
Pinch ground cloves
Small leaves, real or candy (optional) (see note)
Whole cloves (optional)

1 **To make the bread crumbs:** Set oven to lowest heat setting. Lay bread slices on oven rack and leave door slightly ajar. Allow bread to dry completely but not toast, 45 minutes to 1 hour (thin-sliced bread will go faster.) Place dried bread slices in bowl of food processor fitted with a metal blade, and process into very fine crumbs. (You may have to process batches several times to get the crumbs fine enough. Make sure no clumps remain.)

2 In a large, heavy-bottomed pot, place the honey, spices, and red food coloring, "if thou wolt have it Red." Bring to a boil over high heat while stirring occasionally, then immediately reduce heat to low and simmer for 2–3 minutes, or until mixture reaches 240°F.

3 Add 2½ cups bread crumbs and stir quickly, adding more bread crumbs as needed, until mixture becomes stiff and difficult to stir. Remove from heat and allow to cool for 10 minutes.

4 You can either roll out the dough and cut into shapes, or roll into balls (see note).
   To make shapes: Using a rolling pin, roll dough between two sheets of wax paper or parchment, into a ¼-inch thick rectangle. Remove one sheet of paper, flip dough onto a lightly greased baking sheet (you can use cooking spray), and remove rest of paper. Set aside for an hour or two to let the flavors mingle. Then, use a sharp knife to cut gingerbread into small squares (or diamonds, hearts, leaf shapes, etc.). Sprinkle the tops with the sugar and cloves and, if desired, decorate each piece with small nontoxic leaves attached with a clove. **To make balls:** Combine sugar and ground cloves in a small plate. Roll dough into bite-size balls, and coat with the sugar-clove mixture. Set aside for an hour or two to let the flavors mingle.

Sara Gruen

Jerry Bauer

Inspiration

I draw inspiration from everywhere: all the books I've read over the course of my lifetime, snippets of conversation I overhear in restaurants or on the street, things I see on the news or read about in magazines, and, of course, things I've experienced personally. My fiction is a crazy quilt of everything I've encountered in life magnified through the lens of an overactive imagination.

Readers Should Know

I wrote half of *Water for Elephants* in a walk-in closet. I had stalled out about halfway through writing the book and realized I was employing all my favorite writing-avoidance techniques. I painted the walls of our family room five times and was spending altogether too much time on eBay. I didn't have a wireless Internet connection at the time, so I asked my husband to move my desk into our unwired closet and went in there each morning with my laptop, the dog, and a cup of tea. I opened my file on the theory that if I stared at it long enough without any other distractions, something would happen. Fortunately, I was right, and I staggered forth with a finished book four-and-a-half months later.

Readers Frequently Ask

People often ask how I manage to write with three children. The answer is that I make the most of school hours, have a very helpful husband, and a high tolerance for mess.

Influences on My Writing—Too Many to Count!

Every book I've ever loved. Every short story I've ever loved. Margaret Atwood, Ernest Hemingway, James Herriot, Anna Sewell, E. L. Doctorow, Alice Munro, Elizabeth Strout, Jane Austen, all of the Brontës (except the no-good brother), Yann Martel, and Jonathan Franzen; I could go on for days.

The novelist in my novel *Ape House*, Amanda Thigpen, taught herself how to cook after accidentally giving herself and her husband food poisoning through improvisations with canned soup. Amanda is passionate about cooking, and her novel, *Recipe For Disaster*, prominently features the preparation and consumption of food. Because of her unfortunate last name, Amanda is forced by her (fictional) editor to publish under the pseudonym Amanda LaRue.

AMANDA THIGPEN'S SALMON EN CROÛTE

Makes 4–5 servings

While my own method of administering food poisoning involved summer squash (I'm still not sure how I achieved that), I taught myself to cook the same way Amanda did, by joining the Church of Julia (Child). I pored over her books and followed every direction, even if it involved peeling broccoli. This foundation gave me the courage to adapt and experiment, and I now carry a notepad with me at all times so I can deconstruct and record new and unusual combinations of flavors I encounter at restaurants. The following recipe for salmon is inspired by recipes for vegetarian strudel, Jacques Pepin's sautéed salmon, and, of course, Julia Child's Hollandaise.

This is a perennial family favorite, and definitely not diet food. Leftovers can be brought back to life using 40–60 percent power in the microwave, but we rarely have any.

Note: To switch things up, use puff pastry instead of filo (if you do, skip the sesame seeds and instead decorate with carved and scored pastry leaves, using an egg white as glue and glaze).

The fat-free, high-heat method of sautéing the salmon is adapted from one of Jacque Pepin's recipes. Make sure the skin has been scaled and use salmon skin (cracklings) as a garnish, if you have any left. Ours almost never make it to the table.

To prepare ahead of time, you can sauté the capers and fish, and steam the spinach earlier in the day.

Serve with a mixture of white long grain and wild rice (see recipe) and steamed asparagus, or fiddleheads, if you're lucky enough to find them (both of which present another opportunity to enjoy the hollandaise). Or serve with a simple and lightly dressed mesclun mix salad.

12 ounces prewashed baby spinach

Sea salt, for sprinkling

1 pound side of salmon, preferably wild,
   skin on and scaled (see note)

½ cup (1 stick) melted butter (melt more as
   needed)

Approximately ¼ pound filo dough
   (thawed for a few hours at room temper-
   ature, or in the refrigerator overnight)

1½ tablespoons sesame seeds, for sprinkling

¼ cup drained capers

Hollandaise Sauce (see recipe)

1 Steam the spinach lightly, using as little water as possible. I do it in a Pyrex dish sealed with plastic wrap in the microwave, adding about a teaspoon of water, for approximately 3–5 minutes. If cooking on the stove, sauté spinach in a small amount of butter on medium for 4–5 minutes or until wilted. Line a colander with paper towels and turn the spinach into it. Spread it out and pat the top with other paper towels, drying the spinach as much as possible. While you're making the rest of the dish, periodically flip and daub the spinach, replacing the paper towels as necessary.

2 Set an unoiled nonstick pan on high heat for about one minute, until very hot. Sprinkle sea salt on the skin of the salmon and set it skin side down in the pan (it will hiss dramatically and the edges will contract). Cover, reduce the heat to medium-high, and cook until the center is rare (about 5 minutes). Flip the salmon out onto a plate, skin side up. Remove the skin using a spatula and scrape off any flesh that is stuck to it. Salt the underside of the crisp skin (known as "salmon potato chips" in my house), chop or slice, and set aside for use as a garnish.

3 **Assembling the Masterpiece:** Preheat the oven to 415°F. Brush a rimmed baking sheet with melted butter and place a sheet of filo on it. Brush the sheet with melted butter, place another sheet on top, and repeat until you've used all the filo. Use 8–12 sheets of filo, depending on your preference.

4 Lay the steamed spinach lengthwise along the dough, and top with the salmon. Depending on the size and length of the fish, you may need to slice pieces from the thin end and lay them across the rest of the piece. Try to make a rectangle of even thickness that can be folded within the dough.

5 Fold the filo so that it encases the fish and spinach (you will probably need a spatula). Fold both ends up, and then flip the whole thing over so that the presenting side is seamless (the spinach will be on top after you've flipped it). Brush with the remaining butter, and sprinkle sesame seeds on top. Bake for 25 minutes, or until golden and crisp.

6 Sauté the drained capers over moderately high heat until crisp, 3–5 minutes. Set aside half of the capers to mix into the hollandaise, and garnish the salmon with the other half. Garnish with skin cracklings if desired.

7 **Presentation:** Bring the Thing to the table, slice, and serve. Top with a dollop of hollandaise (see recipe).

HOLLANDAISE SAUCE

Makes ¾ cup

Giving credit where credit is due, this hollandaise is
Julia Child's because, frankly, there is no other.

Note: This is the stage I call playing chicken with the egg. You want to heat the egg yolks without scrambling them, so whisk constantly over low heat. Do NOT use a nonstick sauce pan. Use copper if you have it, but do not use nonstick. If you scramble the eggs by accident, you can unscramble them through elbow grease by whisking with tiny bits of lemon juice away from the heat. But you won't scramble them in the first place, right?

> 3 egg yolks
> Juice from half a lemon (about 2 tablespoons)
> 4 tablespoons cold butter, divided
> 10 tablespoons melted (but not hot) butter

1 Whisk egg yolks in a sauce pan until creamy. Whisk in lemon juice. Set the pan on the lowest heat, impale the first 2 tablespoons of butter on the end of your whisk, and swirl it constantly around the bottom. (You want to heat the egg yolks enough to cook them but not enough to scramble them. The cold butter gives you a bit of control. Be ready to grab the pan and remove it from the heat and whisk, whisk, whisk if it threatens to scramble, but do not leave it for even an instant during this stage.)
2 When the mixture is thick enough to see to the bottom of the pan each time you whisk, turn off the heat, whisk in the other 2 tablespoons of cold butter to cool the mixture, and then add the melted (but not hot!) butter in dribbles.

LONG GRAIN AND WILD RICE

Makes 5 servings

I can't remember where I learned to do rice this way—I think I was served it at someone's house and asked the hostess—but I can tell you that I've never cooked it any way since (unless, of course, I'm using a completely different type of rice for curry, etc.).

Note: The leftovers microwave up beautifully.

1 cup long grain white rice
⅓ cup wild rice
2⅔ cups chicken broth
3–4 garlic cloves, crushed (more or less as desired)
A generous pat of butter (about 2 tablespoons)
Juice of half a lemon
2 tablespoons coarsely chopped flat-leaf parsley
Sea salt to taste
Freshly ground pepper to taste

1 Place long grain and wild rice, broth, garlic, butter, and lemon juice in a medium sauce pan. Bring to a rolling boil, then reduce heat to the lowest setting, cover, and simmer for about 20 minutes.
2 When dimples appear on the surface of the rice, add parsley, stir, and remove from heat. Allow to rest while you finish up the rest of the dinner. Add salt and pepper to taste.

MERRAN NEVILLE'S PAVLOVA

Makes 8–10 servings

The recipe for pavlova comes from Merran Neville, a dear family friend, and the first time she served this to me I thought I had died and gone to heaven. It is my favorite dessert of all time, and so easy to make. All my children ask for pavlova instead of birthday cake and I oblige, sticking a single candle in the middle of the whipped cream. The only caveat is that the berries must be ripe. I try to combine as many types of ripe berries as are available, but another good combination is sliced ripe peaches and blueberries.

FOR THE PAVLOVA
4 large egg whites
Pinch of salt
½ teaspoon cream of tartar
1 cup sugar, divided
1 teaspoon cornstarch
1 teaspoon cider vinegar
½ teaspoon vanilla extract

FOR THE TOPPING
1 cup whipping cream
1 tablespoon sugar
½ teaspoon vanilla extract or liqueur
* (Gran Marnier is especially good)*
Ripe berries (a mixture of raspberries, blue-
* berries, and sliced strawberries is good)*

1 Preheat oven to 285°F. Line a baking sheet with parchment paper.
2 **To make the pavlovas:** In electric mixer's large bowl, use the whisk attachment to beat the egg whites with salt and cream of tartar until stiff but not dry. Beat in ½ cup sugar, until the mixture is thick and holds shiny peaks.
3 Mix the cornstarch with the remaining ½ cup sugar. Fold this gently into the egg whites with a rubber spatula.
4 Add the cider vinegar and vanilla extract, and fold them gently into the egg whites until just mixed.
5 Pile the mixture in an 8-inch mound on the baking sheet. Bake for about one hour, until the outside crust is firm but the inside is still soft. The peaks will start to turn golden.
6 Let cool for ten minutes on a wire rack, and then invert gently onto a second rack and let cool thoroughly. Remove the parchment as soon as it will let you (use a spatula and patience). The pavlova will shrink and crack a little, but will look fine when decorated. Just before serving, invert the pavlova onto a serving dish.
7 **To make the topping:** Whip the cream until thick, and then fold in the sugar and the vanilla or liqueur. Spread the whipped cream on the pavlova, pile the berries on top, and serve.

Jennifer Haigh

Asia Kepka

Inspiration   Each of my novels has come about differently. *Baker Towers* was inspired by a place, my hometown in western Pennsylvania. *Mrs. Kimble* began with a scene I actually witnessed. Years ago, when I was living in Tampa, Florida, I went to the corner store one day and saw a young mother with a small child, falling down drunk at ten in the morning. That memory haunted me for years, and when I sat down to write what would become my first novel, it was the scene I wrote.

....

Readers Should Know   My latest novel is *The Lost Gospel* and, after several years of focusing exclusively on novels, I have recently rediscovered my love of the short story. My story "Beast and Bird" is available on the Amazon Kindle.

I am now at work on a short story collection, tentatively titled *The Beauty Part*. In these stories I will return to Bakerton, Pennsylvania, the fictionalized western Pennsylvania mining town that is the setting for, some might say, the main character of my second novel, *Baker Towers*.

....

Readers Frequently Ask   *"Do you write from your own experience?"*
Nope. I make it all up.
"How do you know when a book is done?"
It's like falling in love—you just know.

....

Setting the Bar   If I had to choose only one influence on my writing, it would be the Irish novelist and short story writer William Trevor. I am awed by his exquisitely simple and beautiful sentences, his deep insight into human nature, his compassion and heart. I'm not vain enough to imagine that my writing resembles Trevor's, but reading him reminds me where the bar is.

Dinah Kimble's Green Salad With Salmon (Gravlax)

Makes 12–16 servings

In my novel *Mrs. Kimble,* Dinah, the last of Ken Kimble's three wives, is trained as a chef. When she first appears as an adult, she is working as *garde manger* at Emile's, a posh bistro in Washington, D.C. As *garde manger,* Dinah is responsible for dishes that are served cold: raw oysters, salads, and smoked salmon, among others. Once a week she prepares gravlax, salmon cured in the traditional Swedish manner. Gravlax is traditionally made with dill, an herb Dinah and I don't especially like. Here is our version.

This is a variation on the classic gravlax recipe that appears in Irma S. Rombauer and Marion Rombauer Becker's *The Joy of Cooking* (Scribner, 1997). I have made it this way for years.

Note: This recipe takes three days to prepare.

1¼ cups raw sugar, such as turbinado or demerara

¾ cup kosher salt

½ tablespoon freshly ground black pepper, plus extra for dusting

About 2 pounds very fresh salmon (filleted by a fishmonger into two equal fillets, skin on)

1 cup chopped fresh cilantro leaves

1 tablespoon lemon-flavored vodka (or 1 tablespoon vodka plus ½ teaspoon grated lemon peel)

18–24 cups salad greens, for serving (I like a mix of spinach and arugula)

Freshly ground black pepper to taste

Vinaigrette (see recipe)

---

1 In a large bowl, mix sugar, salt and pepper. Place salmon fillets on a flat surface, such as a cutting board, skin side down. Rub dry mixture onto salmon, covering flesh side completely. Place cilantro on the flesh side of one of the fillets, and sprinkle with vodka. Lay the other fillet, flesh side down, on top of the herb-covered fillet.

2 Wrap fish tightly in plastic wrap. Lay salmon package in a baking dish and top with a plate weighted down with two or three heavy cookbooks (you can also use cans or other heavy objects). Place in refrigerator.

3 Each morning and evening, open the package, baste the fish with any liquids it has exuded, close the package, and turn it over. The fish is ready when its flesh is opaque, usually after 3 days.

4 Unwrap salmon, wipe off dry mixture and cilantro from fish with a paper towel, and detach skin. Slice each side on the diagonal, starting from the tail end. The gravlax should be sliced thinly at an angle.

5 Serve over salad greens with a dusting of black pepper and vinaigrette (see recipe).

VINAIGRETTE

Makes about 2 cups

1¼ cups sesame oil
½ cup plus 2 tablespoons rice wine vinegar
2 teaspoons lime juice
Sugar to taste (about ½–¾ teaspoon)

Place all ingredients in a medium bowl and whisk gently to combine.

Joanne Harris

Lorne Campbell

Inspiration   The inspiration for my books is often drawn from the places and people of my childhood, from members of my family, and from people I have met on my travels. A number of them are set in France, where I still have a number of relatives and where I spent my holidays as a child. Because of this, French food and culture have all played a significant role, especially in some of my earlier novels. I have also drawn extensively on my experience as a teacher in Yorkshire, and on my lifelong interest in aspects of belief, folklore, and fairytale.

....

Readers Should Know   I may still be best known for my 1999 novel *Chocolat*, which was made into a film in 2001 starring Juliette Binoche and Johnny Depp. Since then I have published seven more novels, a collection of short stories, and two cookbooks.

....

Readers Frequently Ask   Many book clubs still ask me about the movie adaptation of *Chocolat*, even though I wasn't responsible for the screenplay. I did enjoy the process of filming, though; I was on set for much of the time, and found it to be a tremendous experience to work and meet with all the artists. Of course, I might have made a few changes to the script if I'd been in charge, but the result looked gorgeous, and the casting was impeccable!

....

Books That Have Influenced My Writing

- Ray Bradbury's *Something Wicked This Way Comes*, for its fabulously dynamic prose and its flawless evocation of childhood.
- Mervyn Peake's Gormenghast trilogy, a brooding, complex masterpiece of neo-Gothic fantasy.
- Vladimir Nabokov's *Lolita,* the most perfect novel of rapture and anguish, by one of literature's greatest stylists.

LENTIL AND TOULOUSE SAUSAGE CASSEROLE

Makes 6 servings

This is a family recipe that was originally published in *My French Kitchen* by Joanne Harris and Fran Warde (HarperCollins, 2003).

There's no better way to get into the atmosphere of the location than through its traditional recipes. This casserole, *Lentilles-Saucisses à l'Ancienne* is an old, old recipe from the Toulouse region in which my grandfather was born. My readers have visited the region many times before in my books, including *Chocolat*. It's an old favorite: easy to make, completely stress-free, and very versatile. It's great with country bread and strong red wine if you want a hot meal in a hurry.

Note: Toulouse sausages are made with pure pork and a generous amount of garlic. They vary from shop to shop according to personal recipes, so keep trying until you find your perfect one. If you prefer, use any of your other favorite sausages. The sausages will cook in the casserole, but if you prefer you can brown them in a skillet before baking.

Lentilles du Puy, small green lentils with a tender skin, are prized produce items. Originally grown in the volcanic soils of Puy in France, you can find them in gourmet or specialty stores.

The cooking of the lentils varies depending on the type of lentils you use. French lentils require longer cooking time than the lentils commonly found in grocery stores. This recipe calls for soaking lentils overnight.

11 ounces lentils, preferably green lentilles du Puy (see note)

2 tablespoons olive oil

2 medium onions, diced

3 celery stalks, chopped

2 garlic cloves, crushed, peeled, and chopped

3 large tomatoes, peeled and chopped

2 teaspoons tomato paste

3 sprigs of thyme

1 bay leaf

¾ cup red wine

2 cups water

6 Toulouse or other favorite cooked sausages (1½ pounds) (see note)

Large bunch flat-leaf parsley, chopped

Salt to taste

Ground black pepper to taste

1 Place lentils in a large bowl and cover with at least 2 inches of water. Soak overnight. Drain and set aside.

2 Preheat oven to 400°F. Heat the olive oil in a large flameproof casserole; add the onions, celery, and garlic and sauté for 5 minutes. Add the tomatoes, tomato paste, thyme, and bay leaf. Mix and cook for 5 minutes.

3 Remove from the heat, add the lentils and red wine, stir well, and pour in enough water to cover (about two cups). Place the sausages on top, cover and bake until lentils are tender, approximately 30–50 minutes (see note).

4 Stir in the parsley and season with salt and pepper to taste before serving.

GÂTEAU LAWRENCE

Makes 10–12 servings

This is a family recipe that was originally published in *My French Kitchen*
by Joanne Harris and Fran Warde (HarperCollins, 2003).

One of the reasons I wrote my cookbook was because so many of my readers kept writing
to ask me for chocolate recipes. Here's one of my favorites, used in the book and the film
version of *Chocolat* and invented by my brother Lawrence.

Note: This is a rich cake. If you find, as I do, that the chocolate icing seems a little too
much of a good thing, try drizzling the warmed apricot jam over the cake just before serving. The sharp tang of the fruit makes a wonderful contrast to the dark chocolate. Bliss!

FOR THE CAKE
*6½ ounces bittersweet (70 percent cocoa)
  chocolate*
*¾ cup (1½ sticks) unsalted butter, at room
  temperature*
⅔ cup sugar
*1⅔ cups (7 ounces) finely ground almonds
  (grind in a food processor or blender)*
4 large eggs, separated

FOR THE ICING
*3½ ounces bittersweet (70 percent cocoa)
  chocolate*
3 tablespoons unsalted butter
*6 tablespoons apricot jam, warmed
  (optional)*

1 **To make the cake:** Preheat oven to 300°F. Line the bottom of a 10" springform pan with parchment paper. Chop the chocolate into small pieces and melt in a heatproof bowl over a saucepan of simmering water. Remove from heat and cool until tepid.

2 In an electric mixer's large bowl, blend the butter and sugar until soft and creamy. Add the melted chocolate, ground almonds, and egg yolks and beat until evenly blended.

3 In a separate bowl, beat the egg whites until stiff. Add to the cake mixture, and use a rubber spatula to quickly fold in until evenly mixed. Pour batter into the prepared pan and bake for 35–40 minutes. A light crust will form on the top and the middle should still be a little squishy.

4 Leave to cool for a few minutes before carefully removing the sides. Cool cake on a wire rack. Slide a long knife underneath the cake to release the parchment from the bottom of the cake pan, but leave the cake on the paper.

5 **To make the icing:** Melt the chocolate and butter together in a heatproof bowl over a pan of simmering water. Stir. Spread evenly over the top of the cake and leave to set. Slide the cake off the paper and onto a serving platter. Drizzle apricot jam over the cake just before serving, if desired.

Katherine Howe

Laura Dandaneau

Inspiration

In 2005, my husband and I moved into the second floor of a little fisherman's house in Marblehead, Massachusetts, that was first built in 1705. I was studying for my PhD qualifying exams at the time, and I started telling myself stories as a distraction from the stress of my academic work. Historical fiction is rather magical that way; who among us hasn't wondered what it would feel like to be transported to a different time? As I wiled away hours at my desk in this funny antique house, where no angle was ever at ninety degrees, I started imagining myself in that same room at different moments in time. What would be in the room with me? How would it smell? Who would be there, and what would they be doing? The story for *The Physick Book of Deliverance Dane* started in just these kinds of ruminations. Someone in that very room, when it was brand new and still smelled like freshly cut pine, had probably been present at the Salem witch trial. What kind of world had that person lived in? How did that world feel different from mine? Most of my work evolves from thought experiments just like this one.

Readers Should Know

I am currently at work on another novel which, like *Physick Book,* will be a story of one of the more macabre corners of New England's past. The novel will take place in Boston in the nineteen teens, a time when the city was starting to look like its modern self but was still very much locked in the nineteenth century. Horse-drawn carts jostled with new electric automobiles; Bostonians poured into the subway to get to work, but still traveled across the ocean by steam ship. The face of the city was changing, growing more crowded, vibrant, and diverse. It was also the end of the spiritualist movement, when many people were passionately curious about the nature of consciousness, of death, and the state of the soul in the afterlife, questions that would grow even more acute after our entry into the Great War. *The Scrying Glass* will visit one Back Bay family caught in the middle of this historic upheaval, and will ask: if you can see death coming, what do you choose?

Readers Frequently Ask By far the most common question that I am asked, perhaps because *Physick Book* is such a magical story, is whether or not I myself believe in magic. Unfortunately, I have a rather opaque response, which is that there are a number of different points of view represented in the book. There are characters who believe fully in magic; there are characters who are devoutly Christian; there are characters who believe only in the power of the human intellect and will; and there are characters who are still making up their minds. I have had the pleasure of meeting readers who respond to each one of these points of view. My fear is that sharing my own opinion would somehow imply that there is one way of reading the story that is more correct than others. For me, the most wonderful thing about fiction is that it creates so many opportunities for discussion, for thought, and for debate, while also having the power to transport us to a different time and place. Different readers experience books differently. I'm much more interested in hearing what my readers have to say.

....

Influences on My Writing—Unexpected and Otherwise My favorite author by far is Edith Wharton, which might surprise some people. But it's not as surprising a choice as you might think. Her Pulitzer Prize winning novel, *The Age of Innocence*, is in effect a work of historical fiction. It is set in the 1870s, but was written in the 1920s. I admire Wharton's ability to select the one specific detail that can then completely illuminate a given scene, and her facility with writing whole characters who are deeply flawed, even unlikable, but with whom we nevertheless sympathize. I also appreciate that Wharton, like a lot of her contemporaries, also wrote ghost stories. *Physick Book* moves across a number of different genres of fiction, and seeing Wharton do the same makes me feel emboldened to add a fantastical twist to the historical novel.

For my next project, I have been reading other novels of old Boston, such as John P. Marquand's *The Late George Apley*. This story was so moving that I cried at the end despite knowing, from the title, that the main character will die. I have also been revisiting Nathaniel Hawthorne. *The House of the Seven Gables* is another tale that deals with the lasting aftershocks of the Salem witch panic, and which has a decrepit old house acting as one of the main characters. *Physick Book*'s Milk Street house is in some ways like the impoverished little cottage version of Hawthorne's grand, imposing haunted mansion.

FISH HOUSE PUNCH AT
THE GOAT AND ANCHOR TAVERN

Makes 12–16 servings

The colonists who settled North America did not much care for water, as a rule. They drank it when they had no alternatives, but usually preferred something harder, and plenty of it. Apple cider, peach brandy, beer, corn mash, and rum all served to make life a little more pleasurable, and to turn "training days" into very festive occasions indeed. These different liquors would often be served in different combinations. A good example of this is "flip," a concoction of sweetened beer spiked with rum and then heated with a hot iron. But the most long lasting, and infamous, of these recipes dates from the sociable Schuylkill Fishing Company of Philadelphia, circa 1732. When, in *Physick Book*, Prue Bartlett meets Robert Hooper in a Marblehead tavern in 1760 to sell her recipe book, they doubtless sealed the deal with something rather like Fish House Punch.

My mother found this recipe when she was working at the New Haven Historical Society in the seventies, and we make it every year on New Year's Eve. It is delicious and is guaranteed to keep your guest room occupied. I include my own preparation instructions.

Note: Leftovers can be preserved in the refrigerator for at least a few weeks.

Water for making ice (approximately 4 cups)	6 lemons
1½ quarts water (pineapple juice may be substituted for 2 cups of water)	1 quart Jamaican rum (light or dark will work, but I think dark is better)
1¼ cups brown sugar, packed (I prefer dark brown sugar)	1 pint brandy
	Good dash peach brandy (apricot will also work)

1 Fill a medium sized plastic container (approximately 4 cups) with water. Place in the freezer to make ice to serve with the punch.
2 Bring 1½ quarts of water (or water and pineapple juice) and brown sugar to boil in a saucepan. Reduce heat and gently simmer, stirring frequently, for 5 minutes or until the sugar is fully dissolved. Remove the pan from the heat and cool until ready to use.
3 Cut lemons in half. In the most enormous bowl you can lay your hands on, squeeze the lemons, leaving juice, seeds, and most of the rinds in the bowl and set aside. Pour sugar syrup over the lemon juice and rinds.
4 Add rum and brandy. Dash liberally with peach brandy "to make it mellow." Float block of ice in the middle of the punch. Punch should be served cold. Watch out for sudden outbreaks of dancing.

SALAD OF HERBS AND FLOWERS FROM GRANNA'S GARDEN

Makes enough for 4 salad-loving people

Adapted from a seventeenth-century recipe (see below)

When Connie and Liz, the graduate student protagonist of *Physick Book* and her closest friend, first arrive at the strange little house on Milk Street in Marblehead, Massachusetts, they are struck by the wide variety of herbs and plants growing in what is essentially a wild kitchen garden. In colonial America, kitchen gardens and forage would have supplied fresh foods to supplement the heavily salted and preserved staples needed for much of the rest of the year. This first recipe is a kitchen garden and forage salad from the seventeenth century, which will nevertheless be appealing to a modern palate.

Note: Fresh edible flowers such as marigolds, violets, and carnations are available at specialty grocery stores in the produce section. If you can't find edible flowers, you can prepare the salad without them and it will still be delicious. The flowers add a special touch.

Amounts of mint and sage can vary according to taste; don't be afraid to experiment.

2 cups (about ½ head) red leaf lettuce, torn into bite-sized pieces

2 cups arugula

1 cup baby spinach leaves

2 tablespoons chopped fresh mint leaves (see note)

1½ teaspoons chopped fresh sage leaves (see note)

½ cup fresh edible flowers (see note)

1 medium cucumber

Juice of 1 lemon (approximately)

½ teaspoon sugar

6 tablespoons olive oil

3 tablespoons vinegar (I like apple cider vinegar)

2 large eggs, hard-cooked and sliced (optional)

Salt to taste

Freshly ground black pepper to taste

1 Rinse lettuce, arugula, and spinach and pat dry. Combine with chopped herbs and set aside in a salad bowl.

2 Rinse the flowers well, drain, and pat dry. Place them in a small mixing bowl.

3 Peel the cucumber, slice it in half lengthwise, and remove the seeds. Cut cucumber into wafer-thin slices and add to the flowers until they are about equal in proportion. Squeeze fresh lemon juice on to the flowers and cucumbers, just enough to moisten them.

4 Sprinkle sugar over the cucumber and flower mixture and add the mixture to the greens. Toss thoroughly with oil and vinegar.

5 Arrange egg slices around the rim of the salad bowl as a garnish, if desired, and serve with salt and pepper to taste.

This is a recipe for "Sallet of all Kinds of Herbs" as it appears in *A Book of Fruits and Flowers* by Thomas Jenner (1653, reprinted in *The Compleat New England Huswife*, compiled by Elizabeth Stuart Gibson, Albion Press, 1992). Take your Herbs (as the tops of red Sage, Mint, Lettuce, Violets, Marigold, Spinach, & cetera) and pick them very fine in fair water; and wash your flowers by themselves and swing them in a strainer. Then mingle them in a dish with Cucumbers and Lemons pared and sliced: scrape thereon Sugar and put into Vinegar and Oil. Spread your Flowers on top of the Sallet, and take Eggs boiled hard and lay them about the dish.

NANA'S TAPIOCA PUDDING

Makes 4 servings

There is no dessert that speaks of New England more to me than pudding. Connie Goodwin, the protagonist of *Physick Book*, passes a tense lunch with her dissertation advisor Manning Chilton at the Harvard Faculty Club, and prods listlessly at that institution's famous bread pudding. A "hasty pudding," made notorious by the Harvard theatrical club of the same name, is really just a term for boiled cornmeal like a polenta, which can either be eaten warm with molasses or maple syrup, or left to set while cold and then fried in butter. Even our local waterside breakfast spot in Marblehead has a rotating selection of daily puddings, ranging from standards like chocolate to regionalisms like Grape Nut. My great grandmother Nana, a firm New Englander frowning her way through many family pictures, has left behind her armchair in my living room and her recipe for tapioca pudding in my kitchen. (My grandmother on the other side, also a New Englander, detested tapioca pudding, calling it "fish eyes and glue." I rather like it, it must be said.)

Note: Tapioca pudding is delicious either warm or cold. Warm pudding is very good topped with a little heavy cream.

Use less sugar if you prefer a less sweet pudding.

---

2 large eggs
⅓ cup sugar (see note)
2 tablespoons quick-cooking tapioca
2 cups whole milk
¼ teaspoon salt
¾ teaspoon vanilla extract

---

1 Place eggs in a medium bowl. Add sugar and tapioca and beat by hand, or with an electric mixer until light and creamy.
2 Place milk in a large saucepan. Pour egg mixture into milk and allow to sit for 5 minutes. Turn heat to medium and stir constantly while mixture comes to a full boil.
3 Remove mixture from heat, add salt and vanilla, and stir. Pour into serving dish. Cool for 20 minutes. Serve warm or cold. (To serve cold: chill for several hours in the refrigerator, covered with plastic wrap.)

Joshilyn Jackson

Herman Esteves

Inspiration   I'm Southern to the bone, and there is such a strong oral tradition here. I grew up listening to all the storytellers in my family telling and retelling tales that got taller and wider and more epic every time. I think it soaked in.

....

Readers Should Know   When people ask me what kind of books I write, I am very often flummoxed. Certainly I have been influenced by Southern gothic writers, but my books are published as "mainstream fiction." That can mean a huge range of things. I think the best way to describe my work is to call it book club fiction. By this I mean, my novels are character driven, but I love plot. I like twists and turns, but there are also things going on under the story, themes and tropes and images, that can fuel good discussions.

   I write the kinds of books I like to read, and I am a rereader. You could take any one of my novels down to the beach with a rum drink and race through and have a grand time. And if that's all you want, more power to you. Underneath the kissing and the gunplay—and I like to have both, especially within a few pages of each other—I am often asking questions about identity: What makes us who we are? Genes? History? Our choices? I am consistently interested in exploring redemption, the role of women in the arts, and the effects of poverty, be it spiritual or literal.

....

Readers Frequently Ask   Book clubs often ask if all the things that happen to my characters have actually happened to me. No, of course not. If I'd lived through everything that happens to all the people in all my books, I would be in a small soft room with sleeves that wrap around and fasten in the back.

....

Influences on My Writing   I love Flannery O'Connor and Harper Lee, though I hesitate to say they have influenced me. It feels presumptuous. I certainly hope the profound impact their work has had on me shows in my own.

Rose Mae Lolley's Chess Pie

Makes 1 (9-inch) pie; 8 servings

Down here in the South, we have a story about how Chess Pie came into its name. I'm not sure what the country mouse version of an urban legend is—a rural legend? But the story goes, a Yankee fella had a big slice of it at a Southern boarding house, and he liked it so much he asked what the pie was called. The lady of the house said something that sounded to the fella's Connecticut ears like, "It's chess pie." He went home with the recipe and the wrong name. She was actually saying that it wasn't any kind of pie in particular. It was "just pie." With her thick accent, she said it like, "jess pie," and he heard it as "chess."

"Just" Pie is an accurate name for this Jackson family favorite . . . it isn't any specific kind of pie, exactly. It has no fruit or chocolate or any sort of leading flavor. It's just a sweet, rich, gooey, basic pie. Pie reduced to its lowest common denominator.

My narrator in *Backseat Saints*, Rose Mae Lolley, is walking calmly in bow-tipped ballet flats and a swirly cotton skirt toward Death by Marriage. She's lost her brave, fierce self—the one we see in *gods in Alabama*—inside a girl she calls Ro Grandee. Ro is the perfect wife. Cooking is one of the few things she controls, and she makes a version of Chess Pie for her husband while trying to negotiate a truce with him.

The book begins when Rose meets a gypsy at the airport, one who shares her past and knows her future. The gypsy lays out the tarot cards and tells Ro that her beautiful, abusive husband is going to kill her. Unless she kills him first.

That pretty much puts the kibosh on any more baking.

I chose a chess pie for the scene because Rose is from small town Alabama and it is such a quintessentially Southern dessert. My mother always serves it with black coffee to "cut the sweet." It's a simple pie and all recipes for it are pretty similar, but this is the way my great aunt Gladys always made it, and her Chess Pie is the very best I have ever eaten.

Note: I mix this pie by hand, with a wooden spoon for true great aunt Gladys authenticity, but an electric mixer works fine too. I only do it that way because I hate cleaning the mixer.

½ cup (1 stick) softened butter (Do not use melted butter or the pie may not set up properly!)

1 cup granulated sugar

1 cup light brown sugar, lightly packed

1 teaspoon vanilla extract

4 eggs

1 tablespoon white cornmeal

¼ cup buttermilk, evaporated milk, or cream

1 teaspoon to 1 tablespoon distilled white vinegar (if you use buttermilk you will need 1 teaspoon of vinegar, and if you choose evaporated milk or cream you'll need 1 tablespoon)

1 9-inch unbaked pie shell (see recipes, p. 72; 235)

1   Preheat oven to 425°F.
2   Mix the butter, both sugars, and the vanilla in a large bowl. Stir in the eggs. Add the cornmeal, buttermilk or evaporated milk or cream, and vinegar. Stir until smooth.
3   Pour batter into pie shell, filling to ¼ inch from top of rim. (You may have some extra batter.) Bake for 10 minutes, then reduce heat to 300°F and bake until the pie sets up. (The pie is done when the top is golden brown and the filling is not loose anymore. A little center wiggling is okay since this is a very gooey pie. Don't shake too hard because the bad news is a chess pie can "fall." The good news is that fallen chess pies taste great!) Some ovens will do the job in 30 minutes, others will take closer to 45.
4   Let cool. Serve with strong black coffee.

Hillary Jordan

SELECTED WORKS

- *Mudbound* (2008)

William Coupon

Inspiration *Mudbound* was inspired by stories about my grandparents' farm, but the novel grew into something much larger than the family drama I'd originally envisioned once my black characters started to speak. Race is America's great unhealed wound, and I believe that the only way to heal it is through fuller understanding. I wanted to paint a vivid picture of how things really were during the Jim Crow era by showing it from multiple points of view: black and white, male and female, educated and illiterate, oppressor and oppressed.

My second novel is set in a right-wing dystopia thirty years in the future. It was sparked by a conversation I had with my uncle about the criminal justice system, but it really caught fire for me during the George W. Bush years. It's about crime and punishment, but also about the erosion of civil and reproductive rights, the dangers of blurring the lines between church and state, and the inevitability of environmental catastrophe if we don't pull our heads out of the sand and act to stop it.

Wherever the Next Word Takes Me I don't outline my books, and half the time I don't know what's happening in the next paragraph, much less the next chapter. I basically pull it out of my brain a sentence at a time.

Readers Frequently Ask

Q: Why did you choose to tell *Mudbound* in six different voices?

A: I wanted to make the process of writing my first novel as difficult as possible.

Q: Do you believe in writer's block and, if so, how do you get past it?

A: We all have days when the writing comes slowly, badly, painfully. Sometimes you have to step away and go refill the well; take a walk somewhere beautiful, see a play, go shoe shopping. But in the end, there's no cure but sitting down with that pristine white page and mucking it up with words.

Q: Did Ronsel Jackson, the black soldier who is victimized upon his return from WWII, really pull through and lead a happy life as you suggest at the end of *Mudbound?*
A: What do you think?

....

The Great Storytellers Who Have Influenced My Writing

The writers I love are first and foremost great storytellers who grab hold of you on page one and don't let go till THE END. To name a few: Austen, for her ability to create perfect snow globes, vivid encapsulations of her world filled with indelible characters. Flannery O'Connor, for the way she uses dark comedy to tackle huge themes and shed light on the human condition. Shakespeare, for the magnificence of his prose and the breadth of his understanding. Faulkner, Barbara Kingsolver, Marilynne Robinson, Styron, Ishiguro, James Baldwin and a host of others have made me the writer I am today. . . .

....

To my knowledge, nobody on my mother's side of the family has ever been thin. This is the Southern side, the side that wore gray in the war (which is pronounced "woe-wah" and refers as a matter of course to The War Between the States). My maternal forebears were Kirkwoods and Betheas and Morrisons and Scarboroughs who hailed from places like Talledega and Charleston and Oxford, Mississippi and who always kept a can of bacon grease on the stove, because almost any Southern recipe that's not a dessert starts with "Heat two tablespoons of bacon grease in a skillet." These were Deep Southerners, people who loved to cook and eat.

Cliché though it may be, it's almost impossible to overstate the Southern zeal for food—especially the rich, luscious, waist-thickening, artery-clogging kind—or the passion we bring to the act of cooking. I remember the tender look on my grandmother's face when she set a platter of fried chicken on the table in front of my grandfather, and how ardently she watched him take that first bite. In my family, cooking is a form of lovemaking.

How much more so, then, must it have been to cook three meals a day on a wood stove in a shotgun shack with no electricity or indoor plumbing? These were the dire circumstances my grandmother found herself in shortly after World War II, when my grandfather moved her and their two young daughters from the comfort of the city to a ramshackle farm in rural Arkansas. *Mudbound* was inspired by stories about that farm and the tumultuous year they spent there. And because it's a Southern story, food (along with floods, family discord, forbidden love, and dead mules) figures prominently in it.

AUNT FAYE'S FAMOUS PEACH CHESS PIE

Makes 1 (9-inch) pie; serves 6 people with self-restraint, 4 in my family

The peach chess pie mentioned in the first chapter narrated by Laura—the heroine of *Mudbound* who ends up rebelling against the traditions of Southern womanhood in which she was raised—is one of the most prized recipes in my family. It comes from Aunt Faye, a genteel Southern lady known for her highly caloric dishes. She wasn't a blood relation, but her husband, Bob Poole, was my grandfather's doctor. This man convinced my grandfather to have stomach surgery after thirty years of painful ulcers and, as a result, allowed him to enjoy food again. Including Aunt Faye's famous pie.

I like to serve this pie when it's slightly warm but not hot, though it's also excellent at room temperature and makes a deliciously naughty breakfast straight out of the fridge.

Note: When separating the eggs, take care not to contaminate the whites with any yolk. If you do, try to fish it out with a piece of eggshell or small spoon. Don't use your fingers; the oil on them will keep the whites from expanding properly. Even a drop of yellow will ruin the meringue so, if you're not sure you've gotten every last bit of yolk, throw out the whites and start over. After separating the eggs (reserving 2 yolks and discarding the third), set the whites aside to come to room temperature. Chilled egg whites won't achieve their full volume, and meringue is all about volume. Aunt Faye held a very dim view of any cook who couldn't make her meringue stand tall.

FOR THE FILLING

3–4 local, in-season peaches (1½ cups' worth of slices), ripe but still nice and firm

½ cup (1 stick) butter, softened

1 cup sugar

2 large egg yolks (see note)

½ cup plus 2 tablespoons all-purpose flour

Pinch salt

FOR THE CRUST

1 (9-inch) frozen pie crust (Aunt Faye will never know, and neither will your guests. If the store's out, or if you simply must make your own, I like Martha Stewart's recipe, or see recipes on p. 72; 235).

FOR THE MERINGUE

3 large egg whites, at room temperature (see note)

½ teaspoon cream of tartar

5 tablespoons sugar

1 Set rack in middle of oven. Preheat oven to 350°F.

2 **To make the filling:** Peel and pit the peaches and cut into wedges about ½-inch thick. Set aside.

3 In large bowl of electric mixer, cream the butter and sugar. Add egg yolks and beat to combine. Add flour and salt and beat to combine. Add sliced peaches and stir in by hand (batter will be thick). Spoon evenly into frozen pie shell.

4 Place pie in oven. Cooking time is about 50 minutes. The pie is done when it's golden brown on top, there's no liquidy jiggling, and a knife stuck in the center comes out clean.

5 When the pie is almost cooked, make the meringue: Beat the egg whites at medium speed until frothy. Add the cream of tartar, increase speed to high, and beat until stiff. Add the sugar a tablespoon at a time, beating continuously. The meringue is done when it makes stiff, shiny peaks (check by lifting up the beaters) and doesn't feel grainy when rubbed between your fingers.

6 Remove pie from oven. Spoon the meringue onto the piping hot pie and sculpt it using a small spatula or the back of a spoon so that you have tall, magnificent peaks (they may curl over slightly, but that's just fine). Bake for an additional 10 minutes or so, until the meringue is lightly browned overall, and the peaks are a darker brown.

7 Allow to cool on a wire rack. When you slice the pie, the meringue will be at least twice as tall as the filling if you've done your job right, and you'll stand a little taller too, knowing that you would have earned Aunt Faye's respect.

Catfish Benedict

Makes 4 servings

Recipe courtesy of Brian Kaywork, Executive Chef
of the Rhinecliff Hotel in Rhinecliff, New York

The Delta is almost as renowned for catfish as for cotton, and this fish is mentioned several times in *Mudbound*. Laura, the heroine of *Mudbound*, would have fried it (and you can't go wrong with fried catfish), but I wanted a more modern twist. So I asked my friend Brian Kaywork, the very talented chef of the Rhinecliff Inn, to create a recipe. He may be a Yankee, but the Catfish Benedict he came up with can only be described as heaven on a plate.

Note: Preparation time for this dish is about 1 hour.

Clarified butter is pure butterfat, made by removing the milk solids and water from butter. To clarify butter: Melt 1½ sticks of unsalted butter slowly in a small saucepan. Remove from the heat and allow to cool a bit; the milk solids will sink to the bottom. Skim any foam off the top and discard. Pour off the clear liquid—this is the clarified butter—and leave behind the milk solids.

White Lily all-purpose flour, long a staple of southern baking, produces light, fluffy biscuits. Unfortunately, it can be difficult to find outside the South. You can substitute a combination of ½ cup all-purpose flour, such as Pillsbury, and ½ cup cake flour.

If you can't find crawfish, you can substitute ½ pound medium shrimp in the shell or ⅓ pound precooked, shelled shrimp. (If you use precooked shrimp, skip the poaching process and just add the shrimp to the completed hollandaise sauce.) For frozen, precooked shrimp or crawfish, defrost in advance, allow to reach room temperature, and pat dry thoroughly before adding to sauce.

Time this recipe carefully. I use one double boiler working for the hollandaise, one pan for the poached eggs, and one sauté pan for the spinach *cooking at the same time*. That should mean that everything will be finished at the same time.

FOR THE CRAWFISH

¾ cup (1½ sticks) unsalted butter, melted
    and clarified (see note)
½ pound crawfish (see note)

FOR THE BISCUITS

1 cup all-purpose flour (preferred brand is
    White Lily) (see note)
1 teaspoon baking powder
¼ teaspoon kosher salt
2 tablespoons unsalted butter, cut into
    ½-inch pieces
2 tablespoons plus 2 teaspoons heavy
    cream
⅓ cup buttermilk
2 tablespoons butter, melted, for brushing
    on top

FOR THE CATFISH

10 ounces catfish fillet, cut into 4 portions
¼ teaspoon salt
Pinch freshly ground black pepper
Pinch seafood seasoning, such as Old Bay

FOR THE POACHED EGGS

4 cups water
2 tablespoons white vinegar
4 large eggs
Salt to taste
Freshly ground black pepper to taste

FOR THE SPINACH

1 tablespoon olive oil or butter
½ pound baby spinach
Salt to taste
Freshly ground black pepper to taste

FOR THE HOLLANDAISE

2 large egg yolks
1 teaspoon white vinegar
1 teaspoon fresh lemon juice
1 tablespoon water
A few dashes hot pepper sauce
Pinch salt
Pinch freshly ground black pepper

1 Preheat oven to 400°F.
2 **To poach the crawfish:** In a 12-quart pot, heat the clarified butter to 160°F and try to maintain this constant temperature. Place the crawfish in the butter and cook for 8–10 minutes, maintaining a constant low temperature. Strain the crawfish, reserving the butter. When cool, peel the crawfish, pat the tail meat dry, and reserve it.
3 **To make the biscuits:** Combine the flour, baking powder, and salt in a large bowl. Using a pastry cutter, 2 knives used in scissor fashion, or your fingertips, cut butter into the flour until pea-sized (it is key to the recipe to have pea-sized pieces). Add the cream and buttermilk, and stir lightly with a fork until a sticky mass forms. Turn onto a floured surface, and fold gently 2–3 times. Use a good bit of flour and only a couple of folds. Be sure not to overwork the biscuits: do not knead, only fold the mixture. The dough should be smooth and cohesive when done. Press dough until it's 1½–2 inches

thick. Use a 3- or 4-inch round cookie cutter or glass to cut dough into rounds (you should get 2 or 3 biscuits). Bake on ungreased baking sheet for 13–15 minutes, until golden brown. Remove from oven and brush the tops with melted butter. Allow to cool on baking sheet.

4 **To prepare the catfish** (the catfish can be baked in the same oven as the biscuits, space permitting): Season the fish on both sides with salt, pepper, and seafood seasoning. Place on oiled nonstick pan or preheated cast-iron skillet, and bake in oven for approximately 10–12 minutes, until fully opaque. Turn the oven off, cover the fish, and keep warm in the oven for no longer than 15 minutes.

5 **To prepare poaching liquid for eggs:** Place water and vinegar in a 3-quart shallow pan and bring to just under a boil.

6 While water is heating, prepare the spinach: Heat oil or butter in medium saucepan over medium heat. Add spinach and sauté until wilted. Season with salt and pepper to taste. Set aside, covered, to keep warm.

7 **To poach the eggs:** The water should be at 170°F. Crack each egg into a small cup with a handle. Lower lips of the cups into the water at the same time, and gently tip the eggs into the water. Be sure not to break the yolks as you are placing in the water! You should see the egg whites envelop the yolks and the eggs will float to the top. Cook for approximately 4–5 minutes. The whites should feel and appear firm and the yolks should have a little "give" to them. Using a slotted spoon, remove eggs to a clean dish towel to remove excess water. If the eggs are done before the rest of the dish, no problem! Keep the eggs on the towel, then assemble the dish and place the eggs back into the water to reheat. Season with salt and pepper before layering on dish.

8 **To prepare the hollandaise sauce:** Warm reserved butter in a small saucepan. Place egg yolks, vinegar and lemon juice in top of a double boiler or a heatproof bowl set over a pan of gently boiling water. Whisk together. Slowly add the melted butter with constant whisking. After half of the butter is incorporated, add the tablespoon of water, and then add remaining melted butter. Control the temperature of the hollandaise by removing it from the double boiler or pan if it seems too hot. Water can be added (just a little!) if the hollandaise appears too thick. Remove from heat and add the crawfish tails, hot pepper sauce, salt, and pepper. Cover and keep in a warm spot.

9 **To assemble the dish:** Split 2 biscuits and place biscuit halves on individual serving plates. If necessary, trim bottom surface of catfish fillets to ensure they will lie flat. Build the Benedict in this order: biscuit, spinach, catfish, egg, and then top with hollandaise. Season with salt and pepper to taste, and serve.

HILL'S FRIED CHICKEN

Serves 3–4, or 1 grad student for the better part of a week

I included a recipe for fried chicken because it is, for me, the ultimate Southern comfort food. It's what I make whenever I'm feeling blue or missing my family. And unlike my heroine, Laura, I don't have to kill, disembowel, and pluck a chicken to get it. If I did, I'd undoubtedly be a lot thinner.

---

1 small (3½-pound) broiler-fryer chicken, cut into 8 pieces

Salt to taste

Freshly ground black pepper to taste

3–4 cups canola oil or solid vegetable shortening (the latter is best, but it has those wicked trans fats)

½ cup all-purpose flour

½ cup rice flour

1–2 tablespoons Tony Chachere's Creole Seasoning (or make your own mixture of equal parts salt, pepper, paprika, cayenne pepper, garlic powder, and cumin)

---

1 Put on some appropriate music, e.g., John Lee Hooker, Muddy Waters, or Keb Mo. Pour yourself a beer or a Jack & Coke.
2 Wash chicken and dry well with paper towels, removing any excess skin or fat (but don't remove all of the skin). Season generously with salt and pepper and let sit at room temperature for half an hour.
3 In a large, preferably cast-iron skillet, heat the oil or shortening on medium-high to about 350°F (hot enough that a pinch of flour dropped into it makes a robust sizzle). The liquid should cover the chicken about two-thirds of the way but no more.
4 As the oil or shortening heats, mix the flours and seasoning together in a large resealable plastic bag. Add the dark meat (drumsticks and thighs) and shake until well-coated. Shake off excess flour and place skin side down in the pan. (If you're cooking more than one chicken for a large group, resist the urge to hurry the process by crowding the pan.) Fry until skin is a lovely crisp brown, 7–9 minutes, then turn and fry the other side, 4–6 minutes.
5 Place chicken pieces on a wire rack set over a jelly roll pan to drain, or on a plate covered in paper towels. Coat and fry the white meat pieces next, 10–12 minutes per side for the breasts (longer if they're very thick) and slightly less for the wings.
6 Think of Dixie, and not your arteries, as you savor every last succulent bite.

Kathleen Kent

SELECTED WORKS

* *The Wolves of Andover* (2010)
* *The Heretic's Daughter* (2008)

Deborah Feingold

Inspiration I grew up hearing stories about Martha Carrier, my grandmother from nine generations back on my mother's side who was hanged as a witch in Salem in 1692. I was always fascinated by the events leading up to the witch trials, but also with the many family tales about the Carrier family's life in seventeenth century New England. I was certain that someday I would weave history and family legend together into a work of fiction, one that that now exists in *The Heretic's Daughter*.

....

Readers Should Know Wherever possible, I tried to use actual names, dates, and places to bring authenticity to my work. *The Wolves of Andover*, the prequel to *The Heretic's Daughter*, is the story of Martha's husband Thomas Carrier who, according to family legend, lived to 109, stood seven feet tall, and was one of the executioners of King Charles I of England. As with the first novel, I used both fictitious and true-to-life characters to develop a story of intrigue, one that includes spies, assassins, heroes, and villains.

....

Readers Frequently Ask The over-arching theme of *The Heretic's Daughter* is about the Salem witch trials. However, the heart of the book is a coming-of-age story about a daughter learning to appreciate the strength of her difficult mother who unflinchingly defends her innocence through the growing witch hysteria. Many people have asked if the character of Martha was modeled after anyone in particular in my family. With a great deal of pride, I answer that she is a composite character, built from the words and deeds of the ferocious Carrier women I have known.

....

Authors That Have Influenced My Writing My favorite books as a young adult were by Charles Dickens. His characters, richly drawn from his own experiences in the back alleys and poor-houses of London, always seemed to reverberate with a profound sense of both the sublime and the ridiculous. And, despite having to sleep with the light on, I often read the works of Edgar Allan Poe for his atmospheric descriptions of the supernatural and the darker side of the human experience.

FLORENCE CARRIER'S COWBOY CAKE

Makes 12–16 servings

The Heretic's Daughter is my first novel. The story is based on family legends passed down through nine generations and on the historical events of the Salem witch trials. I first heard of my ancestor Martha Carrier from my maternal grandmother. She always insisted that there were no such things as witches, only ferocious women. She would have known, as she was a dead shot with a rifle and rode wild horses on the farm where she grew up. The strong women in my family not only influenced the kind of stories I've chosen to write, but gave me the courage to write them in the first place.

I have always been struck by the remarkable courage and fortitude of the Colonial women of New England; how they endured the many physical challenges of day-to-day life while still managing to care for and feed their large families in the most Spartan of conditions. They had no electricity, obviously, or refrigeration, and they were entirely dependent on what they could grow and preserve. Sarah, the main character in *The Heretic's Daughter*, is taught by her mother Martha to cook at a young age, a valuable life lesson that becomes essential when Martha is taken away to jail, accused of being a witch. Sarah, a young girl of ten, is left to care for her brothers and baby sister. During the seventeenth century, the Carrier women would have made Johnny Cakes from corn mash in a pan suspended over an open hearth.

I remember my grandmother as a wonderful cook, often using simple, home grown ingredients from her own garden to create deeply satisfying and delicious meals that could best be described as comfort food.

Following is the recipe for Florence Carrier's Cowboy Cake, a modern take on the Johnny Cakes that Martha might have taught Sarah to make. They are best when shared with the ferocious women in your life.

2 cups light brown sugar, well packed

⅔ cup solid vegetable shortening or butter

2½ cups all-purpose flour

½ teaspoon ground cinnamon

½ teaspoon ground nutmeg

½ teaspoon salt

½ teaspoon baking soda

2 teaspoons baking powder

2 large eggs (eggs can be lightly beaten into
    buttermilk or sour milk)

1 cup buttermilk or sour milk

1 Preheat oven to 350°F. Lightly butter and flour two 9" round cake pans.

2 Using a pastry blender or fork, blend brown sugar and shortening or butter. Set aside ½ cup mixture for topping.

3 Sift flour, cinnamon, nutmeg, and salt together (or mix well). Place in the medium bowl of an electric mixer, and add sugar and shortening mixture and blend well. Add baking soda, baking powder, eggs and buttermilk or sour milk and blend well. The batter will be thick.

4 Divide batter between two cake pans and sprinkle with reserved topping. Bake for 30 minutes, or until a toothpick inserted at center of cake comes out clean.

5 The cake can be served warm or at room temperature, like a coffee cake (Mom said her mother always served it right out of the pan with a cake knife, hence the name "cowboy cake"; you could cook and eat out of the same pan).

Janice Y.K. Lee

- *The Piano Teacher* (2009)

Amy K. Boyd

Inspiration
I'm often inspired by a single image—a woman in an antiseptic supermarket, pushing an empty cart at 2 A.M., a couple fighting in the garden of a country inn—and set out to explore how those people got to that moment. I will often have the last line of the story before anything else. *The Piano Teacher* came from a short story about an English newlywed who was teaching a young Chinese girl the piano. I saw her sitting beside the student on a stool, a little uncomfortable, a little unknowing. From that, a whole world emerged.

The Piano Teacher is being translated into twenty-five languages around the world and it makes me smile to think of a French woman, a Brazilian man, and a Taiwanese college student all reading about these characters that were known only to me just a few years ago.

Readers Frequently Ask
They mostly want to know how I came to write the book, how I chose the era. But like anything that takes a long time and a great deal of work, it's hard to look back and see how it all started. *The Piano Teacher* was at first a short story about Claire and Locket set in the 1970s. Then I started reading about the war in Hong Kong, so I moved it back to that time. More people were born and started to interact. There were many factors involved, over many months and years. The birth of a book is hard to describe. Like childbirth, you tend to forget about the pain and the labor in the afterglow of the actual product.

My Favorite Authors
I have so many favorite writers but Jeffrey Eugenides, Michael Cunningham, and Amy Bloom (see page 7) are on the top of my list. I wouldn't say that they have necessarily influenced me, more that they have inspired me by producing truly great writing that makes reading a transcendent experience.

INDONESIAN GINGER CHICKEN

Makes 4-6 servings

From *The Barefoot Contessa Cookbook* by Ina Garten (Clarkson Potter, 1999)

I make this dish often because it's easy and delicious. It's a real marriage of East and West, with the ginger and the soy sauce, and the honey and the chicken. It's a mix of sweet and sour, much like Trudy Liang of *The Piano Teacher*, although I doubt you'd ever catch her in a kitchen. Researching a wartime novel made me aware of how precious food is when society breaks down. If distribution channels fail, it gets dire very quickly. Descriptions of meals during wartime were enticing because you got the sense that food was so dear. I describe rice dotted with salted pork, or tins of bully beef and condensed milk guarded like treasure. Somehow the tastes always seemed more potent in this time of scarcity and fear. In the high times before the war, however, there was also the exotic. Trudy might have eaten bear's paw or monkey's brains and, in one scene, she tells of taking the Japanese to dine on baby mice in Macao, reportedly a delicacy at that time.

This chicken is always moist and the perfect combination of sweet and savory. I often glop the sauce over everything else on the plate because it is so addictive. It's perfect for a book club because you make the sauce the night before, marinate the chicken, and put it in the oven before the book club arrives. After that, there's nothing for you to do except sniff the tantalizing aroma emanating from the oven as you sip wine with your friends.

I would serve it with rice pilaf and a crisp green salad.

Note: You can prepare the marinade in the morning and marinate the chicken throughout the day (5–8 hours) and still achieve excellent flavor, although it won't be quite as strong.

> *1 cup honey*
> *¾ cup soy sauce*
> *¼ cup minced garlic (8–12 cloves)*
> *½ cup peeled and grated fresh gingerroot*
> *2 small chickens (3½ pounds each), quartered,*
>   *with backs removed*

1 Combine honey, soy sauce, garlic, and ginger in a small saucepan. Cook over low heat until the honey is melted. Place chicken skin side down in a large, shallow baking pan, and pour on the sauce. Cover the pan tightly with aluminum foil. Marinate overnight in the refrigerator (see note).

2 Preheat oven to 350°F.

3 Bake for 30 minutes, uncover the pan, turn the chicken skin side up, and increase temperature to 375°F. Continue baking for 30 minutes, or until the juices run clear when you cut between the leg and the thigh and the sauce is a rich dark brown.

SINGAPORE SLING

Makes 1 drink

"What would an evening be like without drinks?" Trudy Liang of *The Piano Teacher* might wonder as she stirred a pitcher of these Singapore Slings, an iconic cocktail that originated in the famously atmospheric Raffles Hotel in colonial Singapore around 1910. There, languorous women lounged as they tried to beat the heat with icy drinks under slowly undulating fans. Life in Singapore and Hong Kong was much the same; privileged expatriates made the rounds of their favorite haunts, until the Japanese invaded in World War II and their way of life was interrupted. Trudy and Will might have gone to Singapore to visit friends, and found their very same world taking place in another country. This drink takes me to a lobby with tall ceilings, palm fronds, and wicker chairs.

Note: Bénédictine is a sweet French herbal liqueur created from twenty-seven plants and spices.

> *1½ ounces gin*
> *½ ounce cherry brandy*
> *¼ ounce orange-flavored liqueur, such as Cointreau*
> *¼ ounce Bénédictine (see note)*
> *4 ounces pineapple juice*
> *1 tablespoon fresh lime juice*
> *2 teaspoons grenadine syrup*
> *1 dash aromatic bitters*
> *1 ounce club soda*
> *Slice of pineapple, for garnish*
> *Maraschino cherry, for garnish*

1 Fill a cocktail shaker half full with ice cubes. Add the gin, cherry brandy, orange-flavored liqueur, Bénédictine, pineapple juice, lime juice, grenadine, and bitters.
2 Shake well, then strain into an ice-filled tall glass. Top with club soda. Garnish with a slice of pineapple and a cherry on a toothpick, and serve with tiny umbrellas.

Elinor Lipman

Gabriel Amadeus Cooney

Inspiration What inspires a particular novel? I can say that I start with just a glimmer of an idea, usually a first sentence that intrigues me enough to lead me forward. And then another impulse kicks in: I want to write the damn thing so I can find out for myself what happens to these people I've generally grown very fond of.

....

Looking Ahead I try to write 500 words a day, not counting the long breaks between books. A long time ago I got good advice from Tracy Kidder: to be working on and committed to a new project as the latest is being published. It seems the older I get the more easily I am distracted. On occasion, I've literally tied myself to the chair at my computer.

....

Readers Frequently Ask I'm often asked what happens to characters after the book ends. Even though I'm tempted to say, "Uh, well . . . nothing. They're fictional characters," I still try to indulge the reader because it means that the characters have become real people with lives that continue after the last page. Oh, and often I get feedback about the movie version of *Then She Found Me*, my first novel. Many think that the book itself should have been the screenplay and did NOT like the changes. Because I loved the movie, I try to explain that any adaptation should be viewed as a movie based on characters *suggested* by the novel, and cannot be a carbon copy. Readers can be unbelievably loyal to the original text!

....

Influences on My Writing I have two, the first of which is *Happy All the Time* by Laurie Colwin. After reading it for the first time—and I hadn't written anything yet—I wanted to try my hand at something that could be so smart and funny all at once. The second book is *Anne Sexton: A Self-Portrait in Letters*. I read that over a long weekend, and came away (after reading about her workshop at Boston University, taught by Robert Lowell) thinking I should find myself a workshop, too, as a way to get started. I did, in 1979 at Brandeis University Adult Education, and that was where I caught the fiction bug.

KATHLEEN'S VEAL MARENGO FROM *THE LADIES' MAN*

Makes 4 servings

Here is the recipe I've been making for years, adapted from Craig Claiborne's
The New York Times International Cookbook (Harper & Row, 1971).

Whereas other authors might set their scenes in battlefields or bedrooms, I often send my characters to restaurants, which is my idea of a good time. Many of my characters cook, and most are enthusiastic eaters. Not that I admit to autobiographical touches in my novels, but I did assign to Kathleen in *The Ladies' Man* something I do in real life: grade recipes. Dishes don't reappear unless they get an A. Dishes good enough for company have to get an A+. Kathleen's most famous dish was just an unglamorous stew-like thing she made for her sisters, but it became a little famous when the casserole dish that was holding its leftovers was used to near-concuss romantic villain Harvey Nash.

Note: This dish simmers for several hours, so plan ahead.

You can substitute another cut of veal as long as it can be cut into cubes.

2 pounds veal, from the leg, cut into 1½" cubes (see note)

1 teaspoon salt for the meat, plus more for seasoning

¼ teaspoon freshly ground pepper for the meat, plus more for seasoning

¼ cup butter or olive oil

2 onions, chopped (doesn't have to be too fine)

2 garlic cloves, minced

¼ cup all-purpose flour

1½ cups chicken stock

½ cup white wine

1 cup canned diced tomatoes, drained

2 sprigs parsley, plus chopped parsley, for garnish

1 rib celery, sliced crosswise

1 bay leaf

½ teaspoon chopped fresh rosemary, or ¼ teaspoon dried rosemary

3 small (2-inches in diameter) yellow onions, quartered (or more if you'd like)

Buttered noodles, for serving

1 Pat the meat dry and sprinkle with the salt and pepper. In a medium skillet, heat butter or oil over high heat and fry the veal, a few pieces at a time so they're not touching, until browned on all sides.

2 When all the veal has been browned, return it to the skillet and lower the heat to medium. Add the chopped onions and cook until onions are lightly browned, about 3 minutes. Add the garlic and stir until it's fragrant. Stir in the flour and cook until that's lightly browned. Gradually stir in the chicken stock and white wine and bring to a boil. Add the tomatoes, parsley sprigs, celery, bay leaf, rosemary, and salt and pepper to taste. Cover and cook over low heat for 1 hour, careful that it doesn't burn.

3 Add the quartered onions, cover, and cook for 45 minutes longer. Meanwhile, prepare the buttered noodles.

4 Sprinkle with chopped parsley and serve over noodles.

MY MOTHER'S NOODLE KUGEL

Makes 6–8 servings

Natalie Marx, the narrator of *The Inn at Lake Devine*, is an aspiring chef. When tragedy strikes at the once-restricted hotel, she helps by cooking, and her idea of a little revenge cooking is to make noodle kugel and brisket. I was thinking of my mother's noodle pudding, which is her mother's recipe, and probably her mother's recipe before that. Noodle puddings are either the sweet kind or the savory kind depending on where one's European roots are, and this is definitely the sweet kind. Still, my mother (and Natalie) served it as a side dish with the main meal. This is simple and takes no skill, but it's delicious and custardy. The topping (just milk and an egg) makes no sense at the prep stage, but it blends in and works fine in the finished kugel.

FOR THE CASSEROLE
2 tablespoons butter, melted

1 8-ounce container cottage cheese (my
    mother used Hood's small curd)

½ cup sugar (or less, depending on taste)

2 large eggs (her trick to a good custard was
    to beat the eggs only lightly)

1 teaspoon vanilla extract

½ cup whole milk

½ cup raisins

8 ounces wide egg noodles, cooked

FOR THE TOPPING
1 large egg

1 cup whole milk

Ground cinnamon and sugar for sprinkling

Crushed cornflakes (optional)

1 Preheat oven to 350°F. Grease a 9" × 13" × 2" glass baking dish.
2 **To make the casserole:** In a large bowl, combine melted butter, cottage cheese, sugar, eggs, vanilla, milk, and raisins. Add the cooked noodles and stir in gently, then pour mixture into the prepared baking dish.
3 **To make the topping:** Beat egg, stir in milk, and pour over top of pudding. Sprinkle with cinnamon and sugar and top with a few handfuls of crushed cornflakes. (I don't do the cornflakes.)
4 Bake 45 minutes. Serve warm. (It's also delicious cold the next day for breakfast.)

Laura Lippman

Jan Cobb

Inspiration My inspiration comes primarily from my hometown, Baltimore, which fascinates me. It's such an odd mix of dualities. North, south. Rich, poor.

....

The Mystery Misnomer I write crime novels, a term I prefer to "mystery" because the latter implies a whodunit and my books don't always fit into that model. I am often inspired by real crimes, but I don't feel that my stories are "ripped from the headlines" or based on these crimes. Instead, I like to explore the themes and issues raised by certain crimes.

....

Readers Frequently Ask The question I receive most often, hands down, is why Baltimore cops use the vernacular "a police." (I am a police, I am a murder police, He's a good police, etc.) I don't know why they speak this way, only that they do. Others are concerned about coarse language, but I'm afraid that police procedurals without coarse language would be inherently false. I try to reply to all signed e-mails I receive, even the unkind ones.

....

Influences on My Writing I'm a lifelong reader, and much has influenced me. But I particularly liked Maud Hart Lovelace's "Betsy-Tacy" books. Which, not incidentally, are filled with delicious-sounding food.

Although I write about the quintessential Baltimorean, private detective Tess Monaghan, I sometimes feel I have just as much in common with her WASPy best friend, Whitney Talbot. And while Whitney is often mocked for her poor palate and general lack of interest in food, she prizes a good martini and the proper accompaniments. The martini recipe is my father's, slightly adjusted (I use less vermouth and better gin). The origins of the salmon dish, which my mother gave me in college, are now lost, but the cheese straws are credited to my great aunt Effie. One can buy commercial cheese straws, and I often do, but none compare to Aunt Effie's, who was a character in her own right, as brave and funny as Tess (and a much better cook). I've destroyed two cookie presses so far, working with this thick, heavy dough, but that's the price you have to pay. Come to think of it, a cookie press would make an excellent weapon in a mystery. . . .

SALMON SPREAD

Makes about 2½ cups

I first made this recipe when I was twenty-one and the final step called for making an actual ball and rolling it in slivered almonds and parsley. I never made that work and no one has ever complained.

1 14.75-ounce can of red salmon, drained, large bones removed

8 ounces cream cheese, at room temperature

½ teaspoon Worcestershire sauce

2 tablespoons lemon juice

1 tablespoon prepared horseradish

2 tablespoons grated onion

1 tablespoon chopped fresh parsley, plus parsley sprigs for garnish

½ teaspoon salt

Combine all ingredients in a medium bowl. Mix until very smooth (a wooden spoon works just fine). Chill thoroughly. Garnish with parsley sprigs, and serve with crackers or crudités.

AUNT EFFIE'S CHEESE STRAWS

Makes approximately 3 dozen (3-inch) crackers

Note: Commercial cheese straws tend to be cylindrical, but our family recipe yields more of a ridged, rectangular cracker, about 1 inch wide and 2–4 inches long. You will need a heavy-duty cookie press to make these crackers.

You can make the dough with a food processor or with your hands—literally. The hand method is for the truly intrepid. Personally, I find it's a decent workout.

½ cup (1 stick) unsalted butter, at room temperature

1 8-ounce package sharp yellow cheddar, shredded (about 2½ cups), at room temperature

1½ cups all-purpose flour

¾ teaspoons salt

½ teaspoon ground cayenne pepper

1   Preheat oven to 375°F.
2   Place butter, cheese, flour, salt, and cayenne pepper in the bowl of a food processor. Process until a thick, smooth dough forms, about 1 minute. Or, mash butter and cheese together using your hands. Sift flour, salt, and cayenne pepper together and blend, again using your hands, into cheese/butter mixture. Continue to work mixture with your hands for at least 15 minutes, until it becomes a rich, thick dough and has lost all crumbliness.
3   Fit the disk with the flat, ridged opening into the cookie press. Scoop a portion of the dough into the cookie press. Press dough into rectangles, 2–4 inches in length, on an ungreased baking sheet. (In an emergency, you can pinch off pieces of dough and flatten them with the bottom of a juice glass which has been greased and lightly floured. I've done this when my cookie press has broken midway through a batch.)
4   Bake for 20–28 minutes. Timing varies wildly. Look for light browning on the bottom, and no browning (or barely any) on the tops. Remove to wire rack and allow to cool.

THEO LIPPMAN JR.'S
FAVORITE MARTINI

Makes 1 drink

Note: My father started making this drink in the 1960s, long before the explosion of specialty martinis and 12-ounce martini glasses to accommodate them. Choose a smaller cocktail glass for this classic drink.

> *½ ounce dry vermouth*
> *2 ounces gin*
> *Small wedge of lemon*

1 In a shot glass that holds up to two ounces, pour ½ ounce of dry vermouth. Pour this into a martini glass and swirl to coat the inside of the glass. Pour half the vermouth back into the bottle, and half into a cocktail shaker filled with ice cubes.
2 Add 2 ounces of gin to the shaker. (Yes, that's an 8 to 1 ratio. Why not just start with an 8 to 1 ratio? I think the swirl of gin adds a little extra and, besides, my father believes that it's important to have an anal retentive martini ritual.) Shake, and strain into the glass. Rub the lemon wedge around the rim of the glass, squeezing gently, then drop it into the drink.

Margot Livesey

Rob Hann, Retna Ltd.

Inspiration *The House on Fortune Street* had several inspirations: my love of nineteenth century literature, my fascination with how people's lives change over time, a brief encounter with someone, like my character Cameron, whose desires have no place in this world.

....

What Keeps Me Writing? I have two very hard working sisters in Scotland; one runs a market research company, the other is the head teacher in a primary school. They are both ardent readers and when I write I'm always trying to keep them awake at night a little bit longer.

....

Readers Frequently Ask Was Eva, from my novel *Eva Moves The Furniture*, based on a real person? Yes, on my mother. I know very little about her, though, so my character is largely (and lovingly) imagined.

....

Books That Have Influenced My Writing *Great Expectations* by Charles Dickens is, as I hope *The House on Fortune Street* makes clear, a huge influence. My dear friend, the wonderful writer Andrea Barrett, guides both my reading and my writing. I grew up reading and watching Shakespeare, and he still remains my benchmark for character, plot, and, above all, language.

ABIGAIL'S PASTA

Makes 4 servings

Abigail's pasta is borrowed from my Edinburgh sister.

Abigail, the owner of the titular house on Fortune Street, learns to make this from her friend Dara's mother, Fiona. She whips this up the unfortunate evening when she drops in to visit Fiona and instead finds herself alone with Fiona's husband Alastair, Dara's stepfather.

I always put in more of my favorite ingredients—anchovies and pine nuts—but somehow it works out.

Note: Tagliatelle works well, but so would linguine or any not-too-chunky pasta. I'm allowing 2 ounces of pasta per person but for guests with hearty appetites, allow a little extra.

> *8 ounces pasta (see note)*
> *4 tablespoons pine nuts*
> *¼ cup olive oil*
> *2 garlic cloves, minced*
> *1 pound fresh spinach, roughly chopped*
> *½ cup raisins*
> *1 2-ounce tin anchovies (chopped if you prefer)*
> *2 tablespoons grated Parmesan cheese*

1 Prepare pasta according to package directions.
2 While pasta is boiling, toast pine nuts in a small skillet over low heat (it's easy to burn them so don't get distracted). Remove from heat and set aside.
3 In a large skillet, heat olive oil over low heat and sauté garlic for 30 seconds. Add spinach and sauté, stirring frequently until spinach is soft and almost completely cooked. Add raisins and stir for a couple of minutes. Remove from heat.
4 Place cooked pasta in a serving dish. Add spinach to cooked pasta and toss. Stir in anchovies (they dissolve but leave a nice sharp taste). Sprinkle with pine nuts and add Parmesan cheese (I always go a little overboard on this). Serve with good bread and lively conversation.

Dara's Carrot and Ginger Soup

Makes 6 servings

From *The Silver Palate Good Times Cookbook*
by Julee Rosso and Sheila Lukins (Workman, 1985)

Dara makes this soup for her father soon after she moves into the garden flat in *The House on Fortune Street*. She hopes this delicious soup will both make the flat seem more like home and impress her father with her adult competence.

6 tablespoons butter
1 large yellow onion, chopped
¼ cup finely chopped fresh gingerroot
3 garlic cloves, minced
7 cups vegetable stock
1 cup dry white wine
1½ pounds carrots, peeled and cut into ½-inch pieces
2 tablespoons fresh lemon juice
Pinch of curry powder
Salt to taste
Ground black pepper to taste
Chopped chives or parsley, for garnish

1 Melt butter in a large stockpot over medium heat. Add onion, ginger, and garlic and sauté for fifteen minutes.
2 Add stock, wine, and carrots. Bring to a boil, reduce heat, and simmer, uncovered, over medium heat until the carrots are very tender, about 45 minutes.
3 Purée the soup in a blender or food processor until smooth (Dara, in London, would have used a mouli).
4 Return to pot, and season with lemon juice, curry powder, and salt and pepper to taste. Garnish with chives or parsley. Serve hot or chilled to appreciative family members and friends.

Gregory Maguire

Andy Newman

Where I Find Inspiration   Two quotes bully themselves forward clamoring for attention: "Gather ye rosebuds while ye may" and "Still will I harvest Beauty where it grows," from Robert Herrick and Edna St. Vincent Millay, respectively. Both quotes suggest the notions of scavenging, salvage, and even theft. I am inspired in writing by my heroes (Maurice Sendak, Tony Kushner, Penelope Fitzgerald, Lucy Boston, and Emily Dickinson to name the first of hundreds who come to mind). The tiniest accident of concurrence—a visual thing, a scrap of memory pasted against a new understanding of human character, a spiral of melody, a dream image only partly recalled—can serve as the sand in the oyster. And so often does; and so efficiently that usually I cannot recall what the original fleck of sand was. Still, I try to pay attention to as much as I possibly can, for my work as well as for my satisfaction in daily life.

....

Readers Should Know   My critical monograph on Maurice Sendak, *Making Mischief*, codifies some of what I mention above in that I itemize his heroes, the sources of some of his images, and I admire what he makes of his particular sand. (Well, Blake is a very fancy bit of grit.) It also reminds me how to work and keep worthy heroes and muses in mind. I'm hard at work on the fourth, and I think final, volume of The Wicked Years, my series that began with *Wicked*. I have several quotes and bits of poetry as epigrams and a couple of CDs of Fauré set aside to listen to. I also have several years' worth of scraps of questions and conceits about the characters in Oz, scraps that have occurred to me at irregular intervals while I was working on other projects.

....

Readers Frequently Ask Readers seem endlessly fascinated about the relationship among the following creations: The *Wizard of Oz*, both the 1900 novel by L. Frank Baum and the 1939 MGM film starring Judy Garland, and the 1995 novel I wrote called *Wicked* as well as the 2003 play based on my novel.

I cannot always answer the questions. What I do find amusing is that some readers (and some reviewers) claim my book is more directly derived from the film, and others insist I follow Baum's inventions rather slavishly. In fact, I tried hard to derive my work in about equal parts from both iterations of the famous story, while at the same time adding novelty and dash of my own (as well as I was able).

....

Influences on My Writing I admire, and constantly applaud the influence of, T. H. White's magnum opus about King Arthur, published in omnibus edition as *The Once and Future King*. I did not see initially that *Wicked* was inspired by his efforts, but I found his taking of a familiar legend—King Arthur and the Knights of the Round Table—and retelling it as if it had never been told before, through his particular sympathetic intelligence and artistry, to be (when I reconsidered it) the book I had read that most prefigured what I hoped to do in *Wicked*.

Also, interesting, isn't it, that *The Once and Future King* inspired a musical (*Camelot*), and so did my novel.

I have never stopped admiring, for its poetry and its moral sensibility, a fine American novel called *Mariette in Ecstasy* by Ron Hansen. I had already written *Wicked* when I read *Mariette in Ecstasy*, but I went on to read Hansen's novel, *Hitler's Niece*, which did much of what I had wanted to do in *Wicked* in a hugely different vernacular. Hansen is a shockingly capable writer who should be known by everyone. I envy and would love to be able to emulate his capacity to render in storytelling the pettiness and weariness of evil as well as its dreadful cost.

Finally, the English novelist Jill Paton Walsh—a friend of mine as well as a hero—wrote a book for teenagers called *Unleaving*. It is now, I believe, out of print, but certainly worth searching for in libraries or on out-of-print websites. Her capacity for articulating a moral conundrum in the most sensuous prose makes her, in this novel especially, a worthy descendent or follower of Virginia Woolf at her best.

....

Of those denizens of Oz, we know a few things. They can sing. They can dance. Some of them can fly. But can they cook?

Dear reader, let us take a voyage deeper into the mysteries of the place. Let's spend a little time with the backstairs support, the scuttlebutts of scullery and buttery. Let's pay some attention to the help behind the curtain. Welcome to the kitchens of Oz.

OH SWEET OZCRUST GLINDA TART* (LUNCH AT SHIZ UNIVERSITY – PART 1)

Makes 6–8 servings

(*No disrespectation intended in the phrase, *Glinda Tart*)

Glinda—you used to know her as Galinda but times change and she moves on, we all move on—replies to our request for a peek in her larder with a little squeal of protest. Then she pushes through the door to see what is there. (She has rarely been behind that door, as frightening things like pots and kettles and chefs are said to lurk within.)

Imagine her surprise, she tells us, to see things laid out so prettily, almost as if by magic, ready for assembly. A half dozen fresh peaches, sliced and arranged in a pretty design on a pink ceramic plate with scalloped edges. A lemon freshly squeezed and its pips removed, its juice waiting in a small cut-glass decanter. And rough but handsome pastry dough, chill to the touch but ready for manipulation on this convenient, broad, and floured board! Why, who knew cooking could be so easy? And such fun! She'll have to have friends over. She leaves the job half-done to go pen a few hundred notes, only to her very very closest friends, to come sample her baking. While she is gone, nameless staff come in and finish the job. Your nameless staff can do it, too. But if you should want to impress someone, anyone, do the whole thing yourself. (Glinda will not be able to visit; she is previously engaged, she urges me to mention. No matter when you write.)

Note: Use our tart dough recipe below or thawed commercial dough (unwrap it, and thump into lumpiness so Munchkins think you made it by hand the day before).

Dough for one 11-inch tart (see note and recipe)
6 ripe peaches or plums (about 1½ pounds of fruit or 3¾ cups), peeled and pitted
¼ cup (½ stick) unsalted butter
¼ cup fresh lemon juice
1 cup sugar, divided
3 tablespoons all-purpose flour
Whipped cream, for topping

1 Preheat oven to 450°F. On a lightly floured board, roll out the dough into an 11-inch circle. Transfer to a cookie sheet (lined with aluminum foil, if you prefer). Chill while preparing the fruit.

2 Cut fruit into wedges (about ½-inch). Melt butter in a large skillet and sauté the fruit over medium heat until soft but not broken up, 10–12 minutes. Sprinkle with lemon juice and ½ cup of sugar. As soon as sugar has dissolved, remove from heat and stir in flour.

3 Remove dough from refrigerator. With a slotted spoon, arrange fruit as attractively as your skills allow in the center of the dough, leaving most of the excess liquid in the skillet. Leave a 1½-inch border around the edges. Sprinkle with remaining ½ cup sugar.

4 Gently fold the border of the pastry over the fruit, leaving the center of the tart uncovered, pleating it to make an edge.

5 Bake for 20–25 minutes. Slide tart from cookie sheet (or remove with foil). Cool before serving. Serve with whipped cream.

Tart Dough

Adapted from *Cucina Simpatica: Robust Trattoria Cooking From Al Forno*
by Johanne Killeen and George Germon (Morrow, 1991)

1 cup all-purpose flour
⅛ cup superfine sugar
¼ teaspoon kosher salt
½ cup (1 stick) cold, unsalted butter, diced
⅛ cup ice water, plus 1–2 teaspoons if needed

1 Place flour, sugar, and salt in food processor. Pulse a few times to combine. Add butter. Pulse 15 times, or until butter pieces are pea-sized.

2 With motor running, add ⅛ cup ice water all at once through the feed tube. Process for about 15–20 seconds, or as soon as dough comes together. Add additional water as needed.

3 Turn dough out onto a well-floured board, roll into a ball, and press into a flat disk. Wrap disk in plastic wrap and chill for at least an hour in the refrigerator before using. Remove dough from refrigerator and allow to sit at room temperature for 10 minutes before rolling. The dough may be refrigerated for up to 2 days, or frozen for up to 2 weeks.

ELPHABA'S LUNCH SANDWICH*
(LUNCH AT SHIZ UNIVERSITY-PART II)

Makes 1 sandwich

(*supplied by the buttery at Shiz University)

Frankly, Miss Elphaba Thropp was not inclined to answer our request to supply a recipe. She has bigger fish to fry, though not literally she hastens to point out. Who knows if any individual fish might open its mouth and remonstrate against the situation in which it finds itself, browning in unsalted butter on a medium-high flame? Downright undignified.

However, spies who like to keep an eye on Elphaba have found the following in the extensive files kept on her in the archives of the Emerald City. They are not sure if there is any deep meaning or seditious intent in this recipe. Specialists from the "There's No Place like Homeland Security" bureau are still studying it, and believe they will be able to file a report within the decade.

1 scoop (2–3 tablespoons) softened goat cheese (was it generously donated or was it— horrors—appropriated from some incarcerated goat? Check this out!)
2 slices white bread
Handful of (your choice) chives, parsley and /or fresh spinach, ripped or chopped in segments large enough to get caught in your teeth
Ground green peppercorns (optional)

1 Spread cheese on one slice of bread.
2 Sprinkle green matter thereupon. If to your taste, add a light ozdusting of ground green peppercorns.
3 Clamp second slice of bread firmly atop the spread.
4 Serve in the freshest wax paper . . . never mind, you're not that hungry.

MADAME MORRIBLE'S
ADORABLE STORABLE SUGAR COOKIES

Makes about 30 2½-inch cookies
(number varies with size of cookie cutter) and 1 cup of frosting

Sugar cookies and butter frosting are from *Kids' Party Cook Book*,
edited by Mary Jo Plutt (Better Homes and Gardens, 1985)

Madame Morrible, notable figure around Shiz University though with Friends in High Places, likes to welcome the students at her seminars and poetry recitals with plates of her favorite treat. She calls them Madame Morrible's Adorable Storables, for with an extra flick and flourish of her wand she can not only whip up several dozen in an instant, she can store them in airtight cannikins where they keep for days and days.

For those less naturally gifted in the magical Arts of Baking, she supplies a traditional recipe below. An extra note: she herself enjoys using cookie cutters with this recipe, as the more regularized the shape, the easier to store—in a box or a sock or something. Her favorite cookie cutter is the one in the shape of a flying monkey. Should you not be able to locate one for your own use, either in an emporium of cookie cutters or borrowed from some better-heeled neighbor, she recommends you take a pair of secateurs, a length of industrial-strength tin, a small but strong hammer, and an image of the flying monkeys from the 1900 edition of *The Wizard of Oz* by L. Frank Baum with illustrations by W. W. Denslow. You can knock out your own homemade cookie cutter almost as easily as you can follow the recipe below. Assignments due on Thursday, no excuses.

Note: To make this a stiffer frosting, which is preferable for piped designs, add more confectioners' sugar. To thin the frosting, add a few drops of water.

To tint the frosting, use paste food color (available at party supply stores) rather than liquid food color as liquid will thin the frosting. Use the tip of a wooden toothpick to add small amounts of the paste, blend, and add more if necessary to achieve desired tint.

FOR THE COOKIES

2¼ cups all-purpose flour

2 teaspoons baking powder

½ teaspoon salt

½ cup (1 stick) unsalted butter, softened

1 cup granulated sugar

1 large egg

2 tablespoons milk

½ teaspoon vanilla extract

FOR THE FROSTING

3 tablespoons butter, softened

2¼–2½ cups sifted confectioners' sugar

2 tablespoons milk, plus additional if needed

¾ teaspoon vanilla extract

1 **To make the cookies:** In a small bowl, stir together flour, baking powder, and salt.

2 In an electric mixers' large bowl, cream butter and sugar on medium speed until fluffy. Add egg, milk, and vanilla extract, and beat well. Gradually add flour mixture and beat until well blended. Cover and chill dough for about 1 hour.

3 Preheat oven to 375°F. Divide dough in half. Roll out half of the dough on a lightly floured surface to about ¼-inch thickness. Cut into desired shapes with cookie cutters or knife, rerolling dough as necessary. Transfer cookies to ungreased cookie sheets.

4 Bake for 8–10 minutes or until cookies are light brown around edges. Remove cookies to a wire rack and let cool completely.

5 **To make the frosting:** In a small mixing bowl, beat butter with an electric mixer on medium speed until light and fluffy. Gradually add about half of the confectioners' sugar, beating well.

6 Beat in milk and vanilla. Gradually beat in the remaining sugar, and then beat in additional milk, if necessary, to make frosting spreadable.

Frances Mayes

John Gillooly

Inspiration   Italy inspires my recent writing, but in my long life reading for me is the most immediate and joyous inspiration. Good books make me want to write and have done so since I was about eight. The two pleasures are completely intertwined.

....

On Writing   I think of myself as an image-based writer. I love the tactile, visual, auditory world and find my ideas work best when I can recreate a sensuous image. I first learned this from Keats, then later from one of my all time favorite writers, Colette.

....

Readers Frequently Ask   "How did you first start writing about Italy?" The answer? I just settled into a house that was at home in the landscape. I thought if I lived there I could be at home, too. Turns out, that was the right instinct. The place itself gave me the five books I have written there. I spontaneously changed from writing poetry to writing memoir. The new life seemed to demand it. I simply could not break off my lines and I soon had to buy a bigger notebook. There's a *plenitude* that I experience living in Tuscany and I think my genre had to accommodate that in a new way.

....

Influences on My Writing   As mentioned, Keats and Colette for their profound grasp of image. Collectively, all the southern writers seeped into my psyche early on. Thomas Wolfe, Flannery O'Connor, Eudora Welty, James Agee, Carson McCullers, William Faulkner, Conrad Aiken, Margaret Mitchell–they all knew that place is fate, that is, *who* you are is *where* you are.

Frances Mayes's
Summer Shrimp Salad

Makes 6–8 servings

This recipe travels happily between my kitchens in Tuscany and North Carolina. I think it's more Southern than Tuscan, but any summer table will definitely be graced by its presence. I prefer wild-caught shrimp. This can be a main course event, served with toothpicks as an hors d'oeuvre, or as a first course. Leftovers can reappear in a frittata or be stirred at the last minute into risotto.

Note: The shrimp must marinate for 24 hours.

For the marinade
¼ cup tarragon wine vinegar or champagne
    vinegar
1 cup extra-virgin olive oil
1 tablespoon good quality mustard
2 garlic cloves, minced
1 teaspoon salt
½ teaspoon ground black pepper
¼ teaspoon ground paprika
Splash of hot sauce
A few sprigs of thyme
1 green pepper, seeded and chopped into
    postage stamp-sized pieces
3 shallots, minced
2 celery stalks, finely chopped

For the shrimp
4 tablespoons butter
2–3 garlic cloves, smashed
1½ pounds medium shrimp, peeled and
    deveined
1 cup chopped fresh parsley, to stir in before
    serving

For the salad
1 large bunch arugula
2 avocados, peeled, pitted, and sliced
1 mango, peeled, pitted, and sliced
Lemon wedges

1 Mix all marinade ingredients in a medium bowl. Set aside.
2 **To prepare the shrimp:** In a medium skillet, melt butter over medium heat. Add garlic cloves and cook, stirring, for 30 seconds. Add shrimp and sauté until no longer gray—sunrise pink!—about 3 minutes.
3 Use a slotted spoon to transfer shrimp to marinade bowl, and combine well. Cover and marinate, chilled, for 24 hours.
4 Before serving, stir the parsley into the marinating shrimp. Spoon shrimp over a platter of arugula, reserving the marinade. Arrange avocado and mango slices around the sides of the platter, drizzle them with a little of the marinade, and add the lemon wedges. Pass the remaining marinade around on the side.

Emma McLaughlin and Nicola Kraus

Victoria Will

SELECTED WORKS

- *Over You* (2011)
- *Nanny Returns* (2009)
- *The Real Real* (2009)
- *Dedication* (2007)
- *Citizen Girl* (2004)
- *The Nanny Diaries* (2002)

Inspiration We have lunch together every day before we start working and we chew over the topics of the day, paying special attention to angles of stories that aren't being addressed. For example, in 2000 we were obsessed that endless stories were running in New York City media about how hard it was for the newly rich to find decent household help, but the help was never interviewed for these reports. So if there's a side of the story that is being underserved, we'll puzzle over that. We often have "a-ha" moments, when one of us will crystallize one of the topics we've been mulling over into a story. Then Nicki gets teary and the hair on Emma's neck stands on end and we know we've found our next book.

....

The Joy of Working with Friends It's hard for us to believe, but this will be our tenth year of writing collaboratively and *Nanny Returns* is our fifth published novel. A few interesting facts about our partnership:

1. **We have date night.** When in the phase of generating a first draft we try to see each other once a week for a movie or the theater. We always get that delicious high school feeling like it's been FOREVER since we hung out, even though we've talked a minimum of five times on the phone that day. And we won't even count the e-mails.
2. **We have codependent food fixations.** When on tour, one of us will invariably say, "Ooo, do you think they'll have _____ here?" (Fill in the blank with some random local treat.) Invariably "they" will not, and neither will the local diner, bakery, or supermarket. Cut to us trying to construct key lime pie/peanut butter cupcake/baked Alaska from an assortment of over priced stale goods out of a mini bar fridge.
3. **We believe in the Law of Attraction**. Call it what you will—the power of intention, cognitive behavioral therapy, if you build it he will come—but after a decade of partnership we've learned that holding a positive vision is job criteria numero uno.

Readers Frequently Ask *Describe the writing process you have developed.*

We actually stumbled onto a process with our first novel (*The Nanny Diaries*) and, while we have gone on to hone and refine it over the past decade, it has essentially remained the same. Once we have the seed of an idea, we spend several weeks outlining the core elements of the story: primary and periphery characters, each of their arcs, A and B plots, and timeframe. We then break this outline into scenes, each take separate scenes, go off to our own homes and generate them, e-mail them to each other, edit them for each other, and then string them into one document. Once we have this first draft, we sit together and go over it line by line on the computer, on paper, and frequently out loud, until it is ready to go to print. And of course, our editor gets to weigh in at multiple junctures along the way.

How have your lives changed since The Nanny Diaries *became a movie?*

Our lives actually changed the most when the book came out, in that its unexpected success allowed us to leave our "day jobs" and begin to write full time. This is a huge blessing anywhere, but particularly when you live in New York City. Then the working from home thing allowed us to get dogs, who are spectacular. They keep us getting up from the computer and are our mostly companions, to quote Kay Thompson's *Eloise*. When the movie came out our lives changed in that we had the thrill of watching artists we had enormous respect for give life to this story we had written side by side on Nicki's Mac with a package of Oreos. It remains a completely surreal experience for which we are thoroughly grateful.

....

Influences on Our Writing David Sedaris's *Santaland Diaries* was a HUGE influence on us because it was a fresh way of talking about the workplace, with a blend of biting sardonic humor and pathos that resonated with us and helped to inform the voice of Nan, the heroine of *The Nanny Diaries* and *Nanny Returns*. We were also inspired by the naturalistic style of his voice, which made you feel like you were being told a crazy story by your favorite story-teller friend. It had an intimacy and immediacy. It gave us the courage to try writing in our own voices, to capture our story in the rhythms we would tell it to a friend over drinks. We played with stringing words together, italics and capitalization to capture the feeling of a moment—a technique that drove our copy editors crazy but has since been adopted by other writers in our genre.

GRANDMA'S PARK AVENUE PLUM TORTE

Makes 8 servings

From "an ancient *New York Times* recipe" (September 21, 2005)

We found each other at an ATM machine on East 86th Street, slurping the sort of triple caramel something-iattos that could put a girl in a sugar coma until she's retired. We promptly discovered that not only were we both students at NYU, but we were both nannies! And our mad passionate overnight friendship was off and running. Emma's "gig" required her to cook three different three-course dinners a night (macrobiotic for the wife, child-friendly for her charge, and comfort food for the soon-to-be divorced husband) in a galley kitchen with a four-burner stove and no microwave. She did not, however, know a thing about baking, as her employers miraculously didn't "believe" in dessert. Nicki, meanwhile, had managed to dodge elaborate chef responsibilities, *but* had developed the nasty habit of drowning her nannying sorrows in prodigious after hours baking, everything from Krispie treats to a dacquoise, depending on how harrowing the day. Joining forces, we discovered we could throw one heck of a dinner party. In college, boys' behavior is not so far from toddlers' when it comes to social gatherings, so this was a particularly good fit. It was the summer of '95, with record-breaking heat in Manhattan. We'd crack open the vodka, throw in a few ice cubes, and set the oven to preheat.

Five years later we sat down to imagine *The Nanny Diaries*. We were no longer nannies but not yet writers, and we had joined the working drones that ordered in pizza or met each other for cheap sushi. Emma had developed post-traumatic stress from her nanny/chef past and ignored her closet-sized kitchen. Nicki had taken on the gym and her glycemic index and stored shoes in her oven. Clutching mugs in various coffee shops, we imagined the character of Nan's Grandma to represent wealth done right. Grandma is someone who has all the resources that the villains, the X family, also have, at her disposal, and yet she chooses to live a passionate, engaged life. Grandma would support our thesis by showing that it isn't wealth that rotted the Xs, it's the values that informed what they did with it.

We recently wrote the novel's sequel, *Nanny Returns*, which fictionally kicks off twelve years later. Much like our heroine, we, too, are now married and starting families of our own. We have finally learned kitchen moderation. Nicki is still the baker and Emma still the chef and our ovens are getting regular use in the manner in which they were intended. Grandma has once again taken on her life with gusto and we imagine her hosting a reunion for Nan and her college friends, topping off the evening with an elegant and luscious plum tart—Emma's favorite from Nicki's repertoire. May it bring your book group a delicious discussion!

And P.S. If you must know, we still indulge in those triple carmel something-iattos when on tour. So if you see us slurping in O'Hare, don't judge; we've put in our time.

Note: The total time to prepare this recipe is 1 hour and 15 minutes.

Italian prune plums are small and egg-shaped, and their firm texture holds up well when baked. They're available for a few weeks each year, starting in early September. When Italian plums are not in season, you can use any pit fruit, including cherries, larger plums, and peaches. For larger plums and peaches, use about 5 pieces of ripe fruit, and cut each into 6 pieces. One 10-ounce bag of flash frozen berries placed on top of the batter works well, too. Whichever fruit you use, don't be shy; make sure to push the fruit gently into the batter so as to fit in as much as possible.

¾ cup sugar, plus about ½ teaspoon for sprinkling
½ cup (1 stick) unsalted butter, softened
1 cup unbleached all-purpose flour, sifted
1 teaspoon baking powder
Pinch of salt
2 large eggs
12 Italian prune plums, pitted and halved (see note)
About ½ teaspoon sugar, for topping
About ¾ teaspoon cinnamon, for sprinkling

1 Preheat oven to 350°F. Grease sides only of an 8", 9", or 10" springform pan.
2 Cream sugar and butter in bowl of an electric mixer on medium-high speed until fluffy, about 1 minute. Add flour, baking powder, salt, and eggs, and beat well.
3 Spoon the batter into prepared pan, and spread to evenly cover the bottom (a frosting spreader works well). Place the plum halves skin side up on top of the batter (see note). Combine ½ teaspoon sugar (or more, depending on the sweetness of the fruit) and cinnamon in a small dish. Sprinkle mixture over top of batter.
4 Bake for 40–50 minutes, until dough is golden brown. Remove to wire rack and cool for 10 minutes. Remove sides of pan, cool to lukewarm, and serve (the torte stays on the springform base through serving). Or, refrigerate or freeze if desired. To freeze, double wrap the torte in foil after cooling, place in a plastic bag, and seal. To serve a torte that has been frozen, defrost and reheat it briefly at 300°F.

Jacquelyn Mitchard

Liane R. Harrison

The Power of Stories

The world is filled with stories, and these stories are the way we explain ourselves to ourselves, to others, to history. They're the way we tell our children: this is how you came to be born; or this is how your grandmother looked . . . you never met her but she loved to sing the song "Always" to me, just as I sing it to you. In our family, stories told around a table were the way to have power. If you could make someone laugh or cry with a story, that was power. Now, ever since I got hold of a few books when I was a very young girl, maybe twelve, I went nuts over the power of writing them down. These were books like *Gone With the Wind, A Tree Grows in Brooklyn, Marjorie Morningstar*, and (my mother didn't know I found this one) *Another Country*, by James Baldwin. I wanted to write for more than my family. I do this for my living because that response from people, the one I had as a twelve-year-old, is as much power as a human being can have. More than beauty or money or political clout.

If I Wasn't a Writer . . .

If I could have been what I truly wanted to be, I'd have been a singer. My son Martin is a singer and when I hear him sing I think, my goodness, what I do is so pale compared with this. So, to get in the mood to write, I can spend a whole day in the kitchen, baking for the college kids, making a year's worth of spaghetti sauce and applesauce because I won't be coming back to that once I start a novel, and listening to everything from Dusty Springfield to Mirella Freni. And while I'm doing that, I'm talking to the people who will help me shape the authenticity of my story: for this upcoming book, these are a firefighter, a surgeon, a medical illustrator, a feature film maker, and so on. Finally, I turn off the music and, in the silence, write the first sentence: "She was born lucky." (That's the one this next time).

Readers Frequently Ask

Q: Is this book going to be made into a movie like *The Deep End of the Ocean?*

A: I sure hope so!

Q: Why have you written so many books if your first one was so successful?

A: Ummm, see me later for a discussion of college tuition and obsession.

Q: Is it fun to be able to stay home with your kids and make a living too?

A: Fun?

Q: Does writing just flow for you?

A: It does not. I am not a natural.

....

Influences on My Writing

- *In Cold Blood* by Truman Capote. There have never been more elegant sentences. Some were a tad overwrought, but most of them were perfect. Capote found the right word, instead of the right ten words. "Literary" writers of this era need to listen up: just because you can do something does not mean you should do it over and over on the same page.
- *Charlotte's Web* by E. B. White. This is how a story should be structured, exactly this way. This is how emotion should arise naturally from event and how primary and secondary characters come to life through the movement of the tale.
- *Anna Karenina* by Leo Tolstoy. In its time, it was considered a silly piece of romance. Oh, my gosh. Like a few other books, like *Rebecca* by Daphne du Maurier, it was one that nobody (except Dostoyevsky) got, in terms of how amazing a story this was. This is exquisite drama, huge ambition and sweep and, in the way all stories should be, social commentary of the highest order only through the events of the story—not as an exercise in polemic. It's dumb, for my money, to set out to write about "political futility" or "human redemption." It's my belief that stories should teach lessons by accident, not by design. Readers get more from a story that entertains them and moves them and later provokes them to think about their beliefs than from a story that's heavy with symbolism. For example, Bernard Malamud wrote many short stories that were HEAVILY about the human condition. He also wrote the beautiful short novel *The Natural* which was made into a movie with Robert Redford—and which said more about defeat, hope, and redemption than all his other work. Bernard Malamud was at his best writing *The Natural*, not *The Letter*.

NEXT DAY RICE PUDDING

Makes 4 servings

I've never baked Proust's madeleine or even tried any of the recipes from Nora Ephron's *Heartburn*, but one of the happy lessons that the Cappadoras learn early is to guard a great recipe. In *No Time to Wave Goodbye*, Vincent compares Grandma Rosie's recipe for "gravy," which is what Italians call pasta sauce, to such secrets as the recipe for Coca-Cola and Van Gogh's ineffable way of creating the color yellow. In my family, a good recipe needs to be easy, inexpensive, and evoke passionate reactions of joy. My children beg me not to forget the Sierra Secrets or the Tutu cookies at Christmas; my eldest took jars of my spaghetti "gravy" to college; my thirteen-year-old daughter has actually eaten so much of my mustard-and-ketchup meatloaf that she had to lie down for three hours. I created this recipe so that I could make a huge pot of rice for stir-fry one night and have enough left over to make rice pudding chilled for dessert or warm for a cold-weather breakfast the next day.

---

2 cups cooked white rice (it can even be left over from Chinese takeout, but no soy sauce please!)

2 cups milk, nonfat or 2%

1 cup sugar (I use raw or turbinado sugar)

½ teaspoon salt

1 cup golden raisins

¾ teaspoon ground cinnamon

¼ teaspoon ground nutmeg (optional)

¼ cup slivered almonds (not even an option at my house! My kids don't like them but it makes for a more "grown-up" taste)

---

1 In a saucepan, cook the rice and milk together over medium high heat until they boil, stirring nearly constantly until the rice begins to thicken to a pudding-like consistency (this will take a good twenty minutes, so put on some music). Add the sugar and salt and keep cooking until the mixture falls heavily from a spoon (the consistency of very thick waffle batter).
2 Just before removing from heat, add raisins and stir until they heat through.
3 Place pudding in a large serving dish or individual dessert cups and sprinkle with cinnamon, or cinnamon and nutmeg with a dusting (not at my house!) of slivered almonds. Serve warm or cold.

GRANDMA ROSIE'S GRAVY (PASTA SAUCE)

Makes 4 quarts

Grandma Rosie Cappadora is the matriarch of the family in *The Deep End of the Ocean* and Grandpa Angelo was a cook in World War II. This spaghetti sauce, supposedly, is the among the reasons for the success of The Old Neighborhood, the restaurant owned by the Cappadora family in *The Deep End of the Ocean* and *No Time to Wave Goodbye.* My god-mother, Serafina, taught me how to make spaghetti sauce when I was a child. Although I've added ingredients to it on my own (you can throw anything in this, from fresh peas to meatballs to mushrooms), this is a recipe that relies on freshness and the willingness to do just a little bit extra. I make it only once a year, but I make probably fifteen quarts, enough to last through Christmas and to bring the taste of summer into February.

This is a basic marinara sauce that can be served over pasta with Grandpa Angelo's Surefire Army Mess Meatballs (see recipe), as a pizza base, or on rounds of bread with cheese for crostini. It freezes very well.

3 tablespoons olive oil (NOT extra-virgin because it burns)

4–5 garlic cloves, peeled

1½ large yellow onions, chopped

3 celery stalks, chopped

4 pounds large fresh tomatoes (approximately 8 of any kind), washed and chopped into large pieces

3 28-ounce cans whole Roma tomatoes

4 6-ounce cans tomato paste

2 tablespoons dried oregano

1½ tablespoons chopped fresh basil (or ½ tablespoon dried basil)

2 tablespoons chopped fresh parsley (or 1¼ teaspoons dried parsley)

1½ tablespoons salt

1 tablespoon ground black pepper

2–3 tablespoons sugar (to taste, more if sauce is acidic)

Up to 4 cups water

OPTIONAL

1 16-ounce can green peas, drained

2–3 red or green peppers, cored and cut into ½-inch pieces, and sautéed lightly in olive oil

2 ounces sliced fresh button mushrooms, sautéed in olive oil until lightly browned (or canned button mushrooms, drained)

½ cup red wine

Pinch of ground cayenne pepper

1 Heat the olive oil in a large stockpot. Sauté the garlic cloves until they are dark golden and then discard the cloves.
2 Add onion and celery to pot, and sauté until the onions are translucent. Add fresh and canned tomatoes, tomato paste, oregano, basil, parsley, salt, pepper, and sugar. Simmer over low heat for at least one hour, adding up to four cups of water a little at a time to reach desired thickness (it should have the consistency of a chunky soup that can be poured).
3 Pour the sauce into a food processor and process in batches until smooth and thick. Return sauce to pot. If desired, add peas, peppers, and mushrooms, and/or for a spicier sauce, add red wine and ground cayenne pepper. Simmer once more, for about 30 minutes.

GRANDPA ANGELO'S SUREFIRE
ARMY MESS MEATBALLS

Makes 16 (1-inch) meatballs

2–3 tablespoons olive oil, divided (use more if needed)

1 small onion, chopped fine

1 pound lean ground beef

½ teaspoon dried oregano

½ teaspoon garlic salt or ½ teaspoon minced garlic cloves

2 tablespoons grated Parmesan cheese

2 tablespoons ketchup

1 tablespoon mustard

1 teaspoon salt

¼ teaspoon ground black pepper

1 Heat 1 tablespoon olive oil in a small skillet. Sauté onion in olive oil until soft.
2 Using a pastry blender or clean hands, mix the onions, beef, oregano, garlic salt or cloves, Parmesan cheese, ketchup, mustard, salt, and pepper. Form into 1-inch balls.
3 In a cast-iron or other heavy skillet, heat remaining olive oil and sauté meatballs until well-browned, adding a little olive oil if the meatballs begin to stick.

James Patterson

Deborah Feingold

Inspiration I'm infected with the writing bug, and I never want to be cured. I love telling stories that people enjoy. I love giving them plots and characters that light up their minds and take them away from wherever they are. I find the entire process immensely satisfying. Inspiration's not so hard to arrive at when you have a happy compulsion pulling the cart.

No Rest for the Wicked I've got about twenty-seven projects in the works right now. Alex Cross, Lindsay Boxer, Daniel X, Maximum Ride, and some other favorites will be back this year. Plus, a new series just started. Something called *Private*, a detective agency kind of thing; only it's not like your usual sort of detective agency.

Readers Frequently Ask One question I get asked pretty regularly is where I get my ideas from. And I guess my usual reply is from this magical statue I have locked up in my basement. Just kidding. I guess, when you write as much as I do, you just get accustomed to coming up with, and writing down, a lot of ideas.

Influences on My Writing James Joyce's *Ulysses* lit up my mind to the possibilities of the novel. Frederick Forsyth's *Day of the Jackal* lit up my mind to the possibilities of thrillers, and Evan Connell's *Mrs. Bridge and Mr. Bridge* opened my mind to the possibilities of realistic fiction.

ISABELLE'S WACKY CAKE

Makes 9–12 servings

My mother Isabelle, a former school teacher, baked Wacky Cake as a treat for me and my three sisters when we were growing up.

I have not used Wacky Cake in a book yet, so this is the first time my readers will have ever heard of it. As a memory, however, the cake has served me as a great example of kitchen-related family intimacy and, I will confess, I have sometimes used it as a motivational tool for myself. Over the years, I have discovered there is no better way to celebrate a successfully completed manuscript than with a nice healthy slice of Wacky Cake. Preferably à la mode with some Graeter's ice cream. It's a small batch specialty brand I discovered in Cincinnati. Fortunately, you can order it online.

Note: This recipe became popular during the Depression era because it does not require any eggs.

> *1 cup granulated sugar*
> *1½ cups all-purpose flour*
> *½ teaspoon salt*
> *¼ cup unsweetened cocoa powder*
> *1 teaspoon baking soda*
> *1 tablespoon white vinegar*
> *1 teaspoon vanilla extract*
> *⅓ cup salad oil, such as vegetable or canola*
> *1 cup water*
> *Confectioners' sugar, for sprinkling (optional)*

1 Preheat oven to 350°F. Grease and lightly flour a 8" × 8" × 2" baking pan.
2 Sift together sugar, flour, salt, cocoa, and baking soda, and place in a large mixing bowl. Add vinegar, vanilla, oil, and water and stir to combine. Pour batter into prepared pan.
3 Bake for 25–35 minutes, or until toothpick inserted in the center comes out clean. Cool on wire rack. Remove cake from pan and sprinkle with confectioners' sugar, if desired.

Dolen Perkins-Valdez

• *Wench* (2010)

Louie Escobar

Inspiration I am inspired to write stories that need to be told. There are so many out there, and if we don't write and record these stories then the memories will die. I often think of my grandmother's extraordinary life and wish that she had written a journal that I could have and keep. When I began to write, it was so that the generations after me would have a record.

....

Readers Should Know My writing comes from my heart. Many people have called my book, *Wench*, "heartfelt." I take this as the highest compliment. My hope is that I can develop my writing craft enough to clearly tell the stories that haunt my conscience.

....

Readers Frequently Ask The question I receive most often about *Wench* is: "Do Lizzie and Drayle really love each other?" This is a question I asked myself as I began the book. Yet I found that, after finishing the book, I still was never able to answer it for myself. Their relationship is complicated. I leave it to the reader to decide.

....

Influences on My Writing I am influenced by Toni Morrison's bravery, unflinching eye, and incredibly high level of writing craft. I am influenced by Gabriel García Márquez's ability to take on the very biggest themes of human existence. I am influenced by Gayl Jones's beautifully seamless integration of African American idiom and romantic, lyrical prose.

MAWU'S MAGICAL GUMBO

Makes 8–12 servings

Courtesy of Sylvester Thornton

In Part I of my historical novel *Wench*, my protagonist Lizzie meets another slave, Mawu, who makes a stew that, she says, can "soften the white man." Mawu practices hoodoo, an African American folk tradition that uses spells and potions for various magical practices. After the book came out, many readers wrote to me asking what was in Mawu's magical stew. I did not have a recipe in mind at the time that I wrote the book, so I called upon my uncle, Sylvester Thornton, who is the most accomplished cook in my family. The fact that we all respect Uncle Sylvester is a great testament to his skill as I come from a large southern family of men and women in Memphis, Tennessee, who all cook very well. Yet Uncle Sylvester is a true master when he is in the kitchen.

Many cooks in the southern African American tradition learn to cook from their elders. My uncle learned from his mother, Millerine Thornton, and he taught me and my cousins. My mother also gave me many lessons in the kitchen when I was growing up. I was taught to read a recipe, but they encouraged me to bring my own creativity to it. I have always been inspired by the creativity of slave cooks who fashioned an entire cuisine out of meager ingredients. As the old folks would say, they "turned guts into chit'lins."

I hope you enjoy my Uncle Sylvester Thornton's gumbo. My hope is that it will "soften" everyone who eats it.

2 small (4-pound) wild ducks, quartered	½ teaspoon ground black pepper
1 large yellow onion, diced	8 cups chicken broth
¾ cup olive oil, divided	32 ounces frozen okra
1 large red or green bell pepper, diced	5 chopped tomatoes
3–4 celery stalks, diced	1 bay leaf
2 garlic cloves, minced	1 teaspoon dried thyme
1 cup all-purpose flour	Rice, for serving
2 teaspoons salt, plus additional if needed	Chopped fresh parsley, for garnish

1 Place duck in a large stockpot with enough water to cover and boil until tender (about an hour). Add a little of the diced onion to the water.

2 While duck is boiling, prepare the gumbo: In a large (minimum 3-quart) saucepan or stockpot, heat ¼ cup olive oil over medium heat. Add onion, bell pepper, celery, and garlic and sauté until tender, about 10 minutes. Remove from pan and set aside.

3 In the same pan, make a light roux: Pour ½ cup olive oil into pan, add flour and stir constantly over medium heat until golden brown. Add salt and pepper. Gradually stir in chicken broth. Boil until slightly thickened. Roux should have the consistency of a tomato sauce.

4 Add okra, tomatoes, and bay leaf to thickened roux. Simmer on medium heat 25–30 minutes. Add sautéed bell pepper, onion, celery, and garlic.

5 When duck is tender, drain the broth, saving just a bit. Discard onion. Cool duck, and pull apart or cut it into medium pieces before adding to gumbo with reserved broth, thyme, and additional salt and pepper to taste. Cook gumbo uncovered about 30–45 minutes on medium heat. Remove bay leaf before serving.

6 Serve over rice. Sprinkle with fresh parsley.

Tom Perrotta

Roxana Perdue

Inspiration I tend to draw my inspiration from the most mundane sorts of domestic experience. *Little Children*, for example, emerged from the experiences I had as a part-time stay-at-home dad when my kids were little (not that my adventures were quite as exciting as those of my characters). In *The Abstinence Teacher*, a major subplot revolves around youth soccer, which I've spent countless hours watching over the past few years.

From the Page to the Screen Two of my books, *Little Children* and *Election* have been made into excellent movies, and a third, *The Abstinence Teacher*, has been adapted for the screen. I'm a big movie fan, and love the fact that my novels have had such an interesting second life on the big screen.

Writing from the Female Perspective Most book club members are women, and they often seem curious about how a male writer goes about creating female characters like Sarah in *Little Children* and Ruth in *The Abstinence Teacher*. For some reason this seems unusual to a lot of readers, though there's a long history of writers imagining characters across gender lines—think of Tolstoy and *Anna Karenina*, Flaubert and *Madame Bovary*, or Annie Proulx writing *Brokeback Mountain*. My answer is that I just keep my eyes and ears open.

Influences on My Writing

- *This Boy's Life* by Tobias Wolff. A number of my books are about teenagers, and Wolff's memoir of his childhood and adolescence has a been of source of inspiration for me. It's a masterpiece, funny and sad and beautifully told.
- The Rabbit novels by John Updike. Updike's four novels about Harry "Rabbit" Angstrom form an American epic that chronicles the private life of its flawed everyman hero, while also exploring many of the major historical transformations that took place in America in the second half of the twentieth century.
- The stories of Flannery O'Connor. O'Connor stories are like no one else's: funny and bizarre and fearless, soaked in *violence* and religion. I read them as a teenager and haven't gotten them out of my head since.

Like Todd (a.k.a. "The Prom King"), the stay-at-home dad in *Little Children*, I've been known to cook the occasional family dinner. It's a little complicated in our house, though; my son, Luke, and I are carnivores, while my wife, Mary, and daughter, Nina, are vegetarians. Some nights the two parties go in separate directions (chicken for us, risotto for them), and some nights we cooperate (real burgers and veggie burgers). Fortunately, there are a few things everyone can agree on. Here are two of our favorites:

Luke's Pesto

Makes 4 servings

From *The Silver Palate Cookbook* by Julee Rosso and Sheila Lukins (Workman, 1982)

2 cups fresh basil leaves, rinsed and dried
3 garlic cloves, peeled and chopped
1 cup walnut pieces
1 cup olive oil
1 cup grated Romano cheese
1 pound of your favorite pasta

1 Purée basil, garlic, walnuts, olive oil, and cheese in a food processor or blender until smooth.
2 Bring a large pot of water to boil. Cook pasta according to package directions, until al dente. Drain pasta, place in a large serving bowl, and toss pasta with pesto. You know the rest.

NINA'S MINESTRONE

Makes approximately 10 servings

I'm not sure where this recipe comes from. It's just one version of a common soup; the chicken stock keeps it from being purely vegetarian, but vegetable stock can be used instead.

1 large onion, chopped

1 large carrot, peeled and chopped

2 celery stalks, chopped

2 tablespoons olive oil

2 garlic cloves, minced

½ cup tomato sauce

1 teaspoon dried basil

1 teaspoon dried oregano

4 cups chicken (or vegetable) stock

4 cups water

2 chicken bouillon cubes (or salt to taste)

2 cups chopped vegetables (such as green beans, kale, and shredded cabbage)

1 14-ounce can red kidney beans

½ cup small pasta (we like orzo)

Salt to taste

Ground black pepper to taste

Grated Parmesan or Romano cheese

1 In a large saucepan or soup pot, sauté onion, carrot, and celery in olive oil until the vegetables are soft, approximately 8–10 minutes. Add garlic, and sauté for another minute.
2 Add tomato sauce, basil, oregano, stock, water, bouillon cubes, and vegetables. Simmer for at least 45 minutes.
3 Add beans and pasta. Simmer until pasta is soft. Add salt and pepper to taste. Serve with grated Parmesan or Romano cheese. Some fresh bread is always nice, too.

Jayne Anne Phillips

Elena Seibert

The Risk and Joy of Writing For me, writing is about risk and joy; the risk of never knowing where the book will lead and the joy of seeing it through, living with the material for many years until the connection becomes a (spiritual) relationship. Writing is a spiritual practice, actually, in which the writer redeems or saves stories that would otherwise be lost. My books have a core of truth around which the story illuminates and expands. *Black Tickets* looks at the mobility and energized anger of post-1970s America in brief, language-infused stories; *Machine Dreams* tallies the cost of the Vietnam War at home; *Shelter* follows a group of children to a primal wilderness where they confront good (in one another) and evil; *MotherKind* traces a birth/death arc in the lives of one mother and daughter; *Lark & Termite* portrays love as stronger than death, and makes real the connections between parallel worlds linked by the characters.

....

Readers Should Know *Lark & Termite* was a Finalist for the 2009 National Book Award and the National Book Critics Circle Award; the paperback is perfect for book groups. The world of the 1950s, Lark's love for Termite (whose intense perceptions comprise the "living secret" of the novel), the connections between parallel worlds, and the numerous, answered mysteries, make for complex conversations and discussion.

....

Readers Frequently Ask The questions are always different, depending on the book, but many ask where the story started. I wrote an epigraph/disclaimer for my first book, *Black Tickets*, published in 1979 when I was twenty-six, that still holds true: *"These stories began in what is real, but became, in fact, dreams. Love or loss lends a reality to what is imagined."*

....

Influences on My Writing *A Death in the Family* by James Agee; *The Sound and the Fury* by William Faulkner, and *The Collected Stories of Katherine Anne Porter*–all for their language, their knowledge of dimensions beyond life, and their understanding of passion and loss.

Hometown Meat Loaf

Makes 6 servings

My mother's original *Better Homes and Gardens Cook Book*, copyright 1947, is one of my most prized possessions. She married in 1948 (see my novel, *Machine Dreams*) and began raising a family in 1950. The thick book long ago sprung free of its binding and is packed with recipes she wrote out by hand. She gleaned recipes from women's clubs and friends, inherited them from her own mother, or simply invented them. I was surprised to see homemade cards and notes from me (see *MotherKind*) folded into the pages. "Hometown Meat Loaf" was a staple at our house, and it was one way she made sure her children ate oatmeal.

Lark & Termite is about a brother and sister (the title characters) growing up in the late 1950s, in a world full of family secrets. Lark, seventeen, believes that her brother Termite, who doesn't talk or walk, has his own intense perceptions. Their maternal aunt, Nonie, raises them, and her fierce protective love never wavers. Nonie and her longtime boyfriend, Charlie, run a family restaurant that serves up "home cooked" meals. Charlie's meatloaf is a specialty, and it is definitely my mother's recipe, transformed into a basis for argument between Charlie and his penny-pinching mother, Gladdy. Charlie is a beloved character with a complicated history, who watches over Lark and Termite like family.

I like to think of Charlie and Nonie, making this as a Friday night special, while Termite sits on his special stool at the counter and Lark sits beside him, filling the napkin containers.

1½ pounds ground beef (I use organic)
¾ cup quick-cooking rolled oats
2 large eggs, beaten
½ cup chopped onion
1 cup tomato juice
2 teaspoons salt
¼ teaspoon freshly ground black pepper, plus extra for sprinkling
2 slices good-quality Cheddar cheese (medium-thick slices from the deli counter work well)
½ cup ketchup or red salsa

1 Preheat oven to 350°F.
2 Combine beef, oats, eggs, onion, tomato juice, salt, and pepper in a large bowl, using your hands. Pack half of mixture into a 9" × 5" × 3" loaf pan, lay cheese on top, and cover with remaining meat mixture.
3 Sprinkle freshly ground pepper over top, then top with your favorite kind of ketchup or salsa. Bake for 1 hour, or until meat thermometer inserted in center reads 160°F.

Lark and Termite have a brother-sister relationship of uncommon sweetness and depth. Lark, at seventeen, has been her nine-year-old brother's protector, attuned to his wants and needs as Termite is unable to walk or talk. Termite was nearly a year old when "somebody brought him. Not your mother. Somebody brought him for her." Lark tells us he never had a birth certificate. They count the day he came his birthday, but she declares it his birthday when it suits her, with one of her delicious cakes and candles. Lark's second section of *Lark & Termite* ("I decorate the cake …") describes one of her cakes in detail, and ends as she whispers to Termite, "Your birthday, Termite, every day."

Here are two of Lark's cakes, both my mother's recipes from handwritten notes. Food is love, and in Lark and Termite's Winfield, West Virginia, world in 1959, love is always frosted, and the icing is on the cake.

LARK'S WHITE CHOCOLATE-COCONUT CAKE WITH BUTTERCREAM FROSTING

Makes 12 servings

Note: The preparation time for this cake is an hour or so, but the results are worth it!

FOR THE CAKE

2½ cups cake flour

1 teaspoon baking powder

½ teaspoon salt

8 ounces (1⅓ cups) white chocolate morsels

1 cup (2 sticks) unsalted butter, at room temperature

1½ cups granulated sugar

4 large eggs, separated

1 teaspoon vanilla extract

1 cup buttermilk

1 cup chopped pecans

1 cup flaked coconut (sweetened or unsweetened)

FOR THE FROSTING

1½ cups (3 sticks) unsalted butter, at room temperature

2 teaspoons vanilla extract

¼ teaspoon salt

3 cups confectioners' sugar

6 tablespoons evaporated milk

2 ounces white chocolate, in bar form, for decorating (optional)

1 Preheat oven to 325°F. Grease 2 9" round baking pans.

2 **To make the cake:** Sift together the cake flour, baking powder, and salt. Set aside. Place white chocolate morsels in a small, microwave-safe bowl and cover with plastic wrap. Heat in microwave at high power for 30-second intervals, stirring after each interval, until melted, about 1–1½ minutes total. Set aside to cool.

3 In large bowl of an electric mixer, cream butter and sugar on high speed until light and fluffy, about 2 minutes. Reduce speed to medium and add egg yolks one at a time, beating well after each addition. Add melted chocolate and vanilla, and combine. Add ¼ of flour mixture and beat just until incorporated. Then add ⅓ of the buttermilk and beat just until incorporated. Continue alternating the flour mixture and buttermilk, ending with the flour mixture. Gently stir in pecans and coconut.

4 In a separate bowl of an electric mixer, beat egg whites on high speed until stiff. Add egg whites to batter. Fold egg whites into batter by using the edge of a large spatula to cut a path down the middle of the mixture. Then, gently turn half the mixture over onto the other half. Continue to cut down the middle and turn a portion over, only until the egg whites are incorporated. (This technique helps the egg whites retain air for a fluffier cake.)

5 Divide batter evenly between the two prepared pans. Bake for 40–45 minutes, until browned on top and a toothpick inserted in the center comes out clean. Allow to cool for 10 minutes, then transfer cakes to wire rack. Let cool completely before frosting.

6 **To make the frosting:** Beat butter in bowl of an electric mixer on medium-high speed until pale and fluffy, about 2 minutes. Add vanilla and salt and combine. Gradually add sugar, 1 cup at a time, and beat until well blended. Dribble in the evaporated milk, 1 tablespoon at a time, beating until frosting is creamy and smooth. Frosting may be used immediately, kept at room temperature for a few hours, or refrigerated for up to a week. Bring to room temperature before using.

7 **To assemble and frost the cake:** Place one cake layer right side up on cake plate. Spoon frosting on top and spread to cover cake. Place second cake layer right side up on top of the first layer and frost the top and sides.

8 **To decorate the cake, if desired:** Microwave the chocolate bar on high for about 15 seconds to soften (it should not melt). Holding the chocolate with aluminum foil to prevent your fingers from melting the chocolate, use a vegetable peeler to shave curls from the narrow edge of the bar. (If the curls are breaking, heat the chocolate in the microwave for a few more seconds.) While frosting is soft, sprinkle the chocolate curls around the sides of the cake. Curls may be refrigerated until ready to use.

9 Serve on your favorite antique (pedestal) cake plate to show off the gorgeous frosting! As Lark says in *Lark & Termite*, "people ought to see something pretty moving toward them. That way they get time to want what they really can have."

LARK'S APPLE BLACK WALNUT CAKE WITH LEMON GLAZE

Makes 12–14 servings

Note: Black walnuts have a richer and more intense flavor than English walnuts, the ones commonly found in grocery stores. Black walnuts are grown primarily in Minnesota and can be ordered online, or you may substitute English walnuts.

Use firm, tart baking apples, such as Granny Smith or Cortland, for this cake.

FOR THE CAKE
3 cups peeled, cored, and coarsely chopped
*   apples (about 3 medium apples) (see note)*
2 cups granulated sugar
2 cups all-purpose flour
2 teaspoons baking soda
2 teaspoons cinnamon
1 teaspoon salt
2 large eggs

½ cup vegetable oil
2 teaspoons vanilla extract
1 cup chopped black walnuts (see note)

FOR THE GLAZE
2–3 tablespoons fresh lemon juice
1 tablespoon whole milk
2 cups confectioners' sugar

1   Preheat oven to 325°F. Grease and flour a Bundt pan, or spray pan with a cooking spray that contains flour, such as Pam for Baking.

2   **To make the cake:** Combine apples and sugar and set aside. In a separate bowl, sift flour, baking soda, cinnamon, and salt. Set aside.

3   In a large bowl of an electric mixer, combine eggs, oil, and vanilla. Beat on medium speed for 1 minute. Add flour mixture alternately with apples and sugar mixture, beating on medium speed to combine. Stir in walnuts.

4   Pour batter into prepared pan. Bake for 60–70 minutes, or until cake looks dry and nicely browned and has started to pull away from the sides of the pan. Test for doneness with a toothpick (or the clean straw of a broom—my mother's method). Cool cake in pan on a wire rack set over a baking sheet for 10 minutes. Remove cake from pan to cooling rack.

5   **To make the glaze:** Whisk 2 tablespoons lemon juice, milk, and confectioners' sugar until smooth, adding more lemon juice gradually as needed until the glaze is thick but still pourable. Pour half of the glaze over the warm cake and let cool 1 hour. Pour remaining glaze evenly over the top of the cake and allow to set for a few minutes.

6   Transfer cake to pretty platter. Decorate with birthday candles (every day can be a birthday). To serve, slice with serrated knife.

Katherine Russell Rich

Gaspar Tringale

Inspiration In a word, fear. I do best with editors who have gravelly voices and hard, fixed stares. I once had an editor who said, "Really, just take all the time you need." Well, what can I say? Turned out I needed six years.

Making Up for Lost Time I came late to writing; I didn't really begin till I was forty-two. Before that, I was a magazine editor and worked with writers. For years, I didn't really have a whole lot to say. And then when I did, as it turned out, I'd had this twenty-year apprenticeship in writing since I'd spent two decades observing writers up close. I think that helped me skip a certain number of errors. For instance, I knew that if you were going to write a book, you'd better feel a sense of urgency about the subject. Otherwise, you'd be in for a long, long slog. With both my books, *The Red Devil* and *Dreaming in Hindi*, I was urgently obsessed. This sounds pretentious I'm afraid, but with a book I have to feel like what I'm writing about is important. I could be just about to start a novel. I might have the plot and characters, but it won't be until I can feel that this book absolutely has to be written that I'll be able to begin.

The Celestial Tongue Since my book *Dreaming in Hindi* came out, I've been asked "What made you want to learn Hindi?" a lot. The real answer, "I dunno. I just did," makes people squint. So I've come up with a list of the things I've loved about doing it. At different times, and sometimes all at once: I've loved the cadences of the language, the way that the singsong of Hindi reminds me that the language comes out of an oral tradition (as opposed to our Western, written one), out of a culture where most people didn't have books, so that sentences were lilting, had rhymes and repetitions. With that more poetic style of speaking, information is easier to remember. An Indian poet once told me that the ancient medical texts were written in poetry. "Our language is more celestial," he said, referring to the fact that it seems shaped more by nature. I love that celestial tongue for the fact that it has one word for yesterday and today (*kal*), for how in Hindi, night spreads, it doesn't fall. You eat the sun (sunbathe), you eat a beating. I love the way it's allowed me access to people who couldn't speak English and whom I'd never have gotten to meet otherwise: an outcast activist, a middle-aged housewife who'd get so worked up at the fact I was speaking her language with her, she'd haul off and gleefully punch me in the arm. "*Why, these samosas are very good.*" Wham! "*Yes, it sure is hot today.*" Pow! Like getting repeatedly walloped by joy.

Influences on My Writing
I have to say Robert Penn Warren. It was only after I signed a contract to write my first book, *The Red Devil,* that I realized I didn't know how to write a book. I was then struck mute with terror. Luckily for me, the book club I was in at the time chose that moment to read Robert Penn Warren's extraordinary novel, *All the King's Men.* The richness of his language coupled with his surety and the risks he took; it was, all of it, infectious and drained my fear. I just wanted to do what he was doing. Once I started the book, I wrote it in nine months.

MRS. BHARGAV MISTRY'S GUJARATI SALAD

Makes 6-8 servings

In the first half of *Dreaming In Hindi*, a book about a year I spent in India learning to speak Hindi, I write about living with an extended Jain family: two brothers, their wives, five children, and a tiny matriarch. The brothers owned a marble mine and had a sprawling house with many rooms, but everything happened in the kitchen. Afternoons, I'd sit with the wives in the kitchen and watch their choreographed dinner preparations. I'd haltingly answer their questions about life in the United States and when they'd comment, I was lost. I'd be lost during dinner with the children and wives and lost again an hour later, when the men came home and sat down to be served. Day after day, all those hours, everyone spoke to me, ignoring the fact that it was largely a preposterous undertaking. To this day, I marvel at the family's infinite patience with my baby Hindi—they'd speak gently, slowly, repeat things often, as if I were a child. I was cradled by their language, until one day, an astonishing but predictable thing happened: strings of words were suddenly just there, as if I'd known them all along.

It was about then that the wives began hinting broadly that it might be nice if I'd just for once cook them dinner. I suppose I seemed more adult to them, more like a woman, and one thing every woman in India can do is cook. When they'd not-so-subtly suggest this, I'd freeze, stricken, for I deeply wanted to make dinner for them and at the same time, I knew, there was no way to explain that in New York, whence I'd come, people use their slivers of kitchens to microwave, end of story. I'd never learned how to cook anything. So they'd hint and I'd stammer, until finally, the women tried to help me out. I'd made it clear I'd wanted to and now they tried to figure out what was the problem. "*What do you cook at your house?*" they asked, but again, I was at a loss for words. No sense going for the dictionary. "Take out," was not going to be in there.

"*Mexican?*" one of the wives offered helpfully. "*Yes!*" I exclaimed. At home, I had heated up rice. Other times, beans. "*So you can cook Mexican for us here?*" she said, glancing at the stove. Damn. "*No, I need the book,*" I said. "*Book?*" they repeated. "*Yes, I need the book of the kitchen to cook Mexican,*" I said and the senior wife gave me a nice-try smile. "*Good answer,*" I swear she said.

The upshot of this story is that months later, when I met a woman from Gujarat, the wife of the saroda player Bhargav Mistry, who said she'd be glad to teach me to cook, I leaped at the offer. I'd never been so happy to know anything in my life. All of Mrs. Mistry's recipes were magnificent and often intricate, but the one I liked the best, the one I present here, was the simplest.

Note: *Poha*, or white rice flakes, can be purchased at Indian grocers or ordered online.

Pomegranates are in season fall through mid-winter in the United States. After breaking open the fruit, you'll find many arils, or seed casings, which can be consumed raw (including the seed).

You're welcome to adjust amounts of ingredients to suit your taste. When Mrs. Mistry taught me, she'd just say things like, "Add some peanuts, oh, maybe two handfuls." Every time I make this salad, I wing it.

1 20-ounce can pineapple rings, or fresh pineapple, cored
¾–1 cup salted peanuts
1 head of white or red cabbage
1–1½ cups sliced seedless green grapes
¾–1 cup poha (white rice flakes) (optional) (see note)
¾–1 cup pomegranate seeds (see note)
4–6 tablespoons chopped cilantro leaves
Juice of 1 lemon
Pinch of sugar
Salt to taste

1 Slice pineapple rings or cored pineapple into bite-sized pieces, until you have 1–1½ cups. Place peanuts in a small paper bag and use a mallet to smash into pieces.

2 Using a mandoline, food processor fitted with a slicing blade, or box grater, grate the cabbage into long pieces.

3 In a large salad bowl, combine pineapple, peanuts, cabbage, grapes, poha, pomegranate seeds, and cilantro. Add lemon juice, sugar, and salt to taste, and toss. The mix of textures and tastes make this like nothing you've ever tried.

Roxana Robinson

Marion Ettlinger

The Inspiration for Stories versus Novels I usually begin to write
when I find something that disturbs or interests me, something that intrudes on my mind.

I write stories and novels differently. I write stories because of a scene or an exchange, some moment I've seen or heard of, that strikes me as very powerful. I write the story toward that moment. It comes toward the end of a story, and if you read my work you will know it when you reach it, though something else usually happens after it. But that moment is what drives the story.

I write novels differently; I'm not writing toward a moment, and I don't know at all what will happen. I start a novel because of a conflict or a problem that I find compelling. I explore the idea of the conflict, I find the people who are involved in it, I get to know them well, and then I let them deal with the problem. In doing so, they create the narrative. It's a slow, organic process, one that has its own sort of life and direction.

....

Readers Should Know My most recent novel, *Cost*, is about three generations
of a family going through a crisis. I'm interested in the way families respond to each other. I think of the family as being an organic unit, whole and living. I think of it as being like a mobile, a sculpture, delicately balanced, carefully interconnected. Any movement on the part of anyone will have an effect on all the others. One person in crisis sets the whole system into silent, swaying motion.

....

Readers Frequently Ask   Most people ask how I know what it's like to be the characters I write about. One woman called me at home, said she was the main character in my last book, and asked if I'd been stalking her.

It's a hard question to answer; it's hard to say exactly how I get to know my characters. I spend a lot of time with them, in their worlds. And the better I know them, the more I enter their worlds and feel I understand them. Their worlds sort of become mine, particularly toward the end of the process. Then I start living more in their lives than in my own. When it's over I feel sad to let them all go; I'll never live with them again, and I feel a kind of loss.

....

Influences on My Writing   *To the Lighthouse* by Virginia Woolf has probably been the biggest influence on my work. She showed us it was possible to make a small domestic narrative into great literature. She writes about the family: how the members reflect each others' needs and conflicts, about what it's like to be alive, and how it feels and how it looks. Reading her beautiful sentences, you think over and over, Yes! Yes, that's how it is!

Other great favorites include *The Rabbit Quartet* by John Updike. His sublimely elegant language delivers all the mess and complications of real life, and it's driven by deep understanding and compassion. Updike is truly engaged with his characters; he understands them, he sees their flaws and he forgives them. He's a compassionate writer, and for me, compassion is hugely important.

Anna Karenina by Leo Tolstoy is a wonderful, wonderful book delivered so simply, in such small, heartbreaking scenes, each one so beautifully rendered. Plus, it has all the glamorous splendor of prerevolutionary Russia: the balls, the furs, the sleighs, the villa in Italy. The spectacle is mesmerizing. I was put off by it for years because the book is so thick! It's so heavy! It's so Russian! But once I finally began it I realized—it's so easy to read! And it's so riveting, so hypnotizingly engaging. Now I've read it twice, and look forward to reading it many times again. It's like an old friend you know and trust and love.

ARTIST'S SUMMER STEW

Makes 3–4 servings

Julia, from my novel *Cost*, is an artist who spends as much time as possible in her studio. Time in her studio is lost time, and she will forget whatever else is going on. This is very bad for cooking. It means she'll forget whatever is on the stove and let it burn, or forget to even turn it on. When she's alone she hardly cooks at all, though she might make a big batch of lentil soup and eat it for several days. When her family is with her in Maine, she likes making slow-cooked dishes that produce a rich stew of flavors and textures. She can't deal with a lot of last minute steps that involve finishing sauces, but she likes a meal that includes grace notes: fresh chopped herbs scattered on the top of a dish, warm crusty baguettes passed hand to hand, and on the table, a vase of flowers from the meadow.

Here's something she would make. It's a recipe she made up, though it probably has its roots in the cooking of southwestern France, which she admires because it's rich and slow. Serve this dish with a mesclun salad (see recipe) with walnuts and more chopped tarragon sprinkled through it, a warm baguette, and sweet butter. For dessert, another baguette (this one not warmed), some good cheeses, and whatever fruit looked good that day at the market.

1 tablespoon butter

2 medium onions, thinly sliced

6 boneless chicken thighs or 3 boneless chicken breasts (1–1¼ pounds), cut into 3-inch pieces

1½ cups arborio rice

3 cups chicken broth

2–3 tablespoons chopped fresh parsley

Salt to taste

Ground black pepper to taste

2–3 tablespoons chopped fresh tarragon

1. In a big iron skillet, melt the butter over low heat. Add onions, cover with tight-fitting lid, and cook over low heat, stirring occasionally. When they have become translucent (this will take 10–15 minutes, during which time you can run out to the meadow and pick some flowers for the table), remove the onions and set aside.

2. Turn heat to medium, add the chicken pieces, and brown in the skillet. (The browning will also take 10 minutes or so, during which time you can set the table, pour a pitcher of ice water, and make a platter of cheeses for dessert.) You should be nearby during this, so you'll hear and smell if they start to burn.

3. When the chicken is all nicely browned, add the onions, pour in the rice, and stir to coat it with butter. Then add the chicken broth and the chopped parsley, and stir it all. Cover the skillet with a heavy lid, turn the heat down to medium-low, and let it simmer until the rice is soft and the liquid is mostly absorbed, while you take a shower. This will be about 20–30 minutes. Keep checking whenever you can to make sure the heat's not too high or too low. When it's finished, add salt and pepper to taste, and sprinkle the fresh tarragon over it before the last stir.

MESCLUN SALAD AT THE LAST MINUTE

Makes 4 servings

Note: Both walnuts and pine nuts taste good with the mesclun; both are kind of oily and offer a good contrasting crunchy texture to the lettuce, but the walnuts are more visible and so you are more aware of them.

If you're using fresh tarragon, you can either add it to the dressing or sprinkle it on the salad. If you're using dried tarragon, just put it in the dressing. (Dried herbs in salad are scratchy and dry.)

FOR THE SALAD

8 cups fresh mesclun greens, or a combination of mesclun and baby spinach, or a local lettuce on its own

A handful of shelled walnuts or pine nuts (see note)

FOR THE DRESSING

1½ tablespoons balsamic vinegar

1½–3 heaping teaspoons Maille Dijon mustard (this is my favorite ingredient)

¼ cup (or a little less) really good extra-virgin olive oil

⅛ teaspoon dried tarragon or a big handful of fresh chopped tarragon (see note)

1 Wash and drain the lettuce, and spin it dry. Set lettuce in a salad bowl with the nuts on top, in a casual cluster.
2 **To make the dressing:** In an empty glass jar, combine balsamic vinegar, mustard, olive oil, and tarragon. Whisk together gently with a fork. (Don't whip the dressing or shake the jar, because the dressing will thicken and become viscous. Stir it gently, and try to keep it liquid.)
3 Pour the dressing down the inside edge of the salad bowl, so it runs underneath the leaves and pools beneath them. (This dressing is best when brought up from underneath, instead of poured on top, because it can be thick and a bit heavy.) Place a thoroughly dampened paper towel on top of the lettuce to keep it moist, and allow the salad to sit "undressed" until ready to serve. To serve, remove paper towel and toss salad gently, bringing dressing up from underneath, until the leaves are coated.

Stephanie Saldaña

SELECTED WORKS

• *The Bread of Angels: A Journey to Love and Faith* (2010)

Frédéric Masson

Inspiration I am inspired by the people around me and the incredible stories they have to tell. In my memoir *The Bread of Angels*, I take my inspiration from the people I encountered during my year in Syria: my Armenian neighbor, the gossiping Arab Christians who inhabit the streets around me, philosophizing carpet sellers, and Muslim teachers and Christian monks and nuns who live and pray in the Middle East. When I write, I try not only to be honest about my own journeys and struggles, but also to find ways of listening to and learning from the journeys of the people I meet along the way. These days I live between Jerusalem and France, where I've encountered a whole new cast of teachers!

Writing to Heal I have spent much of the last ten years of my life living in countries scarred by conflict and war. And yet I have always encountered the truest moments of beauty in these places. I found love in one of these places. For me, writing is a way of meditating on the beauty I find in the torn cities I've made my home in. I know that it is old fashioned and melodramatic to believe that writing can be a way to heal, but I try to believe that every working day. Maybe the only person I'm healing is myself, but that's a start, at least.

Readers Frequently Ask I am always asked about what happened to my relationship with Frédéric, the French novice monk I fell in love with during my year in Syria. Did we run off together, or did he remain in the monastery to take his final vows? I always tell readers that they have to finish *The Bread of Angels* to find out, right through to the acknowledgments!

I am also often asked whether or not I miss Syria. The answer is yes, yes, yes. I miss Syria every day.

Influences on My Writing One book I have carted all over the world with me is *The Cloister Walk* by Kathleen Norris. She writes movingly about her time as a lay poet living inside of a monastery, inspired by the rhythm of the prayers and the stories of the monks and nuns she meets. She is also extremely funny. I have always struggled with how to live a spiritual life within the chaos of the world, and I go back to her book again and again for answers.

The poet who influenced me the most is probably Czeslaw Milosz, the great modern Polish poet, who described the tragedies of the twentieth century in deep, searing, and beautiful poems. He speaks to my own heart and is a constant reminder that a writer, in all humility, should strive to participate in the act of healing.

Finally, in all honesty, the author who has influenced me the most in the past year is cookbook writer Claudia Roden, whose book *The New Book of Middle Eastern Food* completely changed my life. As I cooked my way through it, she opened up the world of Middle Eastern food in a totally new way and, as a result, Jerusalem came alive to me. Because of her, I know all of the spice store owners, village sellers of greens, vegetable vendors, butchers, and markets in the neighborhoods near where I live.

SYRIAN STYLE *MUHAMMARA* (ROASTED RED PEPPER DIP WITH WALNUTS AND POMEGRANATE SYRUP)

Makes about 2½ cups

Inspired by a recipe in Paula Wolfert's *The Cooking of the Eastern Mediterranean: 215 Healthy, Vibrant, and Inspired Recipes* (William Morrow, 1994)

In my memoir *The Bread of Angels*, I write about the incredible journey I lived during a year in Syria, where I studied Arabic, almost became a nun, explored the Quran with a female sheikh, and found myself in love with a French novice monk who lived in a monastery in the middle of the desert. The backdrop of the story is the city of Damascus, a place of remarkable diversity, full of Muslims, Jews, Druze, Kurds and Armenians, Sunnis and Shiites, and every form of Christianity under the sun. It is a city where every day reveals something magical and unexpected. And it is a city full of remarkable restaurants; gorgeous, tiled Ottoman houses with fountains at the center, where a man plays the *oud* at the front on a stage, and waiters bring out endless plates of delicious appetizers, platters of steaming kabobs, desserts laced with rose water, and delicate mint tea. An average meal can last several hours, and you wouldn't want it to end a moment sooner.

All over the Middle East, meals begin with *mezze,* dozens of small appetizers spread about the table in a dizzying array of flavors: hummus and eggplant dips, cheeses and olives, chopped salads, spicy tomato sauces. In Syria, the first thing I asked at any restaurant is if they offered muhammara, the magical dip consisting of an unlikely mix of roasted red peppers, toasted walnuts, and pomegranate syrup. Syria is famous for its muhammara, and for me it represented everything I loved about the country: exotic flavors, surprising combinations and, more than anything, the blending of spicy and sweet. If life in Syria has a flavor, then it is muhammara.

When I moved to Jerusalem, I couldn't find my beloved muhammara anywhere, and so I decided to learn to make it myself. I never knew that I would love a dip so much that it would lead me to roast my own peppers and toast walnuts, but muhammara is not just any dip. Each time I taste it, I taste Damascus. I hope you do, too. Enjoy!

Note: Muhammara can be prepared countless ways, and no two cooks make it alike. Be sure to experiment with the recipe each time you make it to decide how you like it. Some cooks like it with twice as many roasted red peppers, some like it spicier and pile in the chile peppers, and others double the garlic or leave it out entirely. I always start with the minimum amount of pomegranate syrup, lemon juice, chile pepper, and salt when I begin and then adjust as I go along. It's always delicious!

Muhammara always tastes better the day after you make it, so feel free to make it the night before a party and to let the flavors sit, or to make a double batch so that you can enjoy the leftovers the day after!

Pomegranate syrup is available at Middle Eastern grocers and online.

For the ground hot chile pepper, you can grind hot red pepper flakes or the seeds of whole dried chiles in a spice grinder. Start with the minimum amount and adjust heat to taste.

3 large red bell peppers

¾ cup walnuts

2 garlic cloves, minced

2 slices white sandwich bread, toasted and ground into crumbs in a food processor

1–2 teaspoons pomegranate syrup (see note)

½–¾ teaspoon ground hot chile pepper (see note)

1–2 tablespoons fresh lemon juice

½ teaspoon ground cumin

¼–½ teaspoon salt

2 tablespoons olive oil, plus additional for drizzling

Pita bread, for serving

1 **Roast the red peppers:** If you have a gas range, put the peppers directly on the burners with the flames on high, and rotate them until tender and blackened on all sides. If you have an electric range, place the peppers on a broiling tray covered with foil and broil, turning occasionally, until skin is blackened and blistered on all sides. Place peppers in a bowl, cover tightly with plastic wrap, and let sit for 5 minutes. Remove stems and seeds and peel off blackened skin.

2 Toast the walnuts in a dry, heavy pan over medium heat, stirring frequently, for 1–2 minutes or until fragrant. Remove from pan and pound with a mortar and pestle, or process in a food processor, until they are ground.

3 Put the red peppers into the bowl of a food processor and pulse a few times, then add the walnuts, garlic, bread crumbs, pomegranate syrup, chile pepper, lemon juice, cumin, and salt. Process until combined and then, with the processor on, slowly add the olive oil until you have a smooth paste. Adjust the salt to taste.

4 Serve at room temperature with olive oil drizzled on top, and with squares of pita bread for dipping. Sahteen!–to your health!

Esmeralda Santiago

CANTOMEDIA

Inspiration I'm of the "perspiration, not inspiration" school, believing that if I fill a blank page with enough words, some of them will be useful. Whenever I feel stuck, or uninspired, I scribble random thoughts, complaints, secrets, lists, word doodles, snippets of dialogue, and descriptions of people, places, or things. These scattered seeds upon the page sprout into phrases and sentences like fragile stems that grow to sturdy branches. A leaf appears, and yes, every once in a while, a flower blooms. Even though this is my process, I'm often surprised that writing is hard work and that I must resist the habit of expectations. I certainly shouldn't expect to be inspired every time I prepare to work. Inspiration is a gift as random and surprising as flashes over running water.

....

Readers Should Know I've been writing a novel for five years, and a couple of chapters short of finishing my first draft I had a stroke that robbed me of the ability to concentrate for longer than a few minutes at a time, the ability to read and understand complex sentences in either English or Spanish, the ability to create. Even though my book was outlined, I couldn't get the information that I knew was there from my damaged brain onto a page for about a year. It was a painful, desolate time, especially because there was no obvious physical damage. To everyone else I was fine, but inside I felt confused half the time, and guilty that I'd abandoned my characters. It took me a year to work back to where I was, and I'm happy that my characters' voices were stilled but not silenced. The novel is titled *Conquistadora*, and like my main character, I have learned to conquer a new world by sheer force of will and stubbornness.

....

Readers Frequently Ask My e-mail is a constant delight, because readers send so many touching and emotional messages in response to my work. The most frequent question is about the meaning of the title of my first memoir, *When I Was Puerto Rican*. Readers also want to know where my parents and sisters and brothers now live and what they're doing. After the release of my third memoir, *The Turkish Lover*, readers wanted to know whether I'd stayed in touch with Ulvi. I've included the answers, and others, in a FAQs page on my website (EsmeraldaSantiago.com).

I try to respond to every reader who gets in touch, although sometimes it takes me weeks to do so, depending on my travel and work schedule. Recently, I've "attended" book clubs via phone and video conferences. Now I wish I could taste some of the treats that some of the members bring to the sessions!

....

Influences on My Writing

- Spanish/English Dictionary: I came to the United States from Puerto Rico at thirteen and had to learn English quickly in order to help my mother cope with American culture. Unwilling to lose my Spanish, I kept it alive by reading, even as English has become my literary language. After all these years, it still feels as if I'm thinking in Spanish and writing in English, still interpreting between cultures.
- Abelardo Díaz Alfaro's *Terrazo*, a short story collection published the year before I was born in Puerto Rico. I connected to its stories about rural Puerto Ricans following the invasion of the island by the U.S. Navy that ended the Spanish American War. The stories are filled with sadness, humor, and outrage at the conditions of the rural poor, called *jíbaros*. The style is old-fashioned and sometimes overwrought, but I find beauty in Díaz Alfaro's use of the almost extinct *jíbaro* dialect.
- Edith Hamilton's *Mythology* became my favorite book the first time I read it, and inspires me still. It was one of the first books I read in English cover to cover. There was enough drama and adventure for a lifetime within those pages, and all the convoluted relationships convinced me that there were families crazier than mine.

PUERTO RICAN *PERNIL*

Makes 8–10 servings

I'm not much of a cook, but there's a lot of food in my books and essays. My first memoir, *When I Was Puerto Rican*, begins with me holding a guava in my hand. It represents everything that has been lost and gained with my family's move from Puerto Rico to the United States. In my other books, people connect to each other through food and learn about each other at meals. In *América's Dream*, for example, América Gonzalez discovers just how different her eating habits are from those of her New York employees. In my three memoirs, in numerous essays, and in my upcoming novel, *Conquistadora*, food and cooking are as crucial as the events. Whether or not someone can cook (or can but won't) says much about him or her. What the people in my books eat or don't eat is also important, as well as when and how much, and, of course, where.

For many of us from other countries (or from different regions of the same country), food and its preparation is, at a certain level, ritualistic, a way to remember, celebrate and hold on to our home cultures. I live in the United States and can't travel to Puerto Rico as often as I'd like, but I can slice and fry plantains until they're crispy, dip the warm and fragrant slices into warm olive oil with fresh crushed garlic, salt and pepper, and feel closer to Puerto Rico.

My mother, four of my five sisters, and my five brothers now live in the United States with their spouses and children. Whenever we get together, for celebrations and holiday meals, Mami or one of my sisters will make pernil—pork shoulder that is prepared, rubbed, and marinated overnight before it's roasted for hours, depending on its size. For Puerto Ricans living away from the island, and increasingly those in Puerto Rico, the pernil is the surrogate for the traditional *lechón*—a whole pig roasted on a spit served for Christmas and special occasions.

Before we prepare the pernil, we must make two of the staples of Puerto Rican cuisine: *sofrito* and *adobo*. My earliest olfactory memory is of sofrito sautéed in olive oil until the garlic, onion, green pepper, and *recao* (also known as culantro) mixed and melded into the scent of my mother's love. The proportions of the ingredients for sofrito are as individual as the cook's palate, so I can recognize the smell of Mami's sofrito from my sister's or from mine. The basic ingredients are chopped and then mixed together, but cooks add different components to their sofrito, like tomatoes or fresh oregano. For mine, I add red pepper for color and a bit of sweetness. Traditionally, sofrito requires culantro, which can be found in Caribbean or Asian markets. In this recipe I replace it with cilantro, since it's easier to find, and has a similar but milder flavor.

Sofrito is usually sautéed until the ingredients are fragrant. (To make Puerto Rican beans, cook the sofrito in oil until it smells good, add tomato sauce, salt, pepper, a pinch of oregano, and a bit of cumin.) Sofrito is used to season *arroz con pollo*, fricassees, soups, and stews. As with the following recipe for pernil, sofrito is also used as a marinade for meats.

Pernil is most often served with pigeon peas. It is also served with fried plantains, with boiled and marinated yucca (my favorite), or with marinated green bananas.

Note: Adobo is the second essential ingredient in Puerto Rican cooking. It's always prepared just before used. Like sofrito, cooks individualize their adobo to their palate. In mine, I add cumin.

If you don't have a mortar and pestle to make the adobo, you can use a spice grinder. The idea is that the garlic and other ingredients form a paste. I like pounding it with my mortar and pestle to take out my frustrations as I crush the ingredients.

FOR THE ADOBO

9 garlic cloves, peeled

1 teaspoon peppercorns (or more to taste)

2 tablespoons coarse salt

1 teaspoon dried oregano

½ teaspoon ground paprika

½ teaspoon ground cumin

FOR THE PORK

1 bone-in, skin-on pork shoulder (7½–8½ pounds)

1½ tablespoons olive oil

1½ tablespoons white vinegar

¼–½ cup sofrito (see recipe below)

---

1   Prepare sofrito (recipe below) and set aside. **To make the adobo:** Using a mortar and pestle (see note), pound all ingredients into a paste. Once you've made your sofrito and adobo, you're ready to massage them into the meat.

2   Wash and dry pork. Score all around with a sharp paring knife, making slits deep into the meat. Set aside.

3   Mix the adobo with the olive oil and vinegar, then rub the adobo over the pork roast, making sure that the paste goes deep into the slits.

4 Rub the sofrito over the meat, again, pushing it into the slits. Place the roast in a deep baking pan, fatty skin side up. Cover pan tightly with aluminum foil, and allow to marinate overnight.

5 Remove the pork from the refrigerator 30 minutes before cooking. Discard aluminum foil. Drain any liquid that may have formed overnight and pour over the meat.

6 Preheat oven to 400°F. Cook the pork uncovered, for 1 hour. Reduce oven temperature to 300°F and cook for about another 4 hours, without turning the meat over, until internal temperature reaches 185°F and the meat shreds with a fork. To achieve the much desired crispy, fatty skin, increase the oven temperature to 400°F for the last 20 minutes of cooking.

7 Allow the pernil to rest for at least 20 minutes before serving. Slice with the grain. Serve a bit of the crunchy skin with each portion.

SOFRITO

My mother prepared her sofrito fresh for each meal, but the recipe below will make approximately two cups and any extra can be frozen. Defrost before using.

1 large onion, peeled and quartered
1 large green pepper, seeded and quartered
½ medium red pepper, seeded
6–8 garlic cloves (or more to taste)
1 bunch cilantro, washed, the hard stems discarded

Whirl all ingredients in a food processor until finely chopped.

ASOPAO FOR THE SOUL

Makes 6–8 servings

Comfort food brings you home, engages your senses, nourishes your body and recalls memories. For me, asopao not only brings me home to Puerto Rico, it brings me closer to my mother, who makes the best, most creative asopaos.

Asopao is the Puerto Rican version of chicken soup, but it can be made with shrimp, pork, beef, or gandules (pigeon peas). My uncle once brought Mami a couple of spiny lobsters, and to make sure that she, my uncle, and her eleven children could all have a taste, she made lobster asopao. Today, lobster asopao is not unusual in Puerto Rican restaurants, but they use North American lobster which is meatier and sweeter.

The recipe below for chicken asopao is quite basic. My mother adds pigeon peas, cubed potatoes, and/or sliced carrots. Asopao is served with a dash or two of homemade *pique* (hot sauce) and with a side of crispy fried plantains or slices of garlic bread.

The distinctive golden orange of the asopao is achieved by cooking the *sofrito* in *achiote* oil. Known in English as annatto, achiote is another of the staples in the Puerto Rican kitchen. Annatto seeds are gently warmed in oil until they release their color, then the seeds are strained and discarded. The bright orange achiote oil adds color, and a subtle peppery, nutty flavor to soups, rice dishes, and grilled meats and fish.

Note: The chicken must marinate for at least 30 minutes, and preferably overnight.

My mother chops the chicken into at least 8 pieces so that everyone can get a *presa* (a piece of the chicken). I usually buy thighs and drumsticks because I like the flavor, but I'm giving you her recipe here.

We rinse chicken (and other meat) in lemon juice because of lemon's antibacterial properties and to remove the scent of the meat. The lemon juice also imparts a subtle flavor. It is not necessary though, if the chicken is thoroughly washed.

Short-grain rice is traditionally used in this dish. If you can't find short-grain rice, you can substitute medium- or long-grain rice.

For the adobo

4 cloves garlic

1 teaspoon black peppercorns

1 teaspoon salt

1 teaspoon dried oregano

½ teaspoon paprika

For the chicken

1 3–4 pound chicken, cut up (see note)

Lemon juice, for rinsing (see note)

1 tablespoon white vinegar

4 tablespoons sofrito, divided (see recipe)

For the soup

3 tablespoons achiote oil (see recipe)

½ cup white wine

½ cup tomato sauce

1 cup short-grain rice (see note)

7 cups water

1 tablespoon capers

1 tablespoon Spanish olives, chopped

2 bay leaves

½ teaspoon dried oregano

½ teaspoon salt, plus additional for
   seasoning

Ground black pepper to taste

Chopped cilantro, for sprinkling

1 **To make the adobo:** Pound all the ingredients in a mortar and pestle, or process in a spice grinder, until the adobo forms a paste. Set aside.

2 Rinse chicken pieces in water, then generously sprinkle lemon juice on each piece, and pat dry.

3 Place adobo in a small bowl. Add vinegar and 1 tablespoon of the sofrito and blend well. Rub the mixture over the chicken pieces. Let marinate in the refrigerator for at least 30 minutes, preferably overnight.

4 **To make the soup:** In a stockpot, heat the achiote oil over medium heat. Add remaining 3 tablespoons sofrito. Cook for 2 minutes.

5 Add chicken. Cook, stirring frequently to ensure that all the pieces of chicken are seasoned. Continue cooking a few minutes more until the chicken is opaque.

6 Add the white wine and tomato sauce and stir well, then add the rice, water, capers, olives, bay leaves, oregano, and salt. Return the mixture to a boil, then lower heat and simmer, covered, 20–25 minutes or until chicken is well cooked. Remove bay leaves. Add additional salt and pepper to taste. Spoon into bowls and sprinkle with cilantro before serving.

ACHIOTE OIL

Makes 1 cup

Note: The best sources for annatto seeds are Caribbean and Latin American markets, or online grocery stores.

1 cup olive oil
2 tablespoons dry achiote (annatto) seeds

1 In a medium pan, heat the oil and achiote seeds over medium heat, stirring frequently until the seeds are just beginning to dance and sizzle on the bottom of the pan. (Do not overcook or the seeds will turn black and the oil green and taste bitter.) Remove from the burner, then allow the mixture to cool for 5 minutes. The oil should have a bright, orange color.

2 Pour the achiote oil through a metal strainer into a glass jar. Discard the annatto seeds. Cover jar tightly. The achiote oil can be kept at room temperature for 5 days, longer in the refrigerator.

MY MOTHER'S SWEET COCONUT RICE

Makes 12 servings

Note: Short-grain rice has fat, almost round grains that stick together well when cooked, but you can also use long-grain rice.

I prefer the coconut rice at room temperature.

Some people like to pour the warm rice into ramekins and serve them as individual dishes with a dollop of unsweetened whipped cream. I serve mine plain, with a cup of coffee.

FOR THE SPICE INFUSION	FOR THE PUDDING
1 1½-inch piece fresh gingerroot, unpeeled and sliced in half	1 cup short-grain white rice (see note)
4 2-inch sticks cinnamon	3 cups unsweetened coconut milk
15 whole cloves	1 cup sugar
4 cups water	½ cup seedless raisins
	1 cup unsweetened coconut flakes
	Ground cinnamon, for topping

1   **To make the spice infusion:** Combine the ginger, cinnamon sticks, cloves, and water in a large saucepan and bring to a boil. Lower heat, and simmer uncovered for 30 minutes. Remove solids with a slotted spoon.

2   **To make the pudding:** Place rice in a large bowl, cover with water to about one inch above the rice, and let soak for at least 30 minutes. Drain and add to the saucepan with the spice infusion. Bring to a gentle boil, then immediately reduce heat and simmer, covered, for 10 minutes. Add the coconut milk and sugar. Raise heat to medium until mixture starts to bubble, then reduce heat to low and simmer, covered, for 10 more minutes, stirring frequently.

3   Add the raisins and cook for 5 minutes, continuing to stir. Stir in the coconut flakes, and continue to stir for another 5 minutes, until rice is soft.

4   Spread mixture evenly in 9" × 13" × 2" rectangular glass pan or 12 6-ounce ramekins (see note). Allow to cool for 15 minutes. Sprinkle ground cinnamon on top to taste. Serve at room temperature (see note), or refrigerate and serve cold. When ready to serve, slice into squares.

Lisa See

Patricia Williams

Inspiration In 2000, while researching Chinese opera for an article I was writing, I came across the story of lovesick maidens—Chinese girls in the mid-seventeenth century who loved an opera called *The Peony Pavilion* but were never allowed to see it. These maidens caught "lovesickness" by simply reading the opera, and they would waste away and die. I became obsessed with the true story of three of these lovesick maidens, who were all married to the same man, one right after the other. Together they wrote *The Three Wives Commentary*, the first book of its kind to be written and published anywhere in the world by women. Even though these girls were young—not one of them reached age twenty—what they wrote about love 300 years ago is still absolutely true today. But even though I wanted to write about their lives and explore the different aspects of love, I couldn't figure out how to do it. I tucked all this away in the back of my mind, and I wouldn't use it for eight more years until I sat down to write *Peony in Love*.

A few years later, I was reviewing a book on the history of foot binding that mentioned *nu shu*—the only writing system found that was used exclusively by women in a remote county in southwest Hunan province in China for a thousand years. How could it be that I didn't know about it? I became fascinated. This led me, of course, to write *Snow Flower and the Secret Fan*.

As I wrote the last page of *Snow Flower*, where the narrator, Lily, hopes her words will travel to the afterworld, I finally realized how I could tell the story of the three lovesick maidens. I'd use one voice, the voice of Peony, the first wife, and I'd follow her after she died so she could tell the story of her other sister-wives.

The Uniqueness of Female Relationships
Shanghai Girls is about two sisters who leave Shanghai in 1937 and come to Los Angeles in arranged marriages. Sisters have a unique relationship. A sister is a person who's known you your whole life and therefore knows right where to drive the knife! In *Snow Flower and the Secret Fan*, I wrote about best friends for life. Female friendship is different from any other relationship; it's a particular kind of intimacy. In *Peony in Love*, I wrote about three women married to the same man but also about the relationships among grandmother, mother, and daughter. I'm very interested in the beauty and wonder, as well as the dark shadow side, of female relationships.

Readers Frequently Ask
After reading *Snow Flower and the Secret Fan*, book clubs continually ask: how could a mother bind her daughter's feet? In nineteenth century China, the one thing a mother could do to ensure a better life for her daughter was to help her marry into a better family. If that was the only thing we could do for our daughters today, wouldn't we be tempted to do it?

Book club members are also interested in the very different belief systems portrayed in my novels, especially the idea of the Chinese afterlife as depicted in *Peony in Love*. The Chinese believe that when you die, your emotions travel with you. This is very different from Western beliefs. Male and female readers have opposite reactions to this idea. The men often say they don't like the idea of having the same family in the afterlife. The women, on the other hand, love the idea of staying connected to their families after death. They still get to interfere in their lives! Women who read *Peony in Love* relish this idea of being able to maintain a connection to the people they love on earth, even after death.

Influences on My Writing
Angle of Repose by Wallace Stegner inspired me when I was working on *On Gold Mountain*, the history of my Chinese relatives. The narrator in *Angle of Repose* was also researching his family. Stegner's narrator says of the people he's been investigating, "I want to live in their clothes a while." I feel that way about the research I do, whether it's for fictional characters or real people. I want to live in their clothes for a while, feel what they feel, and live where they live. This brings the characters alive not only for me, but I hope for my readers too.

As a child, every morning I would read "Rikki-Tikki-Tavi" from *The Jungle Book* by Rudyard Kipling before I got out of bed. I loved the idea of being immersed in another culture, but also being able to relate to the people there. Reading that story made this completely different culture real and believable, like I was there in that garden in India.

LISA SEE'S WON TONS

Makes approximately 48 won tons

Food and the Chinese language are the two most important things in Chinese culture and to the Chinese people, so it's no wonder that they both play such important roles in all my books. In *Peony in Love*, food has a greater significance than usual. I don't want to give anything away, but it has to do with the nature of the lovesick maidens and what they were doing (or not doing) in life, as well as the ravenous desires of hungry ghosts.

We've always made won tons in my family. Everyone rolls their own won tons on Thanksgiving in my family. We have a lot of fun, everyone gets their fingers messy, and we come up with some odd shapes. Not to worry though; as long as the won ton is properly sealed, it will cook up just fine.

You can add anything you want to the filling—chopped Chinese mushrooms or garlic, for example—but below are my favorite ingredients. I love fresh ginger and the crunch of the water chestnuts.

If you have extra won tons, you can always make won ton soup. For won ton soup, boil the won tons for a couple of minutes to wash away the flour, drain, and then add them to your soup just before serving.

Note: One pound of ground chicken can be substituted for the pork and shrimp, but the filling will be less moist.

The number of won ton wrappers varies from package to package, but usually they have between 36 and 60 wrappers. I've included an extra package of wrappers in this recipe; the number of wrappers you'll use depends on how plump you make your won tons.

You can serve won tons hot or at room temperature. Won tons also travel well as long as you don't put them in a sealed container. I put them loose in a brown paper grocery bag lined on the bottom with a few paper towels. This helps to soak up any extra oil, keeps the won tons from getting soggy, and you don't have to wash your traveling container!

For an additional dipping sauce option, you can serve ready-made sweet and sour sauce.

FOR THE WON TONS

½ pound lean ground pork (see note)

½ pound uncooked shrimp, peeled, deveined, and minced (see note)

1 8-ounce can water chestnuts, minced

3 scallions, minced

2 tablespoons minced fresh gingerroot

2 tablespoons low-sodium soy sauce

2 packages won ton skins (set aside one wrapper for testing) (see note)

1 large egg, beaten, to seal won tons

Peanut or safflower oil for frying

FOR THE DIPPING SAUCE

¼ cup low-sodium soy sauce

¼ cup fresh lemon juice

Dash of Siracha chili sauce

1 scallion, chopped

1 **To make the filling:** In a medium bowl, combine pork, shrimp, water chestnuts, scallions, ginger, and soy sauce.

2 **To assemble the won tons:** Place won ton wrapper in front of you so that a corner is facing in your direction. Place about a teaspoon of the filling in that corner. Roll this corner toward the middle. Moisten the side corners with a drop of the beaten egg and fold those two ends together to lock the won ton in place. There should be a single layer of won ton skin that curls out the back, like a jaunty scarf. Make sure the filling is sealed inside or the won tons will fall apart during cooking.

3 At this point you can store the won tons in the refrigerator until needed for cooking. When storing, make sure the won tons don't touch each other or they'll stick together.

4 **To make the dipping sauce:** Combine ingredients in a small bowl.

5 **To fry the wontons:** Pour 1–2 inches of oil into a pot or deep-sided skillet. Heat oil over medium heat. Test the oil temperature by tearing off pieces of one won ton wrapper and dropping them in the oil. The wrapper should turn brown quickly but not get too dark. Fry a few won tons at a time in a single layer until golden and crispy. Make sure they don't touch each other, and use tongs to flip them. Don't overcook! Drain on paper towels. Serve with dipping sauce.

THREE GENERATION CURRIED
TOMATO BEEF LO MEIN

Makes 4–6 servings

Food is memory, and many of my memories are linked to food. This recipe has grown and evolved over three generations in my family. My grandfather used to own a restaurant in Los Angeles's Chinatown called Dragon's Den. It was only the seventh family-style Chinese restaurant in Los Angeles. Back in 1936, when Dragon's Den opened, this dish—minus the curry and the noodles—cost just twenty-five cents. The restaurant had closed by the time I was born, but I can remember my grandfather making a version of the Dragon's Den tomato beef at home.

My father first tasted curried tomato beef chow mein (with fried noodles) in a restaurant in San Francisco. He later found it in a café on San Pedro Street, close to Ninth Street, and opposite the wholesale produce market in Los Angeles. He's been perfecting his version ever since. You can use Chinese egg or rice noodles for this dish, but my dad uses angel hair pasta. If I'm not in the mood for noodles, then I just serve the curried tomato beef with rice. My other addition to the recipe is the marinade. It tenderizes the beef and adds a little extra flavor. What I love about this dish is the taste of the tomatoes and vinegar. It's a combination that takes me right back to my childhood. Best of all, this dish is fast, colorful, and combines all the food groups.

Tomato beef is a uniquely Chinese-American dish—symbolic in many ways of America's "melting pot." "Mein" means noodles in Cantonese, but beef and tomatoes are not typical Chinese ingredients. In the past, if you were Chinese and lucky enough to own your own restaurant, you put together ingredients you thought would please your American customers. That's how American tomatoes and beef came to be thrown together with Chinese noodles. For a time, tomato beef chow mein and curried tomato beef chow mein could be found on every menu in Chinese-American restaurants and cafés, such as the Golden Dragon Café and Pearl's Coffee Shop in *Shanghai Girls*. Now you can't even find tomato beef in Chinese restaurants! No one asks for it, orders it, or remembers it. So this truly is a taste of the past, specifically 1950s Chinese America.

Note: There is no right or wrong way to make this dish. It's all about your personal taste and whether you like more vinegar or sugar.

For the more health conscious, you can substitute chicken for the beef. My dad fries boneless, skinless chicken thighs until they're done enough to cut them up easily. Then he adds them back to the wok after the onion and bell pepper to cook a bit more.

Some people like to add the noodles to the wok and toss them with the other ingredients. Transfer to a platter and sprinkle with cilantro.

FOR THE MARINADE

2 teaspoons soy sauce

1 teaspoon dry sherry

1 teaspoon sesame oil

½ teaspoon salt

Black pepper to taste

1 teaspoon cornstarch

FOR THE NOODLES OR RICE AND STIR-FRY

1 pound flank steak, cut into ¼-inch strips against the grain (see note)

1 pound pasta of your choice, or 1 cup rice

2–3 tablespoons canola oil

1 medium to large onion, cut into 1-inch squares

1 green bell pepper, chopped into 1-inch squares

1 tablespoon Madras curry powder

3–6 tablespoons white vinegar (see note)

1–3 teaspoons sugar (see note)

4 Roma tomatoes, quartered

2–3 tablespoons coarsely chopped cilantro leaves, for garnish

1 In medium bowl, combine soy sauce, sherry, sesame oil, salt, pepper to taste, and corn-starch. Add sliced beef, and let marinate for 20 minutes.

2 Heat water in a large pot and cook the noodles of your choice or rice according to package instructions. When done, drain the noodles or rice and put them on a platter (see note).

3 While noodles are cooking, heat oil in a wok or frying pan over high heat. When oil is hot and smoking, add the beef and stir fry until browned but not fully cooked, about 4 minutes. Add the onion and bell pepper. After they've cooked for a while but are still crisp (3–4 minutes), add the curry powder, vinegar, and sugar. Add tomatoes and cook until just heated through. (You don't want the vegetables to lose their shape. They should remain whole and crisp.) Taste for flavor. The sauce should be strong, because it will be toned down by the noodles or rice.

4 Pour the curried tomato beef on top of the noodles, sprinkle with chopped cilantro, and serve.

Garth Stein

Frank Huster

Inspiration   When I hear the voice of a character or several characters, I get really excited about finding their stories. For me, it isn't so much creating, but rather discovering or excavating the backgrounds and lives of these characters. I know my story will work when I start talking about it with my wife and she gets a little spooked. "They're here," she says. And they are here. We can feel them. They are showing me the way; they are telling me what they will do next. When they start telling me how the story goes, I know I have it, and then I get very excited about writing.

....

The Drama of Everyday Life   My writing tends to grapple with families in crisis: in *Raven Stole the Moon* a woman struggles with her grief over the death of her young son; in *How Evan Broke His Head and Other Secrets*, a musician must reveal his secret—he has epilepsy—to a teenage son he has never met; and in *The Art of Racing in the Rain*, a man must choose between his racing career and custody of his daughter in the wake of his wife's death. My interest is not in every day life, but in the dramatic moments, the moments when people are forced to act even when they might not want to. My goal is to capture these moments in an honest and humorous way that inspires people and highlights the drama of our everyday lives.

....

Readers Frequently Ask   Everyone wants to know about the stuffed zebra that figures prominently in *The Art of Racing in the Rain*. I rarely speak about the zebra. Some things about books are fun to learn from the authors of those books; some things are more fun to puzzle out for oneself. I think all Zebronic themes fall into the latter category.

....

Theatrical Influence My writing has been mostly influenced by the theater. I have always acted, and I wrote a play that was produced in Los Angeles a few years ago, titled *Brother Jones*. I very much enjoy the immediacy of drama that comes to life on stage. Therefore, my greatest influences are Tennessee Williams, Eugene O'Neill, Tom Stoppard, Sam Shepherd, Bertolt Brecht, and others in the theater. I look forward to writing more plays in the future.

ENZO'S PANCAKES

Makes 16–18 medium pancakes

My childhood dog was an Airedale terrier named Muggs, to whom I dedicated my book. She loved pancakes more than any other food, and, in fact, her last meal was "hotcakes," as my mother calls them. My current dog, Comet, was cut from the same cloth apparently, because she loves pancakes as well; in our house, Sunday is Pancake Day, and I know it is Comet's favorite day of the week. I am not above stealing from my own life for my books, so it was a no-brainer for me to give Enzo, the narrator of *The Art of Racing in the Rain*, this passion for pancakes.

When trying to think of a recipe that reflected some part of my book, I had to go with our Sunday pancakes. Enzo has some dietary peculiarities: he loves pancakes and bananas; peperoncini upsets his stomach; he enjoys cookie batter when he can get it. If you want to go completely crazy with these pancakes, add a mashed banana—Enzo's second favorite food!

My wife, Drella, and I discovered this recipe many years ago, when my two older boys were on a gluten- and casein-free diet. We absolutely loved the flavor of all the different flours. Several years ago, after my kids were liberated from their dietary restrictions, we kept making this recipe though we now usually use cow's milk and real eggs instead of their substitutes. Still, these pancakes can go either way and are equally delicious.

If you try this recipe, I hope you keep in mind the tastes of your personal Enzo—dogs love pancakes!

(Thanks to Gifts of Nature, an all natural baking mix company, Bette Hagman and, of course, Drella.)

Note: We use cow's milk now, but you can easily use rice milk or another milk substitute, to make it casein-free. If you do so, reduce the sugar by a teaspoon. Egg substitute is totally acceptable as well.

Bette Hagman's flour mix is available online or in natural foods stores.

These pancakes won't bubble as visibly as flour pancakes, so you need to watch the doneness by lifting the edge of your pancakes with a spatula. If the batter gets too thick, thin with a little water. If they end up gummy, your griddle is too hot!

For waffles, add ¼ cup milk or water, 1 egg, and 2 tablespoons oil, and use a waffle iron. Yum!

2 cups Drella's Modified Flour Mix (see recipe), or Bette Hagman's 4 Flour Blend (see note)

½ teaspoon salt

1 tablespoon baking powder

4 teaspoons sugar

2 large eggs

¼ cup neutral oil (grape seed oil or canola oil)

1¾ cups milk or milk substitute

¼ cup water

Butter or oil, for greasing griddle

1 In a large mixing bowl, combine flour mix, salt, baking powder, and sugar. In a medium bowl, beat eggs lightly. Add oil and combine, and then add the milk and combine.

2 Add dry ingredients to wet and mix until smooth. Let sit for 5 minutes. Add up to ¼ cup water, as needed to thin batter to pourable consistency (it all depends on humidity, temperature, air density, dark matter, $E=MC^2$).

3 Heat a griddle or skillet over medium heat. Grease lightly with butter or oil. Ladle enough batter onto the warm griddle to make a thin pancake of desired size. Cook on both sides, turning once. Remove when lightly brown on both sides.

DRELLA'S MODIFIED FLOUR MIX

Makes enough flour mix for 1½ pancake recipes

Note: These flours are available at any natural foods store, or online.

½ cup brown rice flour

½ cup teff flour

⅝ cup white rice flour

¼ cup tapioca starch

¾ cup potato starch

1 teaspoon xanthan gum

In a large bowl, combine the ingredients. Sift, and store.

Hannah Tinti

Linda Carrion

SELECTED WORKS

- *The Good Thief* (2008)
- *Animal Crackers* (2004)

Inspiration   I'm inspired by history. I grew up in Salem, Massachusetts, the town famous for the witch trials and as the birthplace of Nathaniel Hawthorne, so stepping into a different time period is quite natural for me. Most of the houses in my neighborhood were built in the 1700s and 1800s, and it was not unusual to have a back staircase, fireplaces in nearly every room, low ceilings, or small, latched pantry doors. Whenever my family worked outside in our small garden, we were constantly digging up things from the past—fragments of blue and white china plates, broken clay pipes, or crushed shells that used to line the path to a neighboring carriage house. Once, my grandmother found a Spanish reale, a gold coin, from the 1700s. This unearthing of tangible history, and being conscious every day of the people who have lived in places before you, is something common in Europe and other parts of the world. In America, however, it is more unusual. In any event, it made a lasting impression on me, and has certainly wound its way throughout my novel, *The Good Thief.*

....

The Magic of Wishing Stones   Whenever I visit a book club to talk about my novel, *The Good Thief,* I bring a wishing stone as a gift to the readers. A wishing stone is a rock, usually found near water, with an unbroken white line circling it completely. It is good for making one wish come true. I would collect them when I was a child. Later, I was reintroduced to them at an important time in my life. At the beginning of T*he Good Thief*, Ren, a young orphan living in New England, comes into possession of one. He makes a wish, and this wish reverberates throughout the rest of the book, as do the stones themselves.

In my novel, I tried to capture a spirit of old-fashioned storytelling, where a hero with a true heart could win out in the end. Book clubs have told me this is one of the reasons they enjoyed *The Good Thief*—it reminded them of why they became readers, too. Just as I passed my wishing stones on to them, they have been passing *The Good Thief* on to their friends and families. A few have sent me letters, or even mailed me wishing stones in return. I have these stones lined up on my desk, and they remind me every day that the best part of writing a book is also the best part of reading one: sharing it with another person.

....

Readers Frequently Ask   Most people ask me what my writing process is like. I try to follow my intuition, sitting quietly and letting things come. It's a bit like using a divining rod. Often I don't realize what I'm doing until after the words are on the page. Later, I go back and try to make sense of it. The editing process is where most of the work is done, but I discovered long ago that I need to be open and trust my sub-conscious. When I was a little girl, I went net-casting on a fishing boat. The men threw a net overboard, dragged it a hundred yards, then pulled up what they caught into a big tank onboard. They tossed things over that they didn't want, and kept the fish they did. I remember that the water seemed so clear and empty, but when the fishermen pulled the net on board it was full of the strangest things I'd ever seen; bizarre creatures from the bottom of the sea. Novels seem to be like this: casting a net through a writer's mind and pulling the unexpected into the light.

....

Influences on My Writing   Three books that have greatly influenced my writing are *Great Expectations* by Charles Dickens, *Treasure Island* by Robert Louis Stevenson, and *Jane Eyre* by Charlotte Brontë. My mother was a librarian, and she had me reading these classics at an early age. I always wanted to write a book similar to the stories that made me fall in love with reading as a little girl. My novel, *The Good Thief,* is an homage to these great works.

MRS. SANDS'S APPLE CRUMBLE PIE

Makes 1 (9-inch) pie; 8 servings

Adapted from Jennifer Verrill Fadddoul's recipe (*Boston Globe*, November, 2008)

Several pies appear in my novel *The Good Thief*, which is set in New England in the 1800s. One pie comes at the beginning of the book, when Ren, a young orphan boy with a missing hand, is dreaming of the mother who will adopt him. He imagines a perfect dinner, and a pie cooling on the windowsill as she waits for him to arrive home. But this fantasy is smashed when a conman named Benjamin Nab arrives at the orphanage and claims Ren as his long lost brother. Benjamin takes Ren on an adventure across New England, thieving and scamming people along the way, and it isn't until they reach the factory town of North Umbrage that Ren meets a potential mother figure. On the outside, Mrs. Sands does not seem very sweet as she is loud and gruff and shouts all the time. But she soon wins the boy over with her warm heart and delicious cooking. There is a celebratory picnic at the end of the novel when they have formed an adopted family, and Mrs. Sands serves apple pie with cream.

I grew up in New England, and there is nothing like a crisp fall apple. I love to go apple picking, but I always feel torn once I have my bag of apples: do I make an apple pie or an apple crumble? A few years ago this recipe appeared in *The Boston Globe*, and I realized that I could have both. The author of the recipe is Jennifer Verrill Faddoul, who runs Verrill Farm with her parents, in Concord, Massachusetts. My family made her Apple Crumble Pie for Thanksgiving, and it was an enormous hit. Now, we make it every year.

Note: The secret to a good apple pie and/or crumble is to use many different kinds of apples. I usually take one from every pile at the grocery store or the farmer's market. I also add some freshly squeezed lemon juice to the apples and toss them in it before adding them to the pie. Lemon juice adds a bit of brightness and a nice tangy flavor that gives the pie that little something special.

FOR THE PIE CRUST

1⅛ cups flour, plus flour for sprinkling the
   board
⅛ cup granulated sugar
¼ teaspoon salt
½ cup (1 stick) cold unsalted butter, cut up
⅛ cup cold water

FOR THE CRUMB TOPPING

1 cup all-purpose flour
¼ cup granulated sugar
¼ cup light brown sugar, packed
½ cup (1 stick) unsalted butter, cut up

FOR THE FILLING

3 pounds baking apples (about 8–9
   medium apples) such as Cortland,
   Northern Spy, Jonagold, Rome, Baldwin
   (or a combination; see note), peeled,
   cored, and sliced
1–2 tablespoons freshly squeezed lemon
   juice (optional)
½ cup granulated sugar
2 tablespoons all-purpose flour
½ teaspoon ground cinnamon
Pinch of ground nutmeg

1 **To make the crust:** In a food processor, pulse the flour, sugar, salt, and butter until the mixture resembles coarse crumbs. Add the water and pulse again until dough just begins to come together, but doesn't form a ball.

2 Turn the dough out onto a lightly floured board, and knead gently until it comes together. Flatten into a disk and wrap in plastic. Refrigerate at least 1 hour or overnight.

3 **To make the crumb topping:** In a food processor, pulse the flour, granulated and brown sugars, and butter until the mixture forms coarse crumbs. Do not overwork the mixture. Transfer to a bowl, cover, and refrigerate.

4 **To make the filling:** In a large mixing bowl, toss the apples with the lemon juice, if desired. Add the sugar, flour, cinnamon, and nutmeg. Toss well and set aside.

5 Preheat oven to 375°F. Remove dough from refrigerator. On a lightly floured board, roll the dough into a 12-inch round. Carefully transfer dough to 9" pie pan, and gently press it into the bottom. Fold the rim of pastry under itself around the edges. Crimp the border.

6 Mound the apple filling in the pastry. With your fingers, spread the topping evenly over the apples.

7 Bake the pie for 1 hour or until the fruit is bubbling around the edges.

Adriana Trigiani

Timothy Stephenson

Inspiration   Everything! There is nothing more inspiring than walking down a street in New York City.

....

Readers Should Know   I love my work. The process is so rich. I'm alone in a room, trying to create something wonderful.

....

Readers Frequently Ask   The big question is "where do your ideas come from?" It's so funny—I don't think of that part of the creative process as a challenge, rather, my energy goes into how I can serve these characters in an imagined world.

....

Influences on My Writing   I return to *Walden* by Henry David Thoreau time and time again. There is wisdom in every sentence. The essence of the message is to live simply, survive by the labor of your own hands, and be responsible to yourself and to your world.

Charlotte Brontë's title character in *Jane Eyre* is my favorite character in all of literature because she does the right thing and follows her inner compass. Here's Jane, a poor orphan who has no connections, and she lives her life by a decent moral code, even when she has every right to be bitter and awful because she has been mistreated.

The great playwright/screenwriter Ben Hecht wrote *Charlie: The Improbable Life and Times of Charles MacArthur*, the biography of his best friend and fellow writer. It's written with wit, love, and a clear eye for the truth. A must read.

PIA'S CRABBIES

Makes 6–8 servings

During the Christmas dinner scene in my novel *Rococo*, Bartolomeo's Aunt Edith barely makes it though the front door before she demands a serving of these crab delights!

Credit for these savory snacks belongs to my sister, Pia, the ultimate party hostess. Through the years she collects, invents, and reinvents recipes to please the crowds. We can't make enough crabbies when we have a party. They are delish. Enjoy!

½ cup (1 stick) butter, softened
1 cup (4 ounces) shredded mozzarella cheese
1 cup soft pimento cheese spread (store bought or see recipe)
2 tablespoons mayonnaise
1 garlic clove, minced
8 ounces lump crabmeat
4 English muffins, split
Ground paprika, for sprinkling
Salt to taste
1 cup (4 ounces) shredded Cheddar cheese

1   Use a fork to mash together the butter, mozzarella, and pimento cheese spread in a large bowl. Add the mayonnaise, garlic, and crabmeat. Mix well.
2   Toast the English muffin halves, if desired. Spread mixture on the muffin halves, and sprinkle with paprika. Salt to taste. Sprinkle the cheddar cheese on top. Place the muffins on a cookie sheet and broil until tops are golden, approximately 1 minute. Cut each crabbie into quarters, and serve.

PIMENTO CHEESE SPREAD

Makes 1 cup

Note: Pimento cheese is a staple in the South, and is commonly served on crackers or crudités, or as a sandwich spread. You can double the recipe if you want some leftovers.

4 ounces good-quality sharp white Cheddar cheese
2 ounces Monterey jack cheese
1 small garlic clove
1 tablespoon sliced pimentos, drained
3–4 heaping tablespoons mayonnaise

1 Cut the Cheddar and Monterey jack cheeses into large chunks. Place the cheese chunks, garlic, and pimentos into the bowl of a food processor, and pulse long enough to roughly chop. (Do not purée.)
2 Transfer the mixture to a medium bowl and stir in the mayonnaise. Cover and chill. Remove from refrigerator 20–30 minutes before using.

COUSIN DEE'S PEANUT BUTTER BALLS

Makes 7 dozen (1-inch) candies

My "Cousin Dee" wasn't kidding when she sacrificed more than an afternoon in the kitchen to whip up these goodies! Dee Emmerson, an Alabama girl I met at the Milbank Boarding House for women in 1983, almost got evicted from her apartment when she poured the excess hot paraffin down her kitchen sink and clogged her building's plumbing. Ah well, a small price to pay for the best candy you'll ever taste. This treat has been a favorite of everyone I know, including the characters of my novel *Big Cherry Holler.* When the children of Big Stone Gap compete on the *Kiddie Kollege* there is no sweeter treat to ease their loss than a bite of a peanut butter ball!

Here goes, and don't think there won't soon be a bed for peanut butter ball-aholics at Betty Ford. You can't eat just one.

Note: Paraffin wax, also called Baker's Wax or Cooking Wax, is commonly used to seal canning jars, make fruits and vegetables shiny and appealing, and give candy a glossy finish as well as keep it from melting at room temperature. It IS edible, and can be purchased in the canning section of grocery stores. (Gulf Wax is a popular brand.) Paraffin is flammable when overheated, so heat it gently in the top of a double-boiler, only to the point where it is melted. Do not melt it in a saucepan over an open flame.

Choose a natural peanut butter with a generous layer of oil on top, as the oil will moisten the crumb mixture. If you find your crumb mixture is slightly dry, roll the balls very gently between your palms to prevent crumbling.

You can substitute 12 ounces of bittersweet chocolate, chopped, for the semi-sweet morsels.

2 cups natural unsweetened crunchy peanut butter (see note)

4 cups confectioners' sugar

2 cups graham cracker crumbs

1 cup (2 sticks) butter, melted

3 ounces paraffin wax (see note)

12 ounces semi-sweet chocolate morsels (see note)

1 Line two cookie sheets with wax paper. In a large bowl of an electric mixer, blend peanut butter, sugar, graham cracker crumbs, and butter. Roll into 1-inch balls (see note), and place on the cookie sheets.

2 In a double boiler or heatproof bowl set over simmering water, melt paraffin wax and chocolate morsels, stirring until smooth. Remove pan from heat.

3 Toss several balls at a time into the melted chocolate mixture. Use spoon or tongs to coat balls completely, then use tongs to remove candies to cookie sheets and let harden for 10 minutes.

ADRIANA'S LIMONCELLO

Makes 8 servings

Juggling a dying business, a new love, and a large family is never easy, especially when you are eighty! This is why Gram (of my novels *Brava Valentine* and *Very Valentine*) enjoys an occasional Italian cocktail to unwind.

Like Gram, we love a cocktail at our house. We also love a digestif, and thankfully limoncello works either way. For Italians, the lemon is the fruit of the gods. Enjoy this—because we sure do!

Note: The limoncello takes at least 4 days to make.

Use organic lemons, if possible, to prevent any chemicals from entering the drink. If you can't find organic lemons, scrub the lemons thoroughly to clean them of any residue.

> *6 medium lemons (see note)*
> *1 750 ml bottle vodka (80 proof; get the best stuff—Gram uses Grey Goose)*
> *1 cup water*
> *1 cup sugar*
> *Large glass jar with a lid (like the old jar you used to make Sun Tea in)*

1 Grate the lemon peel using a microplane grater or the fine blade of a box grater. You should have about ⅓ cup of peel. (Try to avoid peeling the white pith as it will add bitterness to the drink.) Set aside the grated peels. To save the juice for another recipe, squeeze the meat of the lemons and set aside the juice. (Gram doesn't like to waste; you don't need the juice, but you can use it on chicken cutlets or something else.)

2 Back to the limoncello. Pour the vodka into the jar and add the grated peels. Seal the jar tightly. Let this jar sit for 3 days until the peels of the lemons become pale.

3 Then, make a simple syrup: Boil water in a small saucepan, stir in the sugar, then reduce heat and simmer until sugar is dissolved and mixture becomes syrupy, about 5 minutes. Allow to cool. Once the simple syrup has cooled, pour it into the jar with the vodka and peels. Put the lid back on the jar and let it sit overnight.

4 The next morning, pour the mixture through a strainer. Throw out the peels. Transfer the limoncello to a pretty container. Put it in the fridge or, for best flavor, store it in the freezer in a nonglass container that has some room for expansion. It won't freeze because of the alcohol in it, and it tastes best when it's good and cold.

Monique Truong

Damijan Saccio

Inspiration
I always think about food. What to eat, when to eat, where to eat? My books are, therefore, understandably about food and about the characters' particular relationship with food. That is my way into their stories, which then end up being about many other things as well: language, the search for identity, the meaning of home, the definition of family. Yet, the seeds for my books have all been edible ones. That is how they first get my attention and spark my imagination. I am now working on a third novel that is about hunger, and hopefully other things as well.

....

Readers Should Know
I write very slowly. I have been accused of writing slower than turtles making love (though a rougher word was used than "making love"). I have no idea how turtles make love, but I am sure that the effort, no matter how protracted and cumbersome, must be worth it to them. I blame my lack of speed on my unbending belief in the carefully crafted sentence: First the sentence has to be structurally sound, and then it has to be beautiful, which is not the same as saying overly wrought or needlessly decorative. Beautiful, I think, often comes down to word choice, and the clarity and the candor that can result from finding exactly the right words.

....

Readers Frequently Ask
Readers of *The Book of Salt* most often want to know whether I am a cook. The answer is a resounding yes (You could even add a "hallelujah!" before that yes). Cooking, or rather the techniques and the sensibilities of an avid cook, was one of the few things about my first novel that I did not have to research. I have been cooking and reading cookbooks since I was seven years old. While I had to research the types of dishes that Bình, who is the live-in cook for the American writer Gertrude Stein ("Rose is a rose is a rose") and her lover Alice B. Toklas in their Paris home, would have cooked, I otherwise felt free to draw upon my own experiences in the kitchen. For example, though I have never killed a pigeon with my bare hands (or in any other manner!),

when I wrote the passage in which Toklas teaches Bình the technique, I knew that the fingertips of a cook can often "see" much better than the eyes. (Think about sorting dried beans or fresh cranberries and how your eyes can deceive you about the quality of what is in front of you. It is only when you plunge your fingers into the bowl that you can finally locate the hidden pebble or the soft and wilted berry.)

....

A Major Influence on My Writing
Gabriel García Márquez's writing engages all of the senses. I never feel as if I am on the surface of his narratives. I am never looking in, a pane of glass between them and me. I am inside of them. I smell the scent of bitter almonds. I see the house filled with yellow butterflies. I hear "the desolate breath of the sea." I taste the artificial sweetener that he so aptly describes "as a sad sweetness . . . something like a ringing but without bells."

BÒ KHO

Makes 4–6 servings

Adapted from *Into the Vietnamese Kitchen: Treasured Foodways, Modern Flavors* by Andrea Nguyen (Ten Speed Press, 2006)

My first novel, *The Book of Salt*, was about Bình, a young, gay Vietnamese man who worked as a live-in cook for Gertrude Stein and Alice B. Toklas in their legendary Paris apartment on the 27 rue de Fleurus. A reporter once asked me which dish I would cook for Stein and Toklas if I had the chance. I immediately thought of this Vietnamese take on *daube de boeuf* or French beef stew. Bò Kho is a quintessential example of what we now call fusion cuisine.

I knew that Stein and Toklas, or my "Mesdames" as Bình called them, would be tickled by how recognizable this dish was: cubes of tender beef and chunks of carrots in a slow-cooked sauce. But once they take a bite, the stew's complex flavors would make these two ladies swoon with the pleasures of the unknown: five-spice powder, star anise, turmeric, fresh ginger, and lemongrass. I, of course, would offer the stew and the accompanying loaf of French bread to them without a fork or a spoon, and I would invite Stein and Toklas to eat with their hands. Bình, I know, would enjoy the impropriety of it all.

Note: Allow 24 hours for the beef to marinate. (This stew may be made up to 2 days in advance, cooled, and refrigerated. Actually, like all stews, it is best made ahead and gently reheated.)

Chinese five-spice powder and whole star anise can be found in the spice aisle of many grocery stores. You can find fresh lemongrass and Thai basil leaves at Asian markets or specialty grocers.

The lemongrass will come apart during cooking. I don't mind pieces of lemongrass floating in the finished sauce, but if you prefer to contain the stringy pieces, place the lemongrass in a piece of cheesecloth and tie the pouch with clean string before adding to bowl.

For the marinade and meat

2 stalks fresh lemongrass (use only the compact bottom halves of the stalks, discarding the top looser leaves); cut into 3-inch lengths and bruised with a meat cleaver or the bottom of a heavy sauce pan (see note)

3 tablespoons fish sauce

3 garlic cloves, peeled and minced fine or put through a garlic press (but preferably mashed into a paste with a mortar and pestle or the back of a heavy knife)

1½ teaspoons Chinese five-spice powder (see note)

½ teaspoon ground turmeric

1 tablespoon turbinado sugar

½ teaspoon kosher salt

1 teaspoon freshly ground black pepper

3-inch piece fresh gingerroot, peeled and cut into 1-inch chunks, bruised with a cleaver or the bottom of a heavy sauce pan

2 pounds boneless beef chuck, cut into 1½-inch chunks

For the stew

3 tablespoons canola oil, divided

1 medium yellow onion, finely chopped

1 14-ounce can crushed tomatoes

2 teaspoons turbinado sugar

1 teaspoon kosher salt

2 whole star anise (see note)

1 cup beef broth

2 cups water

1 pound carrots, peeled and cut into 1½-inch chunks

Accompaniments

2 loaves French bread, warmed in the oven

1 cup cilantro leaves

⅔ cup Thai basil leaves (see note)

2 limes, cut into small wedges

1 **To make the marinade:** In a large bowl, combine the lemongrass or lemongrass pouch (see note), fish sauce, garlic, five-spice powder, turmeric, sugar, salt, pepper, and ginger. Add the beef, and mix to coat evenly. Cover with plastic wrap and marinate overnight in the refrigerator. Take the meat out of the refrigerator about 30 minutes before proceeding to next step.

2 Remove meat from marinade. Reserve the lemongrass and the ginger from the marinade, and discard any remaining marinade.

3 In a 5-quart Dutch oven or similarly heavy-bottomed pot, heat 1 tablespoon of the oil over medium-high heat until hot but not smoking. Working in small batches, cook several pieces of the beef until well-browned on all sides, 3–5 minutes. (Reduce heat if oil begins to smoke or food begins to burn.) Transfer cooked beef to a clean bowl. Repeat procedure with remaining beef and oil.

4 Lower the heat to medium-low and add onion. Cook, scraping bottom of pan to loosen any browned bits, until onion is fragrant and soft, 4–5 minutes. Add tomatoes, sugar, and salt, and stir to combine. Cover and cook for 12–14 minutes, or until the mixture is fragrant and has reduced to a rough paste. Check occasionally to make sure tomato mixture is not sticking to the bottom of the pan. If it does, add a bit of water to the pan and stir.

5 When the paste has formed, add the beef, the reserved lemongrass pouch and ginger, and star anise. Cook, uncovered, for another 5 minutes.

6 Add the broth and water and bring to a boil. Lower the heat to a simmer and cover. Cook for 1¼ hours or until the beef is close to being done and is chewy-tender. To test for this, press on a piece; it should yield but still feel firm.

7 Add the carrots and return the stew to a lively simmer. Cook uncovered for 30 minutes or until the carrots are tender.

8 Just before serving, taste the stew. Add a bit more salt or fish sauce, if needed. Or if the taste of the tomatoes is too acidic, add a bit of sugar. If the sauce seems overall too strong in flavor, add a bit of water. You are looking for a balance of salty and sweet and savory (in other words, the balance that is the hallmark of many Vietnamese main dishes).

9 Discard the lemongrass, ginger, and star anise, and serve the stew in wide bowls.

10 On the dining table, offer the loaves of French bread (warmed in the oven is best), the herbs, and the lime wedges. Encourage diners to add the herbs according to their taste. Ask your guests to tear the leaves of the herbs into bite-sized pieces before adding them to their bowl. This final touch of freshness (the fragrance of the herbs) and a judicious squirt of lime are very important to this dish.

11 Finally, diners should feel free to eat with their hands as well as with a fork. Tear the hot bread and dip it into the stew's sauce. (The sauce is why many people eat this dish!)

PALMIERS

Makes 3 dozen cookies

I first read about Gertrude Stein and Alice B. Toklas's "experiences with the Indochinese" in *The Alice B. Toklas Cook Book*. First published in 1954, Toklas's book is equal parts entertaining memoir and compendium of recipes. Toklas writes fondly about a cook who had worked previously in the French Governor-General's house in Saigon. She describes how he always made sure that there was a fresh supply of fruit purées, whipped cream, almond paste, and puff pastry dough in the icebox. That way, he could whip up at the drop of a hat (*her* hat, of course) a tray of elaborate French pastries whenever unexpected guests would appear at the front door.

This recipe calls for frozen puff pastry dough, and I am not sure whether Toklas's cook, who was so clearly classically trained, would have approved of such a convenience item. I, who sorely lack the benefit of his time and labor, certainly approve of frozen puff pastry dough. I always feel prepared, a bit privileged, and wholly transported to France whenever I make a plate of these easy but impressive little cookies.

Note: These cookies are mini versions of the American "Elephant Ears."

The puff pastry should be about 9" × 9½" in size. If you use puff pastry that is smaller, gently roll the dough until it reaches this size.

---

2 sheets frozen puff pastry dough, such as Pepperidge Farm, thawed but still very cold
4–6 tablespoons salted butter, melted and cooled
¼–⅓ cup turbinado sugar

---

1 Place rack in center of oven, and preheat oven to 400°F. Cover two cookie sheets with heavy-duty foil or parchment paper. If using foil, spray the foil with a light coating of nonstick cooking spray. Set aside.
2 Working with one sheet of dough at a time (keep the other sheet in the fridge until you are ready to work with it), place a sheet of dough onto a work surface (an inverted cookie sheet makes for an easy to clean work surface). Because the dough is still very cold, you will not need to flour the work surface. Unfold the sheet of dough and brush it evenly with melted butter.
3 Sprinkle turbinado sugar so that it lightly but evenly coats the dough's surface.

4 The dough is rectangular in shape. Roll the two longer sides in (jelly roll style) so that they meet in the middle. Press the two sides together gently so the resulting roll keeps its shape.

5 Use a sharp knife and cut the log cross-wise into ½-inch thick pieces. Don't worry if the pieces get a bit misshapen while you are doing this.

6 Lay the pieces flat on a prepared cookie sheet, about 2 inches apart. Reshape the pieces, if needed. Pinch and press the sides of the two rolls together so they don't unroll during baking. Brush the tops and sides of the pieces with more melted butter. Then, sprinkle a bit more turbinado sugar on top.

7 Bake in oven for 10–13 minutes until their bottoms have turned golden brown and are a bit caramelized. This recipe is rather forgiving, so open up that oven and peek. Don't let these babies burn. Using a small spatula and the tip of a knife to assist, turn the pieces over, one at a time. (Take the pan out of the oven to do this, if necessary. But try to do it as quickly as possible.)

8 Bake for another 4–5 minutes until the other sides are golden and caramelized. Depending on your oven and how evenly it heats, you may need to remove the palmiers as they become ready.

9 Place the palmiers on a cookie rack to cool completely. (Try not to eat them while they are still warm, as they'll be a bit chewy as opposed to crisp on the outside, as they should be when they are completely cool.)

10 Repeat steps with the second sheet of dough.

NOUVEAU-SOUTHERN
SUMMER SQUASH CASSEROLE

Makes 6 servings

Adapted from a recipe from Randy Yates, the proprietor
of the Ajax Diner in Oxford, Mississippi

I set my second novel, *Bitter in the Mouth*, in Boiling Springs, North Carolina, the little town where my parents and I first lived when we came to the United States in 1975 as refugees from the Vietnam War. I borrowed the southern locale from my own life, but otherwise the similarities between the novel's main character, Linda Hammerick, and me end there, more or less. Linda has a neurological condition that causes her to taste many of the words that she hears and speaks. She is a mystery to herself and, as it turns out, to us as well.

Casseroles were the bane of Linda's childhood, but when she returns to Boiling Springs for the funeral of a beloved family member, she makes sure that summer squash casserole is offered at the luncheon held in his honor. The dish, like so many of the foods and flavors in Linda's life, is significant for reasons that she alone can understand. (Though in this instance, her best friend Kelly also knows what "squash" has to offer.)

Needless to say, the classic southern cook would not use Parmesan cheese for the topping and would opt instead for Ritz or Saltine cracker crumbs. Linda Hammerick is not a classic southern character, so this casserole is very much in her spirit and in her honor.

Note: I recommend using a substantial bread, such as a ciabatta, to make the crumbs. If you are using very fresh or very soft bread, such as supermarket sandwich bread, you may need to toast slightly before processing.

As the author of a novel titled *The Book of Salt*, I have some definite opinions about salt. I recommend that you use *flor do sal* from Portugal. Like all *fleur de sel* (the French name for this type of sea salt), it is flaky and delicate and has a lower salinity level than kosher or regular table salt. Flor do sal also has a gentle, almost sweet, after taste. I find this very pleasing and addictive. I know that the prevailing advice is never to cook with fleur de sel but rather to sprinkle it on right before serving as a finishing touch. I think this has to do more with cost than flavor. Flor do sal is expensive and will undoubtedly bankrupt me. I urge you to try cooking with a really beautiful delicate salt such as a flor do sal at least once, and see whether you will return to the sensible and the economical.

The most important thing, though, is to cook with the salt that you know best. There are significant variations in the salinity level of salts and whether the salt melts immediately or melts slowly into the food. Therefore, a teaspoon of kosher salt is not the same as a teaspoon of flor do sal. So, perhaps, the last thing to say on this topic is the first piece of advice that all cooks should learn and heed: you must taste your food as you are cooking it!

This is a rich, buttery dish. Use the lesser amount of butter if you prefer a lighter version.

3 slices white bread (see note)

3½–5⅓ tablespoons salted butter (see note)

1 medium yellow onion, sliced into ¼-inch-thick half moons

2¼ pounds fresh summer squash, sliced crosswise into ½-inch thick coins (about 8 cups squash coins)

1¼–1½ teaspoons kosher salt or flor do sal (see note)

1 teaspoon freshly ground black pepper

½ cup freshly grated Parmesan cheese

1 Preheat oven to 375°F.
2 Make the fresh bread crumbs (see note): Use a food processor to grind bread (including crust) into crumbs. You should have about 1 cup. Set aside.
3 In a large frying pan, melt the butter over medium heat. Add the onions and sauté until soft and pale yellow.
4 Add the squash, salt, and pepper. Stir to coat the squash pieces in the butter. Cover, turn down heat to achieve a brisk simmer, and cook for about 15 minutes, stirring once.
5 Remove cover and give a good stir and cook for another 5 minutes uncovered.
6 Add ¾ cup of the bread crumbs and mix well.
7 Spoon mixture into a 2-quart oven-safe pan or casserole (more wide than deep because you will want a lot of top surface to get crispy.)
8 In a bowl, mix the remaining ¼ cup of bread crumbs with the Parmesan cheese. Sprinkle the crumb and cheese mixture on top of the squash.
9 Cover with foil and bake for about 30–35 minutes. (This dish, despite the addition of the Parmesan cheese, is an old-school southern vegetable dish at heart, which means that the squash should be very soft and almost about to lose its shape when the dish is done cooking. Aim for a melt-in-your-mouth texture for the squash and a crunch for the topping.)
10 Uncover the dish and bake until the cheese and crumb topping is golden, 5–7 minutes.
11 Let the dish rest for at least 15 minutes before serving.

Thrity Umrigar

Robert Muller

Inspiration Inspiration can come from multiple sources—from a story I may have heard, a chance encounter with someone, an image that has come into my head unprompted, the color of the sky on a particular evening, an idea that I wish to explore further, a question that I want to answer for myself. All I need is a small germ of fact or image or idea and then I can build on that.

....

Readers Should Know Although my books deal with a myriad of issues, they have a few things in common. Almost all of them are concerned with the idea of power—who has it, who doesn't, how it is used by those who do against those who don't. This leads to an examination of class, race, and gender differences. My books also deal with the issue of community—how it is built, what destroys it, why it is important. And in some way or another, I'm interested in talking about love, in all its different forms and complications and how far human beings will go to have it and keep it.

....

Readers Frequently Ask The most common question, hands down, is the very specific question about what happens to Bhima at the end of *The Space Between Us*. I'm constantly amazed and amused by the number of readers who send me desperate-sounding e-mails saying their book club almost came to blows over different interpretations of the ending or begging me to settle the bet that they have taken with another book club member by telling them my interpretation of the ending.

....

Influences on My Writing

- *The Waves* by Virginia Woolf. For its poetic, lyrical, excruciatingly beautiful writing.
- *Midnight's Children* by Salman Rushdie. For its ambition and audacity and for showing me, when I was a young adult, that it was possible to write a novel that was set in my hometown and had Indian characters and street names I was familiar with. Up to that point, I'd only read novels by American and British writers.
- *Beloved* by Toni Morrison. For its righteous anger, its politics, and its humanity.

BOMBAY *BHELPURI*

Makes 4–6 servings

This is a recipe for a snack or street food, known as bhelpuri. This is the quintessential street food in Bombay and often acts as a metaphor for the city. This is because bhelpuri is a mix of many different things: flat *puris*, puffed rice, and deep-fried, thin flour strips known as *sev*. Bombay, too, is a mix of different religions, castes, classes, and cultures, truly a melting pot of a city. Bhelpuri and Bombay, in my mind, are inextricably linked.

Because bhelpuri, with its wonderful mixtures of ingredients, is such an apt metaphor for Bombay, and also because it's such a popular street food in India, many of my novels have references to it. Perhaps the most well-known reference is in *The Space Between Us*, when a pregnant Dinaz has a sudden craving for it and goes to Chowpatty Beach with her husband and mother, Sera. A chance meeting with Bhima and her granddaughter leads to the tragic events that follow.

Although there are many places in Bombay where one can eat bhelpuri, perhaps the most popular are the open-air food booths that line busy, colorful, noisy Chowpatty Beach, the city's largest outdoor food gallery.

Note: Puffed rice, sev, flat puris, red chili powder, and the chutneys can be purchased at an Indian grocer. Make sure to use the red chili powder found at an Indian grocer, as it has a different flavor from typical commercial chili powder.

In place of puffed rice, sev, and flat puris, you can purchase a bag of dry bhelpuri mix. (Be sure to avoid the bhelpuri kits, with dehydrated ingredients.) Simply use 4 cups of the bhelpuri mix in place of the puffed rice, sev, and flat puris.

Assemble the bhelpuri right before you plan to eat it so the puffed rice does not become soggy.

3 cups puffed rice

1 cup sev

Handful of coarsely crushed flat puris

1 medium onion, finely chopped

2 small potatoes, peeled, boiled, and chopped into tiny cubes

3 tablespoons finely chopped cilantro

Pinch red chili powder (optional)

2–4 tablespoons date-tamarind chutney

2–4 tablespoons mint or cilantro chutney

Juice of 1 lime

1 In a large bowl, combine the puffed rice, sev, puris, onion, potatoes, cilantro, and red chili powder, if desired.

2 Add enough chutney so the dry ingredients are moist and flavorful, but not soggy.

3 Sprinkle lime juice to taste, and serve immediately in small bowls.

Abraham Verghese

Inspiration The desire to understand what I am thinking is what inspires the writing. The act is mysterious, and it emerges only in the process of writing.

Readers should know that writing is really all about revision and the finished book in the reader's hand represents one tiny fraction of the pages generated. Hundreds of pages, good pages, gone in the service of not boring the reader.

Readers Frequently Ask Is *Cutting for Stone* autobiographical?

And the answer is no, I was not a twin, or born to doctors, or raised in a missionary hospital. That said, I did use the geography I knew well and I was born in Ethiopia and came to America about the time that Marion does in *Cutting for Stone.*

....

Influences on My Writing

- Günter Grasse's *The Tin Drum*. I loved this novel for its daring point of view, for its acrobatics, for the way it shows how a novel can tell the truth about our world in a manner even more convincing than a factual account.
- Gabriel García Márquez's *Love in the Time of Cholera*. For the delicious language, which I regret I am reading only in translation.
- John Irving's *The World According to Garp*. For the sheer ambition of that book, the wonderful, complete, complex world that he creates.

All three of these recipes are originally from my mother, Mariam Verghese, perfected by her through countless repetitions and passed on to us. The first two are South Indian dishes. The scenes I describe in *Cutting for Stone* of Marion being carried on Almaz's hip while onion is frying and mustard seeds are popping reflect memories of my own childhood in my mother's kitchen, where the Ethiopian maids taught by my (Indian) mother were adept at making these Indian dishes. My mother both taught us how to prepare and helped me write these recipes.

MOM'S BEEF FRY (*IRACHI ULATHU*)

Makes 4 servings

This dish is not only a typical dish from Kerala, but also one that I associate with my mother. No one else makes it better than her. It's a typical South Indian meat dish, the kind of thing that Hema, a Brahmin and a vegetarian character in *Cutting for Stone* would not eat in India but enjoys and craves in Ethiopia, and which Almaz the cook is adept at making. It is served with rice or bread.

Note: You may substitute 4 tablespoons meat masala for the pepper and coriander mixture.

Mariam Verghese adds that by the time you fry the meat, the pepper has lost its intensely spicy quality. However, you might want to add less pepper for a milder dish. She offers some options for finishing the dish: "In Kerala, we add fried coconut slices now (after the dish has cooked). Some folks add a little butter and stir over a low heat for some more time."

3 tablespoons ground black pepper (see note)

2 tablespoons ground coriander (see note)

Small amount of water for paste

1 pound beef tenderloin or sirloin, cut into bite-size cubes

⅓ cup vegetable oil (or more if needed)

A few mustard seeds

1 1-inch stick cinnamon

2 whole cloves

Seeds of 2 cardamom pods (crush pods to release seeds) (optional)

½ cup chopped onion

1 teaspoon chopped garlic

1 teaspoon chopped gingerroot

½ small beef bouillon cube

¼ cup hot water for bouillon cube

Salt (optional)

Butter (optional)

Coconut slices (optional)

1 Place pepper and coriander in a small bowl, and add a small amount of water to make a paste. Place beef pieces into a medium bowl and stir paste into the meat pieces. Set aside for a few hours if there is no hurry to prepare.

2 Heat the oil in a large skillet, add the mustard seeds, and heat until they sputter. Add the cinnamon stick, cloves, and cardamom seeds (if desired). Stir, and then add onion, garlic, and ginger. Continue to stir over low heat until the onions begin to turn brown. Add the beef, and stir-fry for a few minutes.

3 Dissolve the ½ bouillon cube in hot water. Add to skillet, stir, cover, and simmer until the water is nearly gone. Test beef for tenderness and add salt if desired. If satisfactory, remove cover, keep stirring occasionally until the water is completely gone. Add a small amount of butter and/or coconut slices, if desired.

Sister Mary Joseph Praise's *Upma*

Makes 3–4 servings

This would be a typical breakfast dish that Ghosh and Hema and the twins Marion and Shiva (from *Cutting for Stone*) would eat, either with an egg curry or by mashing in some bananas and sugar as something sweet.

Upma is also the sort of simple dish that Sister Mary Joseph Praise, a character central to *Cutting for Stone*, would have learned to make in her mother's kitchen. Upma was probably the first thing she made, and since she joined the convent at a very young age, it might have been the only thing she learned to make.

Note: You can add julienned cooked vegetables to the upma if you like.

You may use commercial ginger paste, found in specialty stores, or make your own. To make ginger paste: Place ⅛ pound peeled and coarsely chopped gingerroot and ¼ cup water in a blender and purée.

Wear plastic or rubber gloves while handling the chiles to protect your skin from the oil in them. Avoid direct contact with your eyes, and wash your hands thoroughly after handling.

1 cup hot wheat cereal, such as Cream of Wheat (semolina or farina)
2 tablespoons vegetable oil
A few mustard seeds
½ cup chopped onion
2 jalapeño chiles, split, with seeds
Dash of ginger paste (see note)
A few curry leaves (optional)
2 cups water
1 tablespoon butter
Salt to taste
A few drops of fresh lemon juice
10 roasted cashew nuts

1 In a medium flat shallow skillet, roast the cereal over low heat, stirring often, until golden in color, approximately 2 minutes.

2 In another medium skillet, heat the oil over medium heat, add the mustard seeds, and heat until they sputter. Add the onion, chiles, ginger paste, and curry leaves, if desired. Continue to stir over medium heat until the onions begin to turn brown at the edges.

3 Add water and butter and stir. Add salt and lemon juice to taste. When the water comes to a boil, reduce the heat and slowly add the cereal, stirring continuously and breaking up any lumps. Turn off the heat.

4 Sprinkle the cashew nuts on top. Cover the dish for a few minutes before serving.

ALMAZ'S ETHIOPIAN *DORO WOT* (CHICKEN CURRY)

Makes 4–6 servings

In *Cutting for Stone*, Hema arrives in Ethiopia after a month-long absence and sends Gebrew to a restaurant to bring back doro wot, which she has been craving. The stoic cook at Missing Hospital would also have regularly made this dish and fed it to the twins. This Ethiopian curry is eaten with *injera*, the pancake like bread. The key to making this dish is *berbere*, a spice mixture (found in Ethiopian stores abroad) that includes chile peppers, pepper ginger, cloves, coriander, allspice, rue berries, and *ajwain.* Berbere is a key ingredient for so many curries (*wot*) in Ethiopia.

Note: Berbere can be purchased online and at local specialty and gourmet food stores.

⅓ cup vegetable oil

2 cups chopped onion

1 medium (4-pound) chicken, skin and fat removed, washed, dried, and cut into large pieces

2 tablespoons garlic paste (puréed garlic), or more to taste

4 tablespoons berbere (more if you like it to be 5 alarm!) (see note)

1 tomato, chopped

2 cups hot water

1 teaspoon salt

Butter (optional)

Hard-cooked eggs (optional)

1 In a deep skillet, heat oil, add onions, and lightly sauté until onions are soft. Add chicken pieces and garlic paste, and cook over medium heat until the chicken is lightly browned.

2 Add the berbere, stirring so that all pieces of the chicken get coated. Add tomato and stir again.

3 Pour in water, bring mixture to a boil, and add salt. Simmer over low heat until the meat is well cooked, approximately 30–45 minutes, depending on the size of the chicken pieces. (In Ethiopia, they say that the woman who loves her husband cooks it slowly so that each piece is tender and the gravy is thick.) You may add a pat of butter and/or hard-cooked eggs during the last 5 minutes of cooking, if desired.

Meg Wolitzer

Deborah Copaken Kogan

Inspiration   *The Ten-Year Nap* was inspired by my thoughts about women who stop working when their kids are born, and then a decade passes and they begin to think about how they want to spend the rest of their lives. I had gotten to know quite a few women who had had a similar experience; I met them through my own children, and was struck by the fact that this phenomenon hadn't often been written about in fiction. It had sometimes been written about in the kind of nonfiction book that took sides in the so-called "mommy wars," a term that makes me highly uncomfortable. As for me, I had no position. A novelist's job, as I see it, is to show "what it's like," and so I set out to do just that, without being judgmental about the complex, overlapping, and sometimes hard-to-choreograph worlds of work and motherhood.

Readers Should Know   I try to write about what I see in the contemporary world, often involving the dynamics between men and women, and among members of a family. Also, when I'm writing, I try to write the book that I would like to find on the bookstore shelf. I write to my own tastes and interests, assuming (I hope, correctly) that they're not all that idiosyncratic or specialized.

Readers Frequently Ask   Readers like to know about how a writer manages to be disciplined. As for me, I try to keep banker's hours, working in my home the way someone might work in an office, with the addition of the fact that I take power naps when needed and don't have to go on corporate retreats. I also never beat myself up when I have a bad work day; instead, I try to remember that there are some times when you're actually working without really knowing it. It almost happens on a cellular level. You're taking in ideas for your novel just by looking around you, and by listening to other people talk.

Influences on My Writing   *Mrs. Bridge* by Evan S. Connell, Philip Roth's novels, and *Death in Venice* by Thomas Mann are all examples of exciting writing, which makes me want to write, or at least want to read.

PATSY'S CASHEW CHICKEN

Makes 2 servings

From *Eat Me: The Food and Philosophy of Kenny Shopsin*
by Kenny Shopsin and Carolyn Carreño (Knopf, 2008)

Shopsin's General Store was my hangout with my friends when I was in my twenties, and this was one of my favorite dishes. Much later, in my forties, I wrote the novel *The Ten-Year Nap*. The women characters in *The Ten-Year Nap*, over the course of a decade, gather frequently at a coffee shop during the day. I wanted to include passages in the book about the collegiality of a group of friends spending time together when their children are still young—strollers in the aisle, baggies of Cheerios at hand, the occasional whip-it-out moment of improvised breastfeeding. I remembered my own earlier experiences, prechildren, at Shopsin's, and I thought about how different my life was then, yet how strong and powerful the connection is between the important friendships of one's twenties and those of one's forties. And in both cases, at least for me, who has always been a food person in addition to a friend, writer, and mother, they involved the consumption of a lot of excellent food.

2 (5–6-ounce) boneless, skinless chicken breasts
All-purpose flour for dredging
2 tablespoons good quality olive oil
½ cup roasted cashew nuts
4 scallions (white and green parts), cut into 1-inch pieces
½ cup soy sauce
Juice of 1 lemon
½ cup chicken stock
Steamed white rice, for serving

1 Cut chicken into 1-inch strips, approximately ⅜ inch thick. Pour flour on a plate or in a small bowl. Dredge chicken in flour and shake off excess flour.

2 Heat olive oil in a large heavy sauté pan over high heat until it's hot but not smoking. Carefully and gently drop chicken in pan, evenly distributing it around the pan. (This can be dangerous because everything is really hot. If you carelessly drop the chicken in, it will splatter on your arms and face.) Let the chicken cook undisturbed for 2–3 minutes. Check the underside of one piece. When it becomes medium brown, use tongs to turn the pieces over.

3 When all of the chicken has cooked on both sides (after about 5 minutes), add the cashews and scallions. Add the soy sauce and lemon juice. Agitate the pan to coat the chicken with the glaze. Pour in the chicken stock, adding more if necessary to cover the chicken, and cook for another 1–2 minutes. Pour the chicken and gravy over the rice and serve.

Acknowledgments

We extend our deepest gratitude to our wonderful agent Joelle Delbourgo, who championed this project from beginning to end. Her advocacy, wisdom, and sound advice have been invaluable. Our editor, Meredith O'Hayre, was passionate about our idea from the beginning, has intelligently guided us every step of the way, and been a pleasure to work with throughout the process.

We are grateful to Chris Duffy of Adams Media for his indispensable help in guiding us through acquiring the various permissions needed to put together a book like this.

We appreciate the assistance and support of the talented Adams Media staff who contributed to the project in many ways. Finally, warm thanks to each of our participating authors. It was a privilege to work with them in creating *Table of Contents*.

We extend our appreciation to the restaurants and chefs who generously shared their recipes:

Erik Goetze and George Mason of Blue Sky Bakery in Brooklyn, New York
Brian Kaywork of the Rhinecliff Hotel in Rhinecliff, New York
Keith Marden of Captain Marden's Seafoods in Wellesley, Massachusetts
Enriqueta Villalobos of the Ventana Inn & Spa in Big Sur, California
Terri Weyland-Henecke and Kathy McCauley of Kathy's Pies in Cedar Rapids, Iowa

Behind the scenes, our devoted corps of recipe testers was critical in helping us perfect these delicious recipes. They donated their time and ingredients to prepare and sample the food and provided invaluable feedback. We are indebted to our testers:

Cheryl Aglio-Girelli, Kay Allison, Linda Bauer, Seth Bauer, Susan Bonaiuto and family, Heidi Brown, Molly Burgess, Laurie Burgess, Lucia Gill Case, Adam Gill Case, Ethan Ceplikas, Jesse Day, Joan Demers, Suzanne Diamond, Mary Kate Dillon, Denise Dirocco, Rebecca Drill, Kim Evans, Jody Feinberg, Elizabeth Freeman and family, Andrew Gelman, Doris Gelman, Loie Gelman, Kim Greenberg, Joyce Montag Greenberg, Holly Hartman, Joe Hutcheson, Louis Hutchins, Susan Katcher, Laura Katz, Jane Levin, Larry Masur, Barbara Matorin, Ana Maria Caballero McGuire, Yael Miller, Rich Moche, Elizabeth Nunberg, Ceci Ogden, Carol Pankin, Allison Pisker, Debbie Pryor, Jayne Raphael, Larni Rosenlev, Tammy Sadok, Judy Safian, Emily Safian-Demers, Abby Schwartz, Daniela Sever, Donna Skinner, Sara Smolover, Dale Sokoloff, Deb Squires and family, and Leslie Zheutlin.

As always, we are grateful for the support of our family and friends.

Vicki: Thanks to my dad, Harvey Levy, and my sister, Larni Rosenlev, for their unwavering support and our Friday lunches that took my mind off recipe testing, and to Zhanna

Volynskaya, cook extraordinaire and loving cheerleader. I appreciate the support and good taste of my teenagers, Aaron, Ben, and Joanna, who were always ready to sample new recipes and offer their honest opinions. Their visits to the kitchen, along with their warm and witty presence, kept me grounded throughout this process.

Judy: Thanks to my sons: Noah for your recipe sampling, feedback, and for sharing your space; and Danny for your excellent palate (and for introducing me to some fantastic New Orleans cuisine.) I am grateful to all of my friends and family who have offered support, encouragement, advice–and excel at recipe testing!

Book and Recipe Pairings

Page number	Author	Book	Featured Recipe 1	Featured Recipe 2	Featured Recipe 3
45	Barbara Delinsky	*Not My Daughter*	Crab and Corn Chowder		
45	Barbara Delinsky	*While My Sister Sleeps*	Hot Mulled Cider		
45	Barbara Delinsky	*Secret Between Us, The*	SoMa Stickies (Sticky Buns)		
117	Joanne Harris	*Chocolat*	Gâteau Lawrence	Lentil and Toulouse Sausage Casserole	
159	Margot Livesey	*House on Fortune Street, The*	Dara's Carrot and Ginger Soup	Abigail's Pasta	
163	Gregory Maguire	*Wicked*	Oh Sweet Ozcrust Glinda Tart	Elphaba's Lunch Sandwich	Madame Morrible's Adorable Storable Sugar Cookies
91	Julia Glass	*Whole World Over, The*	Basque Chocolate Cake with Cherry Preserves		
91	Julia Glass	*I See You Everywhere*	Black Bean Chili with Cayenne-Glazed Tofu		
91	Julia Glass	*Three Junes*	Tourte de Blettes (Apple, Swiss Chard, and Pine Nut Pie)		
177	Jacquelyn Mitchard	*Deep End of the Ocean, The*	Next Day Rice Pudding	Grandma Rosie's Gravy (Pasta Sauce)	Grandpa Angelo's Surefire Army Mess Meatballs

177	Jacquelyn Mitchard	*No Time to Wave Goodbye*	Next Day Rice Pudding	Grandma Rosie's Gravy (Pasta Sauce)	Grandpa Angelo's Surefire Army Mess Meatballs
189	Tom Perrotta	*Little Children*	Nina's Minestrone	Luke's Pesto	
263	Meg Wolitzer	*Ten-Year Nap, The*	Patsy's Cashew Chicken		
141	Kathleen Kent	*Heretic's Daughter, The*	Florence Carrier's Cowboy Cake		
257	Abraham Verghese	*Cutting for Stone*	Mom's Beef Fry (Irachi Ulathu)	Sister Mary Joseph Praise's *Upma*	Almaz's Ethiopian *Doro Wot* (Chicken Curry)
1	Elizabeth Berg	*Open House*	My Favorite Meatloaf		
229	Garth Stein	*Art of Racing in the Rain, The*	Enzo's Pancakes		
61	Chitra Banerjee Divakaruni	*One Amazing Thing*	Amazingly Easy Potato *Parathas* (with Raita)		
61	Chitra Banerjee Divakaruni	*Palace of Illusions, The*	Panchaali's Eggplant *Bharta*		
61	Chitra Banerjee Divakaruni	*Sister of My Heart*	A *Sister Of My Heart* Special: *Payesh* (Bengali Rice Pudding)		
113	Jennifer Haigh	*Mrs. Kimble*	Dinah Kimble's Green Salad with Salmon (Gravlax) (with Vinaigrette)		

123	Katherine Howe	*Physick Book of Deliverance Dane, The*	Salad of Herbs and Flowers from Granna's Garden	Nana's Tapioca Pudding	Fish House Punch at the Goat and Anchor Tavern
7	Amy Bloom	*Where the God of Love Hangs Out*	The Velvet Swing	Idiot-Proof Scrambled Eggs with Lox, Leek and Dill	Red Flannel Hash
39	Helene Cooper	*House at Sugar Beach, The*	Potato Greens	Shrimp Creole	Fried Plantains
233	Hannah Tinti	*Good Thief, The*	Mrs. Sands's Apple Crumble Pie		
35	Chris Cleave	*Little Bee*	Post-Colonial Pie		
107	Sara Gruen	*Ape House*	Amanda Thigpen's Salmon en Croûte (with Hollandaise Sauce)	Long Grain and Wild Rice	Merran Neville's Pavlova
17	Ethan Canin	*America, America*	Anna Sifter's Strawberry Rhubarb Pie		
75	David Ebershoff	*19th Wife, The*	Peaches à la Ann Eliza		
75	David Ebershoff	*Danish Girl, The*	*Kniplingskager* (Danish Lace Cookies)		
185	Dolen Perkins-Valdez	*Wench*	Mawu's Magical Gumbo		
3	Sarah Blake	*Postmistress, The*	Florence (Granny) Blake's Romance Cookies		

11	Jenna Blum	*Stormchasers, The*	Adeline Ellingson's Norwegian Ham Balls	Luverne Joerg's *Rommegrod*	Adeline Ellingson's Potato Salad
21	Kate Christensen	*Trouble*	Mexico City Taco Stand		
21	Kate Christensen	*The Great Man*	Fruit for a Long-Delayed Love Scene		
21	Kate Christensen	*The Epicure's Lament*	Hugo's Neighborly Visit Shrimp Newburg		
27	Jill Ciment	*Heroic Measures*	Rainbow Room's Manhattan	Blue Sky Bakery's Bran Muffins	Blue Sky Bakery's Chicken Garlic Dog Biscuits
53	Anita Diamant	*Day After Night*	Shayndel's Apple Kuchen	Israeli Salad	
53	Anita Diamant	*The Red Tent*	Barley Bread		
67	Heidi Durrow	*Girl Who Fell from the Sky, The*	Heidi's Morning Franksbrød (White Bread)	Mor's *Panekager* (Crepes)	Pecan Pie à la Dane
81	Jamie Ford	*Hotel on the Corner of Bitter and Sweet*	Henry's Favorite *Hum Bao* (Cantonese Barbeque Pork Buns)		
85	Lisa Genova	*Still Alice*	Alice's White Chocolate Challah Pudding (with Raspberry Sauce)	Nana's Cream Puffs	
99	Amy Greene	*Bloodroot*	Appalachian Cathead Biscuits (with White Gravy)		

103	Philippa Gregory	Tudor series and Cousins' War series	Medieval Gingerbread		
129	Joshilyn Jackson	*Backseat Saints*	Rose Mae Lolley's Chess Pie		
133	Hillary Jordan	*Mudbound*	Aunt Faye's Famous Peach Chess Pie	Catfish Benedict	
145	Janice Y.K. Lee	*Piano Teacher, The*	Indonesian Ginger Chicken	Singapore Sling	
149	Elinor Lipman	*Ladies' Man, The*	Kathleen's Veal Marengo from *The Ladies' Man*		
149	Elinor Lipman	*Inn at Lake Devine, The*	My Mother's Noodle Kugel		
153	Laura Lippman	Tess Monaghan series	Salmon Spread	Aunt Effie's Cheese Straws	Theo Lippman Jr.'s Favorite Martini
171	Frances Mayes	*Under the Tuscan Sun*	Frances Mayes's Summer Shrimp Salad		
171	Frances Mayes	*Bella Tuscany: The Sweet Life in Italy*	Frances Mayes's Summer Shrimp Salad		
171	Frances Mayes	*Every Day in Tuscany: Seasons of an Italian Life*	Frances Mayes's Summer Shrimp Salad		
171	Frances Mayes	*In Tuscany*	Frances Mayes's Summer Shrimp Salad		

173	Emma McLaughlin and Nicola Kraus	*Nanny Diaries, The*	Grandma's Park Avenue Plum Torte		
173	Emma McLaughlin and Nicola Kraus	*Nanny Returns*	Grandma's Park Avenue Plum Torte		
193	Jayne Anne Phillips	*Lark & Termite*	Hometown Meat Loaf	Lark's White Chocolate-Coconut Cake with Buttercream Frosting	Lark's Apple Black Walnut Cake with Lemon Glaze
199	Katherine Russell Rich	*Dreaming in Hindi*	Mrs. Bhargav Mistry's Gujarati Sald		
203	Roxana Robinson	*Cost*	Artist's Summer Stew	Mesclun Salad at the Last Minute	
209	Stephanie Saldaña	*The Bread of Angels: A Journey to Love and Faith*	Syrian Style *Muhammara* (Roasted Red Pepper Dip with Walnuts and Pomegranate Syrup		
213	Esmeralda Santiago	*Conquistadora*	Puerto Rican *Pernil* (with Sofrito)	*Asopao* for the Soul	My Mother's Sweet Coconut Rice
213	Esmeralda Santiago	*The Turkish Lover*	Puerto Rican Pernil (with Sofrito)	*Asopao* for the Soul	My Mother's Sweet Coconut Rice
213	Esmeralda Santiago	*Almost a Woman*	Puerto Rican Pernil (with Sofrito)	*Asopao* for the Soul	My Mother's Sweet Coconut Rice

213	Esmeralda Santiago	*América's Dream*	Puerto Rican Pernil (with Sofrito)	*Asopao* for the Soul	My Mother's Sweet Coconut Rice
213	Esmeralda Santiago	*When I Was Puerto Rican*	Puerto Rican Pernil (with Sofrito)	*Asopao* for the Soul	My Mother's Sweet Coconut Rice
223	Lisa See	*Shanghai Girls*	Three Generations Curried Tomato Beef Lo Mein		
223	Lisa See	*Peony in Love*	Lisa See's Won Tons		
237	Adriana Trigiani	*Rococo*	Pia's Crabbies		
237	Adriana Trigiani	*Big Cherry Holler*	Cousin Dee's Peanut Butter Balls		
237	Adriana Trigiani	*Brava Valentine*	Adriana's Limoncello		
237	Adriana Trigiani	*Very Valentine*	Adriana's Limoncello		
243	Monique Truong	*Book of Salt, The*	Bo Kho	Palmiers	
243	Monique Truong	*Bitter in the Mouth*	Nouveau-Southern Summer Squash Casserole		
253	Thrity Umrigar	*Space Between Us, The*	Bombay Bhelpuri		

Recipe Index

General Index

About Judy Gelman and Vicki Levy Krupp

Judy Gelman, a public relations consultant, and Vicki Levy Krupp, a former high school history teacher, have participated in many book clubs. Both are avid readers and cooks. Seeking to combine their passion for books, food, and book clubs, they met over stacks of books and endless cups of coffee at a local sandwich shop, where *The Book Club Cookbook*, the first cookbook designed specifically for book clubs, was born.

They were motivated to write their second book, *The Kids' Book Club Book*, after librarians, parents, and teachers who attended their talks asked for a book for the growing number of youth book clubs across the country. During their eighteen months of research and writing on this trend, they were inspired by the enthusiasm and ideas of youth book club members, and the insights of notable children's authors whom they contacted.

Judy and Vicki have launched two websites, BookClubCookbook.com and KidsBook ClubBook.com, designed to bring authors and book clubs together.

The authors enjoy speaking about food and literature to groups across the country, and appreciate their ongoing conversations, both in person and via their websites, with book and food enthusiasts.

They both live with their families in the Boston area.

About BookClubCookBook.com

Do you thirst for bush tea when you read about Mma Precious Ramotswe's favorite drink in The No. 1 Ladies Detective Agency series? Did descriptions of Afghani culture in The *Kite Runner* by Khaled Hosseini send you hunting for a lamb and rice recipe?

Our website, BookClubCookBook.com features author recipes, book recommendations from book groups around the country, book giveaways, author blogs, newsletters and a directory of authors who will speak to your book club. The books featured on our website do not necessarily have a culinary tie-in: we connect readers with the best fiction and non-fiction titles for book clubs.

Please visit BookClubCookBook.com for news and information about recipes, authors, books, and the book club experience. You can sign up for our newsletter on the home page, and find out where we'll be appearing. We love hearing from book club members! Tell us what you're reading, what book-related foods you or your group has been serving, or what books your group recommends. Through communication with thousands of book club members, we've developed a unique picture of what book clubs are reading and eating, and how food enhances their book club experiences and appreciation of their reading. We're thrilled to share this with you.

Notes on Recipes

Notes on Recipes

Notes on Recipes

Notes on Recipes

Notes on Recipes